Safety Symbols

These symbols appear in laboratory activities.
They alert you to possible dangers and remind
you to work carefully.

General Safety Awareness Read all directions for an experiment several times. Follow the directions exactly as they are written. If you are in doubt, ask your teacher for assistance.

Physical Safety If the lab includes physical activity, use caution to avoid injuring yourself or others. Tell your teacher if there is a reason that you should not participate.

Safety Goggles Always wear safety goggles to protect your eyes in any activity involving chemicals, heating, or the possibility of broken glassware.

Lab Apron Wear a laboratory apron to protect your skin and clothing from harmful chemicals or hot materials.

Plastic Gloves Wear disposable plastic gloves to protect yourself from contact with chemicals that can be harmful. Keep your hands away from your face. Dispose of gloves according to your teacher's instructions.

Heating Use a clamp or tongs to hold hot objects. Test an object by first holding the back of your hand near it. If you feel heat, the object may be too hot to handle.

Heat-Resistant Gloves Hot plates, hot water, and hot glassware can cause burns. Never touch hot objects with your bare hands. Use an oven mitt or other hand protection.

Flames Tie back long hair and loose clothing, and put on safety goggles before using a burner. Follow instructions from your teacher for lighting and extinguishing burners.

No Flames If flammable materials are present, make sure there are no flames, sparks, or exposed sources of heat.

Electric Shock To avoid an electric shock, never use electrical equipment near water, or when the equipment or your hands are wet. Use only sockets that accept a three-prong plug. Be sure cords are untangled and cannot trip anyone. Disconnect equipment that is not in use.

Fragile Glassware Handle fragile glassware, such as thermometers, test tubes, and beakers, with care. Do not touch broken glass. Notify your teacher if glassware breaks. Never use chipped or cracked glassware.

Corrosive Chemical Avoid getting corrosive chemicals on your skin or clothing, or in your eyes. Do not inhale the vapors. Wash your hands after completing the activity.

Poison Do not let any poisonous chemical get on your skin, and do not inhale its vapor. Wash your hands after completing the activity.

Fumes When working with poisonous or irritating vapors, work in a well-ventilated area. Never test for an odor unless instructed to do so by your teacher. Avoid inhaling a vapor directly. Use a wafting motion to direct vapor toward your nose.

Sharp Object Use sharp instruments only as directed. Scissors, scalpels, pins, and knives are sharp and can cut or puncture your skin. Always direct sharp edges and points away from yourself and others.

Disposal All chemicals and other materials used in the laboratory must be disposed of safely. Follow your teacher's instructions.

Hand Washing Before leaving the lab, wash your hands thoroughly with soap or detergent, and warm water. Lather both sides of your hands and between your fingers. Rinse well.

Sound and Light

PRENTICE HALL Science Explorer

PEARSON

Prentice Hall

Boston, Massachusetts
Upper Saddle River, New Jersey

Sound and Light

Book-Specific Resources

Student Edition
StudentExpress™ with Interactive Textbook
Teacher's Edition
All-in-One Teaching Resources
Color Transparencies
Guided Reading and Study Workbook
Student Edition on Audio CD
Discovery Channel School® Video
Lab Activity Video
Consumable and Nonconsumable Materials Kits

Program Print Resources

Integrated Science Laboratory Manual
Computer Microscope Lab Manual
Inquiry Skills Activity Books
Progress Monitoring Assessments
Test Preparation Workbook
Test-Taking Tips With Transparencies
Teacher's ELL Handbook
Reading Strategies for Science Content

Differentiated Instruction Resources

Adapted Reading and Study Workbook
Adapted Tests
Differentiated Instruction Guide for Labs and Activities

Program Technology Resources

TeacherExpress™ CD-ROM
Interactive Textbooks Online
PresentationExpress™ CD-ROM
ExamView®, Computer Test Bank CD-ROM
Lab zone™ Easy Planner CD-ROM
Probeware Lab Manual With CD-ROM
Computer Microscope and Lab Manual
Materials Ordering CD-ROM
Discovery Channel School® DVD Library
Lab Activity DVD Library
Web Site at PHSchool.com

Spanish Print Resources

Spanish Student Edition
Spanish Guided Reading and Study Workbook
Spanish Teaching Guide With Tests

Acknowledgments appear on page 182, which constitutes an extension of this copyright page.

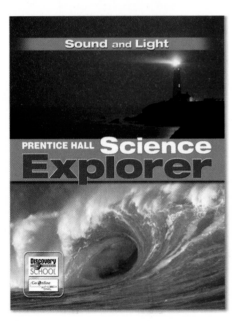

Cover
A lighthouse casts a beam of light across a stormy sea (top). Waves crashing on the North Shore of Oahu, Hawaii, contain tremendous energy (bottom).

ISBN 0-13-201159-X
4 5 6 7 8 9 10   10 09 08 07

Program Authors

Michael J. Padilla, Ph.D.
Professor of Science Education
University of Georgia
Athens, Georgia

Michael Padilla is a leader in middle school science education. He has served as an author and elected officer for the National Science Teachers Association and as a writer of the National Science Education Standards. As lead author of Science Explorer, Mike has inspired the team in developing a program that meets the needs of middle grades students, promotes science inquiry, and is aligned with the National Science Education Standards.

Ioannis Miaoulis, Ph.D.
President
Museum of Science
Boston, Massachusetts

Originally trained as a mechanical engineer, Ioannis Miaoulis is in the forefront of the national movement to increase technological literacy. As dean of the Tufts University School of Engineering, Dr. Miaoulis spearheaded the introduction of engineering into the Massachusetts curriculum. Currently he is working with school systems across the country to engage students in engineering activities and to foster discussions on the impact of science and technology on society.

Martha Cyr, Ph.D.
Director of K–12 Outreach
Worcester Polytechnic Institute
Worcester, Massachusetts

Martha Cyr is a noted expert in engineering outreach. She has over nine years of experience with programs and activities that emphasize the use of engineering principles, through hands-on projects, to excite and motivate students and teachers of mathematics and science in grades K–12. Her goal is to stimulate a continued interest in science and mathematics through engineering.

Book Author

Jay M. Pasachoff, Ph.D.
Professor of Astronomy
Williams College
Williamstown, Massachusetts

Contributing Writers

Rose-Marie Botting
Science Teacher
Broward County School District
Fort Lauderdale, Florida

Edward Evans
Former Science Teacher
Hilton Central School
Hilton, New York

T. Griffith Jones, Ph.D.
Science Department Chair
P.K. Yonge Developmental Research School
College of Education—University of Florida
Gainesville, Florida

Consultants

Reading Consultant

Nancy Romance, Ph.D.
Professor of Science
    Education
Florida Atlantic University
Fort Lauderdale, Florida

Mathematics Consultant

William Tate, Ph.D.
Professor of Education and
    Applied Statistics and
    Computation
Washington University
St. Louis, Missouri

Reviewers

Tufts University Content Reviewers

Faculty from Tufts University in Medford, Massachusetts, developed *Science Explorer* chapter projects and reviewed the student books.

Astier M. Almedom, Ph.D.
Department of Biology

Wayne Chudyk, Ph.D.
Department of Civil and Environmental Engineering

John L. Durant, Ph.D.
Department of Civil and Environmental Engineering

George S. Ellmore, Ph.D.
Department of Biology

David Kaplan, Ph.D.
Department of Biomedical Engineering

Samuel Kounaves, Ph.D.
Department of Chemistry

David H. Lee, Ph.D.
Department of Chemistry

Douglas Matson, Ph.D.
Department of Mechanical Engineering

Karen Panetta, Ph.D.
Department of Electrical Engineering and Computer Science

Jan A. Pechenik, Ph.D.
Department of Biology

John C. Ridge, Ph.D.
Department of Geology

William Waller, Ph.D.
Department of Astronomy

Content Reviewers

Paul Beale, Ph.D.
Department of Physics
University of Colorado
Boulder, Colorado

Jeff Bodart, Ph.D.
Chipola Junior College
Marianna, Florida

Michael Castellani, Ph.D.
Department of Chemistry
Marshall University
Huntington, West Virginia

Eugene Chiang, Ph.D.
Department of Astronomy
University of California – Berkeley
Berkeley, California

Charles C. Curtis, Ph.D.
Department of Physics
University of Arizona
Tucson, Arizona

Daniel Kirk-Davidoff, Ph.D.
Department of Meteorology
University of Maryland
College Park, Maryland

Diane T. Doser, Ph.D.
Department of Geological Sciences
University of Texas at El Paso
El Paso, Texas

R. E. Duhrkopf, Ph.D.
Department of Biology
Baylor University
Waco, Texas

Michael Hacker
Co-director, Center for Technological Literacy
Hofstra University
Hempstead, New York

Michael W. Hamburger, Ph.D.
Department of Geological Sciences
Indiana University
Bloomington, Indiana

Alice K. Hankla, Ph.D.
The Galloway School
Atlanta, Georgia

Donald C. Jackson, Ph.D.
Department of Molecular Pharmacology, Physiology, & Biotechnology
Brown University
Providence, Rhode Island

Jeremiah N. Jarrett, Ph.D.
Department of Biological Sciences
Central Connecticut State University
New Britain, Connecticut

David Lederman, Ph.D.
Department of Physics
West Virginia University
Morgantown, West Virginia

Becky Mansfield, Ph.D.
Department of Geography
Ohio State University
Columbus, Ohio

Elizabeth M. Martin, M.S.
Department of Chemistry and Biochemistry
College of Charleston
Charleston, South Carolina

Joe McCullough, Ph.D.
Department of Natural and Applied Sciences
Cabrillo College
Aptos, California

Robert J. Mellors, Ph.D.
Department of Geological Sciences
San Diego State University
San Diego, California

Joseph M. Moran, Ph.D.
American Meteorological Society
Washington, D.C.

David J. Morrissey, Ph.D.
Department of Chemistry
Michigan State University
East Lansing, Michigan

Philip A. Reed, Ph.D.
Department of Occupational & Technical Studies
Old Dominion University
Norfolk, Virginia

Scott M. Rochette, Ph.D.
Department of the Earth Sciences
State University of New York, College at Brockport
Brockport, New York

Laurence D. Rosenhein, Ph.D.
Department of Chemistry
Indiana State University
Terre Haute, Indiana

Ronald Sass, Ph.D.
Department of Biology and Chemistry
Rice University
Houston, Texas

George Schatz, Ph.D.
Department of Chemistry
Northwestern University
Evanston, Illinois

Sara Seager, Ph.D.
Carnegie Institution of Washington
Washington, D.C.

Robert M. Thornton, Ph.D.
Section of Plant Biology
University of California
Davis, California

John R. Villarreal, Ph.D.
College of Science and Engineering
The University of Texas – Pan American
Edinburg, Texas

Kenneth Welty, Ph.D.
School of Education
University of Wisconsin–Stout
Menomonie, Wisconsin

Edward J. Zalisko, Ph.D.
Department of Biology
Blackburn College
Carlinville, Illinois

Teacher Reviewers

David R. Blakely
Arlington High School
Arlington, Massachusetts

Jane E. Callery
Two Rivers Magnet Middle
    School
East Hartford, Connecticut

Melissa Lynn Cook
Oakland Mills High School
Columbia, Maryland

James Fattic
Southside Middle School
Anderson, Indiana

Dan Gabel
Hoover Middle School
Rockville, Maryland

Wayne Goates
Eisenhower Middle School
Goddard, Kansas

Katherine Bobay Graser
Mint Hill Middle School
Charlotte, North Carolina

Darcy Hampton
Deal Junior High School
Washington, D.C.

Karen Kelly
Pierce Middle School
Waterford, Michigan

David Kelso
Manchester High School Central
Manchester, New Hampshire

Benigno Lopez, Jr.
Sleepy Hill Middle School
Lakeland, Florida

Angie L. Matamoros, Ph.D.
ALM Consulting, Inc.
Weston, Florida

Tim McCollum
Charleston Middle School
Charleston, Illinois

Bruce A. Mellin
Brooks School
North Andover, Massachusetts

Ella Jay Parfitt
Southeast Middle School
Baltimore, Maryland

Evelyn A. Pizzarello
Louis M. Klein Middle School
Harrison, New York

Kathleen M. Poe
Fletcher Middle School
Jacksonville, Florida

Shirley Rose
Lewis and Clark Middle School
Tulsa, Oklahoma

Linda Sandersen
Greenfield Middle School
Greenfield, Wisconsin

Mary E. Solan
Southwest Middle School
Charlotte, North Carolina

Mary Stewart
University of Tulsa
Tulsa, Oklahoma

Paul Swenson
Billings West High School
Billings, Montana

Thomas Vaughn
Arlington High School
Arlington, Massachusetts

Susan C. Zibell
Central Elementary
Simsbury, Connecticut

Safety Reviewers

W. H. Breazeale, Ph.D.
Department of Chemistry
College of Charleston
Charleston, South Carolina

Ruth Hathaway, Ph.D.
Hathaway Consulting
Cape Girardeau, Missouri

Douglas Mandt, M.S.
Science Education Consultant
Edgewood, Washington

Activity Field Testers

Nicki Bibbo
Witchcraft Heights School
Salem, Massachusetts

Rose-Marie Botting
Broward County Schools
Fort Lauderdale, Florida

Colleen Campos
Laredo Middle School
Aurora, Colorado

Elizabeth Chait
W. L. Chenery Middle School
Belmont, Massachusetts

Holly Estes
Hale Middle School
Stow, Massachusetts

Laura Hapgood
Plymouth Community
    Intermediate School
Plymouth, Massachusetts

Mary F. Lavin
Plymouth Community
    Intermediate School
Plymouth, Massachusetts

James MacNeil, Ph.D.
Cambridge, Massachusetts

Lauren Magruder
St. Michael's Country
    Day School
Newport, Rhode Island

Jeanne Maurand
Austin Preparatory School
Reading, Massachusetts

Joanne Jackson-Pelletier
Winman Junior High School
Warwick, Rhode Island

Warren Phillips
Plymouth Public Schools
Plymouth, Massachusetts

Carol Pirtle
Hale Middle School
Stow, Massachusetts

Kathleen M. Poe
Fletcher Middle School
Jacksonville, Florida

Cynthia B. Pope
Norfolk Public Schools
Norfolk, Virginia

Anne Scammell
Geneva Middle School
Geneva, New York

Karen Riley Sievers
Callanan Middle School
Des Moines, Iowa

David M. Smith
Eyer Middle School
Allentown, Pennsylvania

Gene Vitale
Parkland School
McHenry, Illinois

Contents

Sound and Light

Reference Section

VIDEO

Enhance understanding through dynamic video.

Preview Get motivated with this introduction to the chapter content.

Field Trip Explore a real-world story related to the chapter content.

Assessment Review content and take an assessment.

Web Links

Get connected to exciting Web resources in every lesson.

 Find Web links on topics relating to every section.

Active Art Interact with selected visuals from every chapter online.

Planet Diary® Explore news and natural phenomena through weekly reports.

Science News® Keep up to date with the latest science discoveries.

Experience the complete text-book online and on CD-ROM.

Activities Practice skills and learn content.

Videos Explore content and learn important lab skills.

Audio Support Hear key terms spoken and defined.

Self-Assessment Use instant feedback to help you track your progress.

Activities

Turning Down the Volume on Sonic Booms

A sleek white plane swoops high into the California sky. This F-5E navy jet has been specially modified for this test. Its nose tapers smoothly. Its underside curves. The plane reaches supersonic speed—a speed faster than the speed of sound. The aircraft breaks the sound barrier. Sensors on the ground and in nearby planes measure the sonic boom—the sudden, sharp BOOM made when a plane flies faster than sound.

Scientists hold their breath while another plane—an unmodified F-5E jet—flies the same course at supersonic speed. The two planes' sound patterns are different! The test demonstrates that the shape of a supersonic aircraft can reduce sonic booms.

Aeronautics engineer Christine Darden is a national expert on sonic booms. Her team at the National Aeronautics and Space Administration (NASA) has been looking for ways to soften sonic booms. They had predicted that changing the shape of an airplane could soften sonic booms. They had tested models. But this was the first actual test flight based on their work. Fifty years after the first supersonic flight, another significant discovery had been made.

Career Path

Christine Mann Darden grew up in Monroe, North Carolina. She earned a Ph.D. in mechanical engineering at George Washington University in Washington, D.C. For more than 30 years, Dr. Darden was an aeronautical engineer at NASA's Langley Research Center in Hampton, Virginia. She is currently Assistant Director for Planning at Langley.

This modified F-5E fighter jet makes an historic test flight (above). Christine prepares to test a model of the F-5E in the supersonic wind tunnel (right). This tunnel at Langley Research Center is four feet by four feet.

Talking With
Dr. Christine Darden

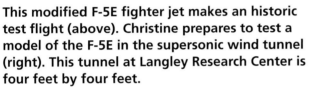

Choosing Engineering

Christine's research in sonic booms is a long way from her first career as a math teacher. In the late 1960s, she taught near the NASA labs in Virginia. At the time, NASA was working on a program to send astronauts to the moon. Christine went to work for NASA as a mathematician.

   She quickly became fascinated with the work of the NASA research engineers. "They were the ones who were working with the really tough challenges of the program," she says. "They were doing the interesting, hands-on work." At the time, there were few engineers in aerospace. Christine decided to get a degree in engineering. She has been at NASA studying supersonic aircraft ever since.

Breaking the Sound Barrier

The sound barrier was first broken in 1947. Since then, people have complained about sonic booms so much that the government has passed regulations. It's now against the law to fly most aircraft at supersonic speeds over the United States.

   "If it is loud enough, a sonic boom can actually break windows and do damage to buildings," says Christine. "People find it very disturbing. Right now, the boom is one of the biggest obstacles to commercial supersonic air service." But what if scientists can find ways to lower the volume of sonic booms?

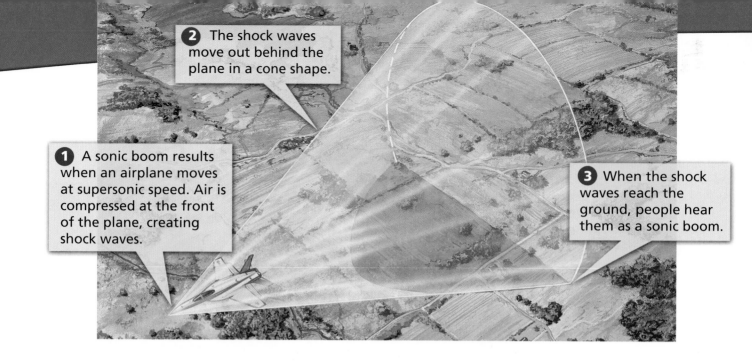

A supersonic aircraft sends out shock waves that people hear as a sonic boom.

What Is a Sonic Boom?

You have probably heard the sound that is made when an airplane breaks the sound barrier. A sonic boom sounds like a clap of thunder or a sharp explosion high in the sky. Just what are you hearing?

"A sonic boom is a compression or pressure wave," Christine explains. "An airplane pushes a wave of air molecules ahead of it as it travels forward, just as a ship's bow pushes out a wave as it moves through the water. Those compressions travel outward from the plane as a shock wave of high pressure. When that shock wave reaches our ears, we hear it as a boom."

"Think of blowing up a balloon," Christine says. "With the balloon inflated, the air on the inside is much more compressed than the air on the outside. When the balloon pops, the compression immediately flies outward in the form of a shock wave."

"Christine's NASA team found that the shape of an aircraft determines the size of the sonic boom it creates."

How Do You Study Sound?

You can't see a sonic boom. So how do you research it? Christine's Sonic Boom Group at NASA investigated the distinctive "sound print" made by aircraft that fly faster than the speed of sound.

"Part of our work is coming up with new ways to observe and measure the phenomenon we're studying," says Christine. "For example, we know that all waves have similar properties. So we look at how waves behave in water to tell us something about how they behave in the air."

How Do You Test Aircraft?

One way to study how supersonic aircraft create sonic booms is to "fly" model aircraft in a high-speed wind tunnel. The scientists place the steel models in the tunnel. They observe how the models behave in winds moving at up to three times the speed of sound. (The speed of sound varies with altitude and temperature. At sea level on a 16°C day, the speed of sound is about 1,207 kilometers per hour.)

Instruments on the sides of the tunnel allow Christine to "hear" the sonic boom created by the model. By adding very fine smoke, she can even watch how the air moves over the plane. "We can actually see the shock wave," she says.

How Can Sonic Booms Be Softened?

Christine's NASA team found that the shape of an aircraft determines the size of the sonic boom it creates. They performed tests with computer programs, on actual supersonic jets, and in wind tunnels. Some experiments showed that angling the wings back sharply reduces the size of the shock wave and the loudness of the sonic boom. Another factor in softening the sonic boom was the overall shape of the plane, especially a sleek, narrow design.

But the same features that make planes quieter also make them harder to fly. "You could put a needle up there supersonically and you wouldn't get a sonic boom," explains Christine. "But you wouldn't have much of an airplane, either."

The test flights of the modified F-5E jet in 2003 took the research out of the laboratory and into the sky. The tests were a milestone in softening sonic booms. Someday, supersonic commercial jets may be allowed to fly across the United States.

Writing in Science

Career Link Christine's Sonic Boom Group at NASA tested the way that changes in an airplane's shape might affect a sonic boom. They set up experiments to test these changes. Now think of different-shaped boats moving through water—a kayak, a tugboat, and a rowboat. Predict the type of wave that each boat will make. In a paragraph, describe ways in which you could test your predictions.

Go Online
PHSchool.com

For: More on this career
Visit: PHSchool.com
Web Code: cgb-5000

Christine is shown here with the modified F-5E jet that she and her team designed.

Characteristics of Waves

Chapter Preview

In this art, colored lights shine on waves moving along spinning ropes. ▶

Lab zone™ Chapter Project

Over and Over and Over Again

Some waves involve repeating patterns, or cycles. Any motion that repeats itself at regular intervals is called periodic motion. The hands moving on a clock, a child swinging on a swing, and a Ferris wheel going round and round are examples of periodic motion.

Your Goal To find examples of periodic motion and describe them

To complete this project you must

● identify examples of periodic motion or events that have periodic characteristics
● collect and organize data on the frequency and duration of each event
● present your findings as a poster, a display, or a demonstration

Plan It! With your group, brainstorm examples of objects or events that go back and forth or alternate from high to low, dark to light, loud to quiet, or crowded to uncrowded. Select at least two objects or events to observe. Record data such as how long it takes for the event to finish and start again or the highest and lowest point of the object's motion. Finally, organize your findings to present to your class.

What Are Waves?

Reading Preview

Key Concepts
- What causes mechanical waves?
- What are two types of waves and how are they classified?

Key Terms
- wave • energy • medium
- mechanical wave • vibration
- transverse wave • crest
- trough • longitudinal wave
- compression • rarefaction

Target Reading Skill

Using Prior Knowledge Before you read, look at the section headings and visuals to see what this section is about. Then write what you know about waves and energy in a graphic organizer like the one below. As you read, continue to write in what you learn.

What You Know
1. Waves are high and low.
2.

What You Learned
1.
2.

▼ **A motorboat making waves**

Lab zone Discover **Activity**

How Do Waves Travel?

1. Fill a shallow pan with about 3 cm of water.
2. With a pencil, touch the surface of the water at one end of the pan twice each second for about a minute.
3. Describe the pattern the waves make. Sketch a rough diagram of what you see.
4. Float a cork in the center of the pan. Repeat Step 2 and observe how the cork moves. Draw a diagram of what you see.

Think It Over
Observing How did the cork move in Step 4? How is its movement similar to the wave's movement? How is it different?

It was a long swim, but now you're resting on the swimming raft in the lake. You hear the water lapping gently against the raft as the sun warms your skin. Suddenly a motorboat zooms by. A few seconds later you're bobbing wildly up and down as the boat's waves hit the raft. Although the speedboat didn't touch the raft, its energy caused waves in the water. Then the waves moved the raft—and you!

You can see and feel the water waves when you're on a swimming raft. But did you know that many kinds of waves affect you every day? Sound is a wave. Sunlight is a different kind of wave. Light, sound, and water waves may seem very different, but they all are waves. What is a wave?

Waves and Energy

A **wave** is a disturbance that transfers energy from place to place. In science, **energy** is defined as the ability to do work. To understand waves, think about the swimming raft. A wave that disturbs the surface of the water also will disturb the raft. The wave's energy lifts the heavy raft as the wave passes under it. But the disturbance caused by the wave is temporary. After the wave passes, the water is calm again and the raft stops bobbing.

What Carries Waves? Most kinds of waves need something to travel through. Sound waves travel through air. Water waves travel along the surface of the water. A wave can even travel along a rope. The material through which a wave travels is called a **medium.** Gases (such as air), liquids (such as water), and solids (such as rope) all act as mediums. Waves that require a medium through which to travel are called **mechanical waves.**

But not all waves require a medium to travel through. Light from the sun, for example, can carry energy through empty space. If light could not travel through empty space, you could not even see the sun! Waves that can travel without a medium are called electromagnetic waves. You will learn more about electromagnetic waves in a later chapter.

How Do Waves Transfer Energy? Although mechanical waves travel through a medium, they do not carry the medium with them. Look at the duck in Figure 1. When a wave travels under the duck, the duck moves up and down. But the duck does not travel with the wave. After the wave passes, the duck and the water return to where they started.

Why doesn't the medium travel along with the wave? All mediums are made of tiny particles. When a wave enters a medium, it transfers energy to the medium's particles. The particles bump into each other, passing the wave's energy along. To understand this, think about how food is passed at a table. You hand the food to the next person, who passes it to the next person, and so on. The food is transferred, but the people don't move. The food is like the wave's energy, and the people are like particles in a medium.

Direction of wave

FIGURE 1
Motion of a Medium
Waves travel through water, but they do not carry the water (or the duck) with them. **Predicting** *If you add a sixth stage to the diagram, which earlier stage should it most resemble?*

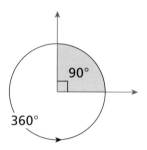
What Causes Waves? Energy always is required to make a wave. **Mechanical waves are produced when a source of energy causes a medium to vibrate.** A **vibration** is a repeated back-and-forth or up-and-down motion. When a vibration moves through a medium, a wave results.

Moving objects have energy. A moving object can transfer energy to a medium, producing waves. For example, you can make waves by dipping your finger in water. Your finger has energy because it is moving. When your finger touches the water, it transfers energy to the water and makes waves. In the same way, a motorboat slicing through calm water transfers energy to the water and makes waves.

Reading Checkpoint What is a vibration?

Types of Waves

Waves move through mediums in different ways. **Mechanical waves are classified by how they move. There are two types of mechanical waves: transverse waves and longitudinal waves.**

Transverse Waves When you make a wave on a rope, the wave moves from one end of the rope to the other. But the rope itself moves up and down or from side to side, at right angles to the direction in which the wave travels. Waves that move the medium at right angles to the direction in which the waves travel are called **transverse waves.** Transverse means "across." As a transverse wave moves, the particles of the medium move across, or at a right angle to, the direction of the wave.

In Figure 2, you can see that the red ribbon on the rope is first at a low point of the wave. Then it is at a high point. The high part of a transverse wave is called a **crest,** and the low part is called a **trough** (trawf).

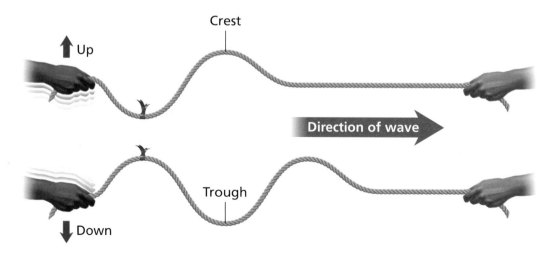

FIGURE 2
Transverse Waves
A transverse wave moves the rope up and down in a direction perpendicular to the direction in which the wave travels.

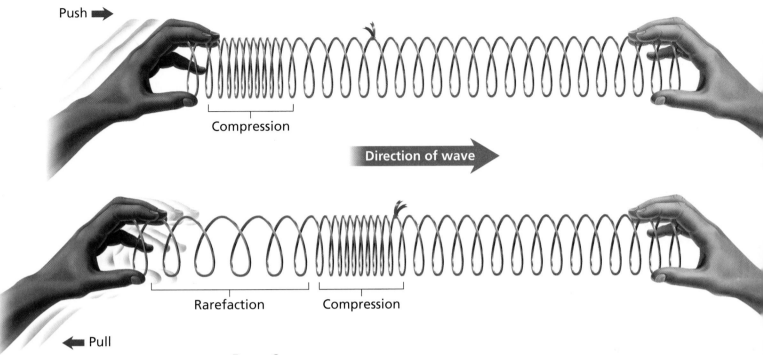

Push ➡

Compression

Direction of wave ➡

Rarefaction   Compression

⬅ Pull

FIGURE 3
Longitudinal Waves
A longitudinal wave moves the coils of a spring toy back
and forth in a direction parallel to the direction the wave
travels. **Comparing and Contrasting** *How do the coils
in a compression compare to the coils in a rarefaction?*

Longitudinal Waves Figure 3 shows a different kind of
wave. If you stretch out a spring toy and push and pull one end,
you can produce a longitudinal wave. **Longitudinal waves**
(lawn juh TOO duh nul) move the medium parallel to the
direction in which the waves travel. The coils in the spring
move back and forth parallel to the wave motion.

Notice in Figure 3 that in some parts of the spring, the coils
are close together. In other parts of the spring, the coils are
more spread out. The parts where the coils are close together
are called **compressions** (kum PRESH unz). The parts where
the coils are spread out, or rarified, are called **rarefactions**
(rair uh FAK shunz).

As compressions and rarefactions travel along the spring toy,
each coil moves forward and then back. The energy travels from
one end of the spring to the other, creating a wave. After the
wave passes, each coil returns to the position where it started.

Sound is also a longitudinal wave. In air, sound waves cause
air particles to move back and forth. In areas where the particles are pushed together, compressions form. In between the
compressions, particles are spread out. These are rarefactions.

Go **O**nline
*SC*i*Links.* NSTA

For: Links on waves
Visit: www.SciLinks.org
Web Code: scn-1511

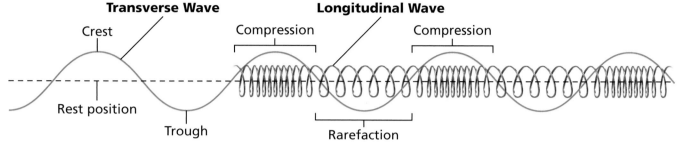

Transverse Wave

Crest

Rest position

Trough

Longitudinal Wave

Compression

Compression

Rarefaction

FIGURE 4
Representing Waves
The compressions of a longitudinal wave correspond to the crests of a transverse wave. The troughs correspond to rarefactions.

Representing Types of Waves You can use diagrams to represent transverse and longitudinal waves. Transverse waves like those on a rope are easy to draw. You can draw a transverse wave as shown in Figure 4. Think of the horizontal line as the position of the rope before it is disturbed. This position is called the rest position. As the wave passes, the rope moves above or below the rest position. Remember that the crests are the highest points of the wave and the troughs are the lowest points of the wave.

To draw longitudinal waves, think of the compressions in the spring toy as being similar to the crests of a transverse wave. The rarefactions in the spring toy are like the troughs of a transverse wave. By treating compressions as crests and rarefactions as troughs, you can draw longitudinal waves in the same way as transverse waves.

Reading Checkpoint **How do you draw the rest position of a transverse wave?**

Section 1 Assessment

Target Reading Skill Using Prior Knowledge Revise your graphic organizer about waves based on what you just learned in the section.

Reviewing Key Concepts

1. a. **Defining** What is a mechanical wave?
   b. **Explaining** How are mechanical waves produced?
   c. **Inferring** A wave moves a floating dock up and down several times, but then the dock stops moving. What happened to the wave?
2. a. **Identifying** What are the two types of mechanical waves?
   b. **Describing** Use a wave diagram to represent the crests and troughs of a wave. Then describe a crest and trough in your own words.

c. **Comparing and Contrasting** How does a transverse wave move a medium? How does a longitudinal wave move a medium?

Writing in Science

Firsthand Account Suppose you are a particle of water in a lake. Describe what happens to you when a motorboat passes by. Be sure to use words like *vibration* and *crest* in your description.

Properties of Waves

Reading Preview

Key Concepts
- What are the basic properties of waves?
- How is a wave's speed related to its wavelength and frequency?

Key Terms
- amplitude • wavelength
- frequency • hertz (Hz)

 Target Reading Skill
Outlining An outline shows the relationship between main ideas and supporting ideas. As you read, make an outline about the properties of waves that you can use for review. Use the red headings for the main ideas and the blue headings for the supporting ideas.

Properties of Waves
I. Amplitude
A. Amplitude of transverse waves
B.
II. Wavelength
III.

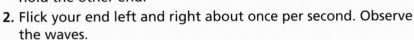

Lab zone Discover Activity

Can You Change a Wave?

1. Lay a 3-meter-long rope on the floor. Hold one end of the rope. Have a partner hold the other end.
2. Flick your end left and right about once per second. Observe the waves.
3. Now flick your end about twice per second. Observe the waves.
4. Switch roles with your partner and repeat Steps 2 and 3.

Think It Over
Predicting What happened to the waves when you flicked the rope more often? Predict how the wave will change if you flick the rope less often than once per second. Try it.

One of the most elegant and graceful Olympic sports is rhythmic gymnastics. A ribbon dancer flicks a stick attached to a ribbon, making waves that travel down the ribbon. Some of the waves are longer, while others are shorter. The rate at which the gymnast flicks her hands affects both the length and shape of the waves in the ribbon.

This is just one of many different kinds of waves. Waves can carry a little energy or a lot. They can be short or long. They can be rare or frequent. They can travel fast or slow. All waves, however, share certain properties. **The basic properties of waves are amplitude, wavelength, frequency, and speed.**

A rhythmic gymnast ▲

Amplitude

Some crests are very high, while others are very low. The distance the medium rises depends on the amplitude of the wave. **Amplitude** is the maximum distance that the particles of the medium carrying the wave move away from their rest positions. For example, the amplitude of a water wave is the maximum distance a water particle moves above or below the surface level of calm water. You can increase the amplitude of a wave in a rope by moving your hand up and down a greater distance. To do this, you have to use more energy. This energy is transferred to the rope. Thus, the more energy a wave has, the greater its amplitude.

Amplitude of Transverse Waves As shown in Figure 5, the amplitude of a transverse wave is the maximum distance the medium moves up or down from its rest position. You can find the amplitude of a transverse wave by measuring the distance from the rest position to a crest or to a trough.

Amplitude of Longitudinal Waves The amplitude of a longitudinal wave is a measure of how compressed or rarefied the medium becomes. A high-energy wave causes more compression and rarefaction than a low-energy wave. When the compressions are dense, it means that the wave's amplitude is large.

FIGURE 5

Amplitude, Wavelength, and Frequency

The basic properties of all waves include amplitude, wavelength, and frequency.
Developing Hypotheses *How could you increase the amplitude of a wave in a rope? How could you increase the frequency?*

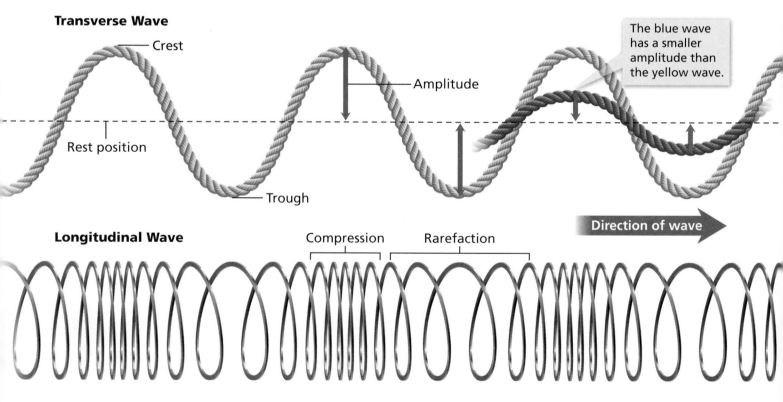

Transverse Wave

Crest

Amplitude

The blue wave has a smaller amplitude than the yellow wave.

Rest position

Trough

Direction of wave

Longitudinal Wave

Compression   Rarefaction

Wavelength

A wave travels a certain distance before it starts to repeat. The distance between two corresponding parts of a wave is its **wavelength.** You can find the wavelength of a transverse wave by measuring the distance from crest to crest, as shown in Figure 5. Or you could measure from trough to trough. The wavelength of a longitudinal wave is the distance between compressions.

Frequency

Wave **frequency** is the number of complete waves that pass a given point in a certain amount of time. For example, if you make waves on a rope so that one wave passes by every second, the frequency is 1 wave per second. How can you increase the frequency? Simply move your hand up and down more quickly, perhaps two or three times per second. To decrease the frequency, move your hand up and down more slowly.

Frequency is measured in units called **hertz** (Hz). A wave that occurs every second has a frequency of 1 Hz. If two waves pass you every second, then the frequency of the wave is 2 per second, or 2 hertz. The hertz was named after Heinrich Hertz, the German scientist who discovered radio waves.

Reading Checkpoint **In what unit is the frequency of a wave measured?**

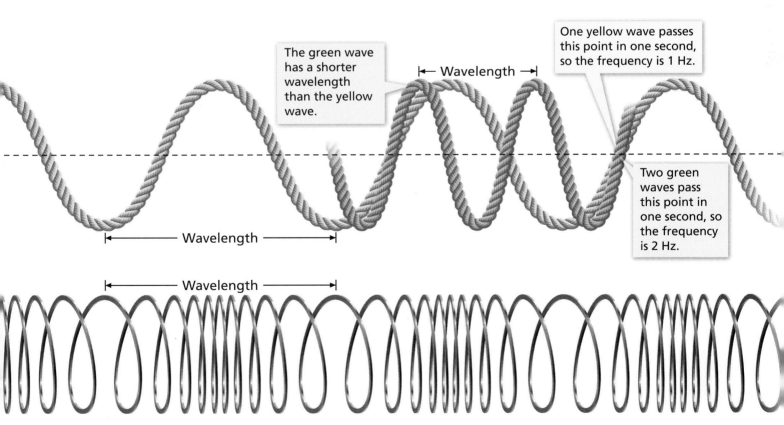

The green wave has a shorter wavelength than the yellow wave.

← Wavelength →

One yellow wave passes this point in one second, so the frequency is 1 Hz.

Two green waves pass this point in one second, so the frequency is 2 Hz.

|← Wavelength →|

|← Wavelength →|

FIGURE 6
Speed of Waves
Light waves travel much faster than sound waves.
Problem Solving *Why do you see lightning before hearing thunder?*

Speed

Imagine watching a distant thunderstorm approach on a hot summer day. First you see a flash of lightning. A few seconds later you hear the thunder rumble. Even though the thunder occurs the instant the lightning flashes, the light and sound reach you seconds apart. This happens because light waves travel much faster than sound waves. In fact, light waves travel about a million times faster than sound waves!

Different waves travel at different speeds. The speed of a wave is how far the wave travels in a given length of time, or its distance divided by the time it took to travel that distance. **The speed, wavelength, and frequency of a wave are related to one another by a mathematical formula:**

$$\text{Speed} = \text{Wavelength} \times \text{Frequency}$$

If you know two of the quantities in the speed formula—speed, wavelength, and frequency—you can calculate the third quantity. For example, if you know a wave's speed and wavelength, you can calculate the frequency. If you know the speed and the frequency, you can calculate the wavelength.

$$\text{Frequency} = \frac{\text{Speed}}{\text{Wavelength}} \qquad \text{Wavelength} = \frac{\text{Speed}}{\text{Frequency}}$$

If a medium does not change, the speed of a wave is constant. For example, in air at a given temperature and pressure, all sound waves travel at the same speed. If speed is constant, what do you think will happen if the wave's frequency changes? If you multiply wavelength by frequency, you should always get the same speed. Therefore, if you increase the frequency of a wave, the wavelength must decrease.

 **Reading Checkpoint** **What is the speed of a wave?**

Math **Sample Problem**

Calculating Frequency

The speed of a wave on a rope is 50 cm/s and its wavelength is 10 cm. What is the wave's frequency?

1 **Read and Understand**
What information are you given?

Speed = 50 cm/s

Wavelength = 10 cm

2 **Plan and Solve**
What quantity are you trying to calculate?

The frequency of a wave = ■Hz

What formula contains the given quantities and the unknown quantity?

$$\text{Frequency} = \frac{\text{Speed}}{\text{Wavelength}}$$

Perform the calculation.

$$\text{Frequency} = \frac{\text{Speed}}{\text{Wavelength}} = \frac{50 \text{ cm/s}}{10 \text{ cm}}$$

$$\text{Frequency} = \frac{5}{s} = 5 \text{ Hz}$$

3 **Look Back and Check**
Does your answer make sense?

The wave speed is 50 cm per second. Because the distance from crest to crest is 10 cm, 5 crests will pass a point every second.

Math **Practice**

1. A wave has a wavelength of 2 mm and a frequency of 3 Hz. At what speed does the wave travel?

2. The speed of a wave on a guitar string is 142 m/s and the frequency is 110 Hz. What is the wavelength of the wave?

Section 2 Assessment

Target Reading Skill Outlining Use the information in your outline to help you answer the questions below.

Reviewing Key Concepts

1. a. **Listing** What are four basic properties of waves?
   b. **Explaining** Which wave property is directly related to energy?
   c. **Comparing and Contrasting** Which wave properties are distances? Which are measured relative to time?
2. a. **Identifying** What formula relates speed, wavelength, and frequency?
   b. **Inferring** Two waves have the same wavelength and frequency. How do their speeds compare?
   c. **Calculating** A wave's frequency is 2 Hz and its wavelength is 4 m. What is the wave's speed?

Math **Practice**

3. **Calculating Frequency** A wave travels at 3 m/s along a spring toy. If the wavelength is 0.2 m, what is the wave's frequency?

Wavy Motions

Problem

How do waves travel in a spring toy?

Skills Focus

comparing and contrasting, classifying

Materials

- spring toy
- meter stick

Procedure

1. On a smooth floor, stretch the spring to about 3 meters. Hold one end while your partner holds the other end. Do not over-stretch the spring toy.

2. Pull a few coils of the spring toy to one side near one end of the spring.

3. Release the coils and observe the motion of the spring. What happens when the disturbance reaches your partner? Draw what you observe.

4. Have your partner move one end of the spring toy to the left and then to the right on the floor. Be certain that both ends of the spring are held securely. Draw a diagram of the wave you observe.

5. Repeat Step 4, increasing the rate at which you move the spring toy left and right. Record your observations.

6. Squeeze together several coils of the spring toy, making a compression.

7. Release the compressed section of the spring toy and observe the disturbance as it moves down the spring. Record your observations. Draw and label what you see.

Analyze and Conclude

1. **Comparing and Contrasting** Compare the waves generated in Steps 1–5 with the waves generated in Steps 6–7.

2. **Classifying** Were the waves generated in Steps 1–5 transverse or longitudinal? Explain your answer.

3. **Comparing and Contrasting** In Step 3 of the procedure, compare the original wave to the wave that came back.

4. **Classifying** Were the waves generated in Steps 6 and 7 transverse or longitudinal? Explain your answer.

5. **Interpreting Data** What happened to the wavelength and frequency when you increased the rate at which the spring toy moved left and right?

6. **Developing Hypotheses** How might you change the amplitude of the longitudinal waves you made?

7. **Communicating** Use your drawings to make a poster that explains your observations.

Design an Experiment

Obtain some different spring toys. Look for different sizes and materials, such as metal and plastic. Design an experiment to test whether the differences of the spring toys result in differences in the waves the springs make. Have your teacher approve your procedure before you carry out the experiment.

Interactions of Waves

Reading Preview

Key Concepts
- How do reflection, refraction, and diffraction change a wave's direction?
- What are the different types of interference?
- How do standing waves form?

Key Terms
- reflection • law of reflection
- refraction • diffraction
- interference
- constructive interference
- destructive interference
- standing wave • node
- antinode • resonance

⊙ Target Reading Skill

Asking Questions Before you read, preview the red headings. In a graphic organizer like the one below, ask a *what, how, when,* or *where* question for each heading. As you read, write the answers to your questions.

Interactions of Waves

Question	Answer
How are waves reflected?	Waves are reflected . . .

How Does a Ball Bounce?

1. Choose a spot at the base of a wall. From a distance of 1 m, roll a wet ball along the floor straight at the spot you chose. Watch the angle at which the ball bounces by looking at the path of moisture on the floor.
2. Wet the ball again. From a different position, roll the ball at the same spot, but at an angle to the wall. Again, observe the angle at which the ball bounces back.

Think It Over
Developing Hypotheses How do you think the angle at which the ball hits the wall is related to the angle at which the ball bounces back? Test your hypothesis.

You slip into the water in your snorkel gear. With your mask on, you can see clearly across the pool. As you start to swim, your flippers disturb the water, sending ripples moving outward in all directions. As each ripple hits the wall, it bounces off the wall and travels back toward you.

When water waves hit the side of a swimming pool, they bounce back because they cannot pass through the solid wall. Other kinds of waves may interact in a similar way when they hit the surface of a new medium. This type of interaction is called reflection.

Making waves in a pool ▶

Reflection

When an object or a wave hits a surface through which it cannot pass, it bounces back. This interaction with a surface is called **reflection.** There are many examples of reflection in your everyday life. When you did the Discover Activity, you saw that the ball hit the wall and bounced back, or was reflected. When you looked in your mirror this morning, you used light that was reflected to see yourself. If you have ever shouted in an empty gym, the echo you heard was caused by sound waves that reflected off the gym walls.

All waves obey the law of reflection. To help you understand this law, look at Figure 7. In the photo, you see light reflected off the surface of the sunglasses. The diagram shows how the light waves travel to make the reflection. The arrow labeled *Incoming wave* represents a wave moving toward the surface at an angle. The arrow labeled *Reflected wave* represents the wave that bounces off the surface at an angle. The dashed line labeled *Normal* is drawn perpendicular to the surface at the point where the incoming wave strikes the surface. The angle of incidence is the angle between the incoming wave and the normal. The angle of reflection is the angle between the reflected wave and the normal line. The **law of reflection** states that the angle of incidence equals the angle of reflection.

Reading Checkpoint **What is reflection?**

FIGURE 7
Law of Reflection
The angle of incidence equals the angle of reflection. All waves obey this law, including the light waves reflected from these sunglasses.
Predicting *What happens to the angle of reflection if the angle of incidence increases?*

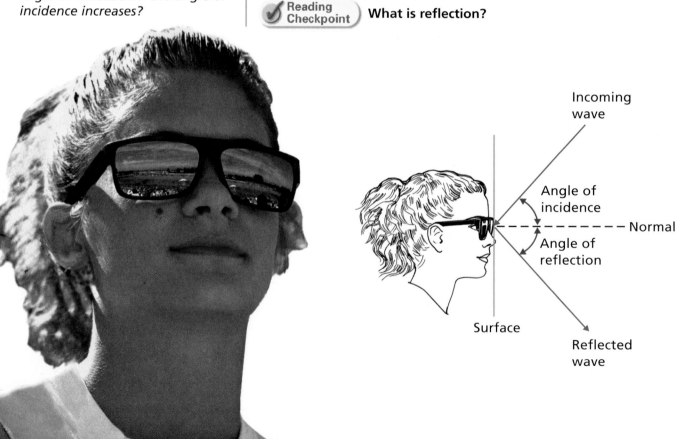

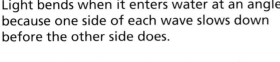

FIGURE 8
Refraction of Light Waves
Light bends when it enters water at an angle
because one side of each wave slows down
before the other side does.

Beam
of light

Air
(fast wave speed)

Wave crests

Water
(slow wave speed)

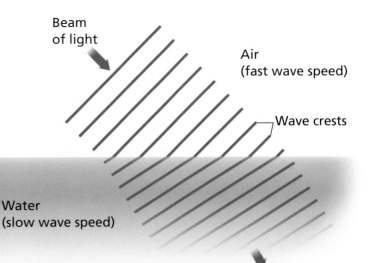

Refraction

Have you ever been riding a skateboard and gone off the side-walk onto grass? If so, you know it's hard to keep moving in a straight line. The front wheel on the side moving onto the grass slows down. The front wheel still on the sidewalk continues to move fast. The difference in the speeds of the two front wheels causes the skateboard to change direction.

What Causes Refraction? Like the skateboard that changes direction, changes in speed can cause waves to change direction, as shown in Figure 8. **When a wave enters a new medium at an angle, one side of the wave changes speed before the other side, causing the wave to bend.** The bending of waves due to a change in speed is called **refraction.**

When Does Refraction Occur? A wave does not always bend when it enters a new medium. Bending occurs only when the wave enters the new medium at an angle. Then one side of the wave enters the medium first. This side changes speed, but the other side still travels at its original speed. Bending occurs because the two sides of the wave travel at different speeds.

Even if you don't skateboard, you have probably seen refraction in daily life. Have you ever had trouble grabbing something underwater? Have you ever seen a rainbow? Light can bend when it passes from water into air, making an underwater object appear closer than it really is. When you reach for the object, you miss it. When white light enters water, different colors in the light bend by different amounts. The white light separates into the colors you see in a rainbow.

 **Reading Checkpoint** When does refraction occur?

Lab zone Skills Activity

Observing

You can simulate what happens as waves move from one medium to another.

1. Roll a drinking straw from a smooth tabletop straight onto a thin piece of terry cloth or a paper towel. Describe how the straw's motion changes as it leaves the smooth surface.

2. Repeat Step 1, but roll the straw at an angle to the cloth or paper.

Describe what happens as each side of the straw hits the cloth or paper. How are your results similar to what happens when waves are refracted?

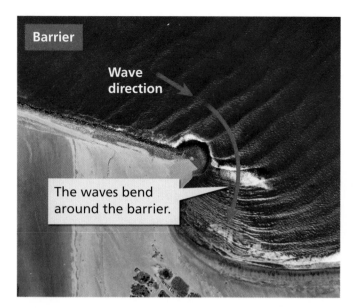

Barrier

Wave direction

The waves bend around the barrier.

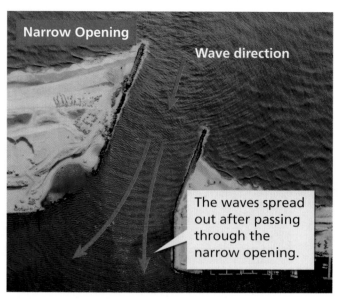

Narrow Opening

Wave direction

The waves spread out after passing through the narrow opening.

FIGURE 9

Diffraction of Water Waves
Waves diffract when they move around a barrier or pass through an opening. As a wave passes a barrier, it bends around the barrier. After a wave goes through a narrow opening, it spreads out.

Diffraction

Sometimes waves bend around a barrier or pass through a hole. **When a wave moves around a barrier or through an opening in a barrier, it bends and spreads out.** These wave interactions are called **diffraction.** Figure 9 shows how waves bend and spread by diffraction.

Interference

Have you ever seen soccer balls collide in a practice drill? The balls bounce off each other because they cannot be in the same place at the same time. Surprisingly, this is not true of waves. Unlike two balls, two waves can overlap when they meet. **Interference** is the interaction between waves that meet. **There are two types of interference: constructive and destructive.**

Constructive Interference The interference that occurs when waves combine to make a wave with a larger amplitude is called **constructive interference.** You can think of constructive interference as waves "helping each other," or adding their energies. When the crests of two waves overlap, they make a higher crest. When the troughs of two waves overlap, they make a deeper trough. In both cases, the amplitude increases.

Figure 10 shows how constructive interference can occur when two waves travel toward each other. When the crests from each wave meet, constructive interference makes a higher crest in the area of overlap. The amplitude of this crest is the sum of the amplitudes of the two original crests. After the waves pass through each other, they continue on as if they had never met.

Reading Checkpoint What is constructive interference?

Destructive Interference The interference that occurs when two waves combine to make a wave with a smaller amplitude is called **destructive interference.** You can think of destructive interference as waves subtracting their energies.

Destructive interference occurs when the crest of one wave overlaps the trough of another wave. If the crest has a larger amplitude than the trough, the crest "wins" and part of it remains. If the original trough had a larger amplitude, the result is a trough. If the original waves had equal amplitudes, then the crest and trough can completely cancel as shown in Figure 10.

Go Online
active art

For: Wave Interference activity
Visit: PHSchool.com
Web Code: cgp-5013

FIGURE 10
Wave Interference

Interference can be constructive or destructive.
Interpreting Diagrams *What does the black dotted line represent in the diagram below?*

Constructive Interference

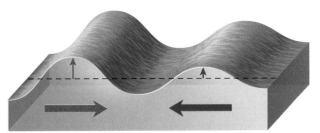

1 Two waves approach each other. The wave on the left has a higher amplitude.

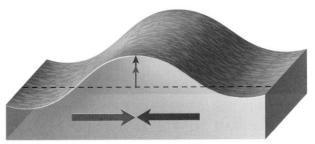

2 The crest's new amplitude is the sum of the amplitudes of the original crests.

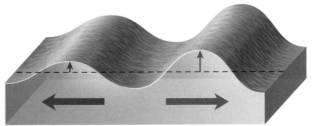

3 The waves continue as if they had not met.

Destructive Interference

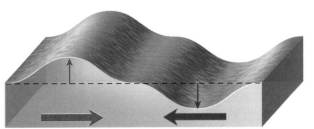

1 Two waves approach each other. The waves have equal amplitudes.

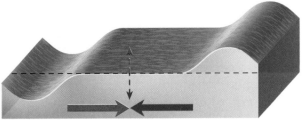

2 A crest meets a trough. In the area of overlap, the waves cancel completely.

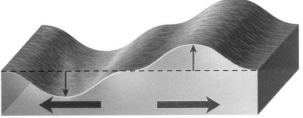

3 The waves continue as if they had not met.

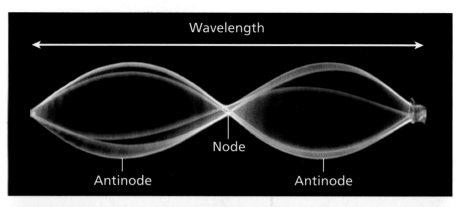

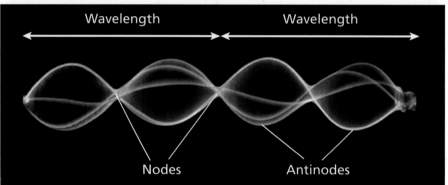

FIGURE 11
Standing Waves
These photos show standing waves in vibrating elastic strings. The photographer used a bright flashing light called a strobe to "stop" the motion.

Lab zone Try This **Activity**

Interfering Waves

1. Place two identical empty bottles near each other. Using a straw, blow gently across the top of one bottle until you hear a sound. Describe the sound.

2. Using two straws, blow across the tops of both bottles at the same time. Describe what you hear.

3. Add a few drops of water to one bottle. Blow across the top of each bottle and note any differences in the sound.

4. Using two straws, blow across the tops of both bottles at the same time.

Observing Describe the sound you heard in Step 4. How did it differ from the sounds you heard in the other steps?

Standing Waves

If you tie a rope to a doorknob and continuously shake the free end, waves will travel down the rope, reflect at the end, and come back. The reflected waves will meet the incoming waves. When the waves meet, interference occurs.

If the incoming wave and a reflected wave have just the right frequency, they produce a combined wave that appears to be standing still. This combined wave is called a standing wave. A **standing wave** is a wave that appears to stand in one place, even though it is really two waves interfering as they pass through each other.

Nodes and Antinodes In a standing wave, destructive interference produces points with an amplitude of zero, as shown in Figure 11. These points of zero amplitude on a standing wave are called **nodes.** The nodes are always evenly spaced along the wave. At points in the standing wave where constructive interference occurs, the amplitude is greater than zero. The points of maximum amplitude on a standing wave are called **antinodes.** These are also the points of maximum energy on the wave. The antinodes always occur halfway between two nodes.

Resonance Have you ever pushed a child on a swing? At first, it is difficult to push the swing. But once you get it going, you need only push gently to keep it going. This is because the swing has a natural frequency. Even small pushes that are in rhythm with the swing's natural frequency produce large increases in the swing's amplitude.

Most objects have at least one natural frequency of vibration. Standing waves occur in an object when it vibrates at a natural frequency. If a nearby object vibrates at the same frequency, it can cause resonance. **Resonance** is an increase in the amplitude of a vibration that occurs when external vibrations match an object's natural frequency.

Resonance can be useful. For example, musical instruments use resonance to produce stronger, clearer sounds. But sometimes resonance can be harmful. Figure 12 shows Mexico City after an earthquake in 1985. Mexico City is built on a layer of clay. The frequency of the earthquake waves matched the natural frequency of the clay layer, so resonance occurred. City buildings 8 to 18 stories high had the same natural frequency. Due to resonance, these buildings had the most damage. Both shorter and taller buildings were left standing because their natural frequencies did not match the natural frequency of the clay layer.

FIGURE 12
Destructive Power of Resonance
In the 1985 earthquake in Mexico City, resonance caused the greatest damage to buildings between 8 and 18 stories tall.
Inferring *Why did taller buildings survive the earthquake?*

 **Reading Checkpoint** How can resonance be useful?

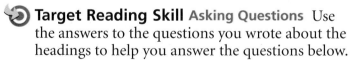

Section 3 Assessment

Target Reading Skill Asking Questions Use the answers to the questions you wrote about the headings to help you answer the questions below.

Reviewing Key Concepts

1. a. Listing What are three ways that waves change direction?
   b. Summarizing How does a wave change direction when it bounces off a surface?
   c. Relating Cause and Effect How does a change in speed cause a wave to change direction?
2. a. Identifying What are two types of interference?
   b. Interpreting Diagrams Look at Figure 10. What determines the amplitude of the wave produced by interference?

c. Predicting Wave A has the same amplitude as wave B. What will happen when a crest of wave A meets a trough of wave B? Explain.
3. a. Defining What is a standing wave?
   b. Explaining How do nodes and antinodes form in a standing wave?

Lab zone **At-Home Activity**

Waves in a Sink With your parent's permission, fill the kitchen sink with water to a depth of about 10 cm. Dip your finger into the water repeatedly to make waves. Demonstrate reflection, diffraction, and interference for your family members.

Making Waves

Problem

How do water waves interact with each other and with solid objects in their paths?

Skills Focus

observing, making models

Materials

- water
- plastic dropper
- metric ruler
- paper towels
- modeling clay
- cork or other small floating object
- ripple tank (aluminum foil lasagna pan with mirror at the bottom)

Procedure

1. Fill the pan with water to a depth of 1.5 cm. Let the water come to rest. Make a data table like the one shown in your text.

2. Fill a plastic dropper with water. Then release a drop of water from a height of about 10 cm above the center of the ripple tank. Observe the reflection of the waves that form and record your observations.

3. Predict how placing a paper towel across one end of the ripple tank will affect the reflection of the waves. Record your prediction in your notebook.

4. Drape a paper towel across one end of the ripple tank so it hangs in the water. Repeat Step 2, and record your observations of the waves.

5. Remove the paper towel and place a stick of modeling clay in the water near the center of the ripple tank.

Data Table		
Type of Barrier	Observations Without Cork	Observations With Cork

6. From a height of about 10 cm, release a drop of water into the ripple tank halfway between the clay and one of the short walls. Record your observations.

7. Place the clay in a different position so that the waves strike it at an angle. Then repeat Step 6.

8. Place two sticks of clay end-to-end across the width of the tank. Adjust the clay so that there is a gap of about 2 cm between the ends of the two pieces. Repeat Step 6. Now change the angle of the barrier in the tank. Again repeat Step 6, and watch to see if the waves interact with the barrier any differently.

9. Cut the two pieces of clay in half. Use the pieces to make a barrier with three 2-cm gaps. Then repeat Step 6.

10. Remove all the clay and add a small floating object, such as a cork, to the water. Then repeat Steps 2–9 with the floating object. Observe and record what happens to the cork in each step.

11. Once you have finished all of the trials, clean and dry your work area.

Analyze and Conclude

1. **Observing** How are the waves affected by the paper towel hanging in the water?

2. **Observing** What happens when the waves strike a barrier head on? When they strike it at an angle?

3. **Observing** What happens when the waves strike a barrier with a gap in it? With three gaps in it?

4. **Making Models** What did the paper towel represent? What did the cork represent?

5. **Applying Concepts** How does the behavior of waves in your model compare to the behavior of waves in a harbor?

6. **Communicating** Evaluate your model. Write a paragraph about the ways your model represents a real situation. Then write a paragraph about your model's limitations.

More to Explore

Predict what would happen if you could send a steady train of uniform waves the length of the ripple tank for an extended time. Use a plastic bottle with a pinhole in the bottom to make a dropper that will help to test your prediction. Get permission from your teacher to try out your dropper device.

Seismic Waves

Reading Preview

Key Concepts
- What are the types of seismic waves?
- How does a seismograph work?

Key Terms
- seismic wave
- P wave
- S wave
- surface wave
- tsunami
- seismograph

Target Reading Skill

Building Vocabulary Using a word in a sentence helps you think about how to best explain the word. As you read, carefully note the definition of each Key Term. Also note other details in the paragraph that contains the definition. Use all this information to write a sentence using the Key Term.

Earthquake damage in Chile in 1960 ▼

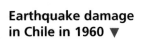

Can You Find the Sand?

1. Fill a plastic film canister with sand and replace the lid.
2. Place the canister on a table with four identical but empty canisters. Mix them around so that a classmate does not know which canister is which.
3. With your fist, pound on the table a few times. Ask your classmate which canister contains the sand.
4. Then stick each canister to the table with some modeling clay. Pound on the table again. Can your classmate tell which canister contains sand?

Think It Over

Inferring Pounding on a table makes waves. Why might the canister with sand respond differently from the empty canisters?

On May 22, 1960, a massive earthquake occurred under the Pacific Ocean about 120 km west of Chile. Traveling underground faster than the speed of sound, earthquake waves hit the coast in less than a minute. Buildings were demolished as the waves shook the ground. But the destruction wasn't finished. The earthquake sent water waves speeding toward the shore at almost 700 km/h. When the waves struck the shore, floods and mudslides killed many people who had survived the first wave of damage. For several more days, earthquakes occurred again and again. All told, thousands of people died and more than 2 million people in Chile were left homeless.

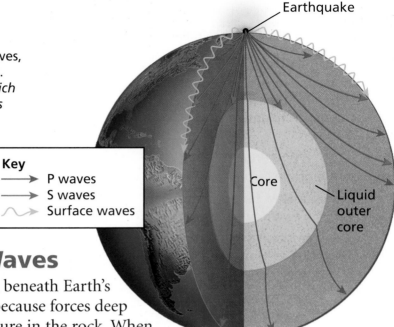

FIGURE 13
Seismic Waves
Seismic waves include P waves,
S waves, and surface waves.
Interpreting Diagrams *Which
kind of seismic wave travels
through Earth's core?*

Key
→ P waves
→ S waves
〰→ Surface waves

Earthquake

Core

Liquid
outer
core

Types of Seismic Waves

An earthquake occurs when rock beneath Earth's
surface moves. This rock moves because forces deep
inside Earth create stress or pressure in the rock. When
the pressure in the rock builds up enough, the rock breaks
or changes shape, releasing energy in the form of waves. The
waves produced by earthquakes are called **seismic waves.** (The
word seismic comes from the Greek word *seismos*, which means
"earthquake.")

Seismic waves ripple out in all directions from the point
where the earthquake occurred. As the waves move, they carry
energy through Earth. The waves can travel from one side of
Earth to the other. **Seismic waves include P waves, S waves,
and surface waves.** Figure 13 shows how each kind of wave
travels through Earth.

P Waves Some seismic waves are longitudinal waves. Longitudinal seismic waves are known as **P waves,** or primary waves.
They are called primary waves because they move faster than
other seismic waves and so arrive at distant points before other
seismic waves. P waves are made up of compressions and rarefactions of rock inside Earth. These waves compress and
expand the ground like a spring toy as they move through it.

S Waves Other seismic waves are transverse waves with
crests and troughs. Transverse seismic waves are known as
S waves, or secondary waves. S waves shake the ground up and
down and side to side as they move through it. They cannot
travel through liquids. Because part of Earth's core is liquid,
S waves do not travel directly through Earth like P waves.
Therefore, S waves cannot be detected on the side of Earth
opposite an earthquake. Scientists on the side of Earth opposite the earthquake detect mainly P waves.

DISCOVERY
CHANNEL
SCHOOL™

*Characteristics
of Waves*

Video Preview
▶ Video Field Trip
Video Assessment

Go Online
SciLINKS
NSTA

For: Links on seismic waves
Visit: www.SciLinks.org
Web Code: scn-1514

Motion of a Tsunami

This graph shows the rate at which a tsunami moves across the Pacific Ocean. Use the data plotted on the graph to answer the following questions.

1. **Reading Graphs** What two variables are plotted on the graph?

2. **Interpreting Data** How far does the tsunami travel in two hours? In four hours?

3. **Predicting** Easter Island is 3,700 kilometers from the earthquake. How many hours would it take the tsunami to reach Easter Island?

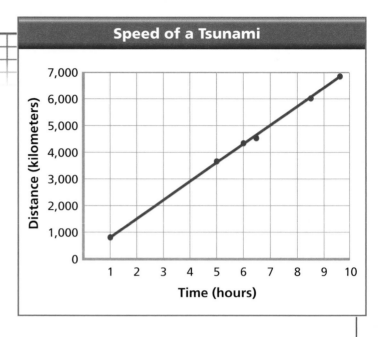

Speed of a Tsunami

FIGURE 14
This map shows the progress of the 2004 tsunami caused by an earthquake near Indonesia.
Classifying What type of wave interference—constructive or destructive—causes tsunamis?

Surface Waves When P waves and S waves reach Earth's surface, they can create surface waves. A **surface wave** is a combination of a longitudinal wave and a transverse wave that travels along the surface of a medium. Surface waves produced by earthquakes move more slowly than P waves and S waves. However, they can cause the most severe ground movements. They combine up-and-down and side-to-side motions, making the ground roll like ocean waves.

Earthquakes that occur underwater, like the one off the coast of Sumatra, Indonesia, in 2004, can produce huge surface waves on the ocean called **tsunamis** (tsoo NAH meez). Tsunamis come in all sizes, from 2 centimeters to 30 meters tall. They can travel thousands of kilometers across the ocean. In the deep ocean, the larger waves are only about 1 meter high. But as they near land, tsunamis slow down in the shallow water. The waves in the back catch up with those in the front and pile on top. Tsunamis caused by the 2004 earthquake near Sumatra traveled as far as 7,000 km across the Indian Ocean to Somalia. Tragically, the tsunamis killed more than 230,000 people worldwide and caused more than $100 billion in home and property damage.

 **Reading Checkpoint** How are tsunamis produced?

Tsunami Surface Waves

India

Africa

Somalia

Sumatra

Tsunami reaches Somalia almost 7 hours after the earthquake occurs.

Underwater earthquake occurs off the coast of Sumatra in 2004.

Detecting Seismic Waves

To detect and measure earthquake waves, scientists use instruments called **seismographs** (SYZ muh grafs). **A seismograph records the ground movements caused by seismic waves as they move through Earth.**

The frame of the seismograph is attached to the ground, so the frame shakes when seismic waves arrive. Seismographs used to have pens attached to the frame that made wiggly lines on a roll of paper as the ground shook. Now scientists use electronic seismographs to record data about Earth's motion.

Because P waves travel through Earth faster than S waves, P waves arrive at seismographs before S waves. By measuring the time between the arrival of the P waves and the arrival of the S waves, scientists can tell how far away the earthquake was. By comparing readings from at least three seismographs located at different places on Earth, scientists can tell where the earthquake occurred.

To find oil, water, and other valuable resources, geologists set off explosives at Earth's surface. Seismic waves from the explosions reflect from structures under the ground. Geologists then use seismograph data to locate the underground resources.

FIGURE 15
Seismologist Studying Data
A scientist studies the arrival time of seismic waves on the printout from a seismograph.

Section 4 Assessment

Target Reading Skill Building Vocabulary Use your sentences about seismic waves to help you answer the questions below.

Reviewing Key Concepts

1. a. **Identifying** What are three types of seismic waves?
   b. **Classifying** Which seismic waves are transverse waves? Which are longitudinal waves?
   c. **Comparing and Contrasting** Why do seismic waves that travel along Earth's surface cause more damage than other seismic waves?
2. a. **Defining** What is a seismograph?
   b. **Explaining** How does a seismograph work?

c. **Interpreting Data** S waves arrive in Los Angeles 3 minutes after P waves. In Dallas, S waves arrive 1 minute after P waves. Which city is closer to the earthquake? Explain your answer.

Lab zone At-Home **Activity**

Sounds Solid Explore how waves travel through different solids. Have a family member or friend tap one end of a table with a spoon. Now put your ear to the table and listen again. What difference do you notice? Repeat the tapping on various surfaces around your home. What observations have you made?

1 What Are Waves?

Key Concepts

- Mechanical waves are produced when a source of energy causes a medium to vibrate.
- Mechanical waves are classified by how they move. There are two types of mechanical waves: transverse waves and longitudinal waves.

Key Terms

wave
energy
medium
mechanical wave
vibration
transverse wave
crest
trough
longitudinal wave
compression
rarefaction

2 Properties of Waves

Key Concepts

- The basic properties of waves are amplitude, wavelength, frequency, and speed.
- The speed, wavelength, and frequency of a wave are related to one another by a mathematical formula:

$$\text{Speed} = \text{Wavelength} \times \text{Frequency}$$

Key Terms

amplitude
wavelength
frequency
hertz (Hz)

3 Interactions of Waves

Key Concepts

- When an object or a wave hits a surface through which it cannot pass, it bounces back.
- When a wave enters a new medium at an angle, one side of the wave changes speed before the other side, causing the wave to bend.
- When a wave moves around a barrier or through an opening in a barrier, it bends and spreads out.
- There are two types of interference: constructive and destructive.
- If the incoming wave and a reflected wave have just the right frequency, they produce a combined wave that appears to be standing still.

Key Terms

reflection
law of reflection
refraction
diffraction
interference
constructive interference
destructive interference
standing wave
node
antinode
resonance

4 Seismic Waves

Key Concepts

- Seismic waves include P waves, S waves, and surface waves.
- A seismograph records the ground movements caused by seismic waves as they move through Earth.

Key Terms

seismic wave
P wave
S wave
surface wave
tsunami
seismograph

Review and Assessment

Organizing Information

Concept Mapping Copy the concept map about waves onto a sheet of paper. Then complete it and add a title. (For more on Concept Mapping, see the Skills Handbook.)

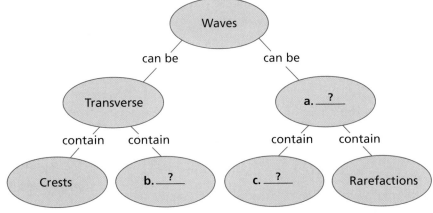

Reviewing Key Terms

Choose the letter of the best answer.

1. A wave transfers
   a. energy.
   b. particles.
   c. water.
   d. air.

2. A wave that moves the medium in the same direction that the wave travels is a
   a. transverse wave.
   b. longitudinal wave.
   c. standing wave.
   d. mechanical wave.

3. The distance between one crest and the next crest is the wave's
   a. amplitude.
   b. wavelength.
   c. frequency.
   d. speed.

4. The number of complete waves that pass a point in a certain amount of time is a wave's
   a. amplitude.
   b. frequency.
   c. wavelength.
   d. speed.

5. The bending of a wave due to a change in its speed is
   a. interference.
   b. reflection.
   c. diffraction.
   d. refraction.

6. The interaction between waves that meet is
   a. reflection.
   b. diffraction.
   c. refraction.
   d. interference.

7. A point of zero amplitude on a standing wave is called a
   a. crest.
   b. node.
   c. trough.
   d. antinode.

8. Seismic waves that do not travel through liquids are
   a. P waves.
   b. surface waves.
   c. S waves.
   d. tsunamis.

Writing in Science

Research Report Write an article for a boating magazine about tsunamis. Include details about what causes them and why they are dangerous. Explain what is being done to help reduce damage from tsunamis.

Discovery CHANNEL SCHOOL

Characteristics of Waves

Video Preview
Video Field Trip
▶ Video Assessment

Review and Assessment

Checking Concepts

9. Explain the difference between transverse and longitudinal waves. Use diagrams to illustrate your explanation.

10. How can you measure the amplitude of a transverse wave?

11. Describe how to measure the speed of a wave.

12. What is the angle of incidence if a reflected wave bounces off a mirror with an angle of reflection equal to 55°?

13. Describe the two types of diffraction.

14. Explain why S waves cannot be detected everywhere on Earth after an earthquake.

Math Practice

15. **Angles** Label a 90° angle on a transverse wave.

16. **Calculating Speed** A wave in a spring has a wavelength of 0.1 m and a frequency of 20 Hz. What is the wave's speed?

17. **Calculating Wavelength** A sound wave has a frequency of 660 Hz and its speed is 330 m/s. What is its wavelength?

Thinking Critically

18. **Applying Concepts** Suppose ripples move from one side of a lake to the other. Does the water move across the lake? Explain.

19. **Comparing and Contrasting** The waves shown below travel at the same speed.
    a. Which wave has the higher frequency?
    b. Which has the longer wavelength?
    c. Which has the greater amplitude?

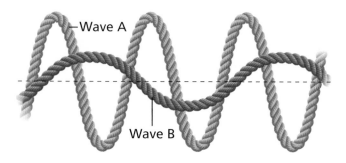

20. **Predicting** One wave has an amplitude of 2 m, and a second wave has an amplitude of 1 m. At a given time, crests from each wave meet. Draw a diagram and describe the result.

21. **Making Models** If you push a shopping cart that has a stiff or damaged wheel, it is difficult to steer the cart in a straight line. Explain how this is similar to refraction of a wave as it enters a new medium.

Applying Skills

Use the illustration below to answer Questions 22–25.

The wave in the illustration is a giant ocean wave produced by an underwater earthquake.

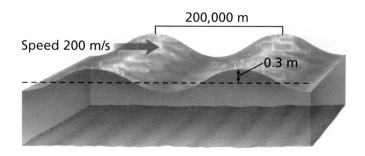

22. **Classifying** What kind of wave is shown in the diagram?

23. **Interpreting Diagrams** What is the amplitude of the wave? What is its speed?

24. **Calculating** Find the frequency of the wave.

25. **Calculating** How long would it take this wave to travel 5,000 km?

Lab zone Chapter **Project**

Performance Assessment Share your examples of periodic motion with your classmates. On your display, highlight the repeating patterns and the frequency of each example. Point out interesting connections. For example, track-and-field practice involves repetitions, as do other sports. Which examples involve waves moving through a medium?

Standardized Test Prep

Choose the letter of the best answer.

1. The speed of a wave in a spring is 3 m/s. If the wavelength is 0.1 m, what is the frequency?
  A 30 Hz
  B 0.3 Hz
  C 30 m/s
  D 0.3 m/s

2. A wave enters a new medium. The wave
  F slows down and bends.
  G speeds up and bends.
  H may slow down or speed up.
  J must always bend.

3. During a storm, a TV reporter says that the ocean waves are 3 meters high. This reported distance equals the distance
  A from one crest to the next crest.
  B from one trough to the next trough.
  C from a crest to a trough.
  D from a crest to the level of calm water.

4. Two waves move in opposite directions as shown in the diagram below. What will be the height of the crest produced when the crests from each wave meet?
  F 20 cm
  G 35 cm
  H 15 cm
  J 5 cm

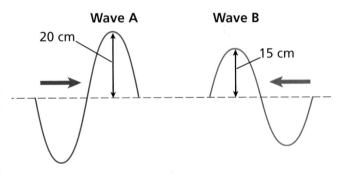

5. In an experiment, you and a friend stand at opposite ends of a football field. Your friend pops an inflated balloon while you observe. Which of the following is a testable hypothesis?
  A If sound travels much faster than light, you will hear the balloon pop before you see it pop.
  B If light travels much faster than sound, you will see the balloon pop before you hear it.
  C If sound and light travel at the same speed, you will see and hear the balloon pop at the same time.
  D all of the above

Constructed Response

6. A large rock is tossed into a pond to produce a water wave. Explain how you know that the wave transfers energy but not matter across the pond.

Chapter

2

Sound

interactive Textbook

In a recording studio, a microphone picks ▶ up sound waves from the singers.

Chapter **Project**

Music to Your Ears

In this chapter you will investigate the properties of sound. You will learn how sound is produced by different objects, including musical instruments. As you work through the chapter, you will gather enough knowledge to create a musical instrument of your own.

Your Goal To design, build, and play a simple musical instrument

Your musical instrument must

- be made of materials that are approved by your teacher
- be able to play a simple tune or rhythm
- be built and used following the safety guidelines in Appendix A

Plan It! Begin by discussing different kinds of instruments with your classmates. What instruments are common in your favorite type of music? Which type of instrument would you like to build? Make a list of materials you could use to build your instrument. Then, design and sketch your instrument. After your teacher approves your design, build your instrument and test it by playing a simple tune.

The Nature of Sound

Reading Preview

Key Concepts
- What is sound?
- How do sound waves interact?
- What factors affect the speed of sound?

Key Terms
- echo
- elasticity
- density

Target Reading Skill
Identifying Main Ideas As you read the Interactions of Sound Waves section, write the main idea—the biggest or most important idea—in a graphic organizer like the one below. Then write three supporting details that further explain the main idea.

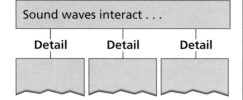

Main Idea

Sound waves interact . . .

Detail	Detail	Detail

Discover **Activity**

What Is Sound?
1. Fill a bowl with water.
2. Tap a tuning fork against the sole of your shoe. Place the tip of one of the prongs in the water. What do you see?
3. Tap the tuning fork again. Predict what will happen when you hold it near your ear. What do you hear?

Think It Over
Observing How are your observations related to the sound you hear? What might change if you use a different tuning fork?

Here is an old riddle: If a tree falls in a forest and no one hears it, does the tree make a sound? To answer the riddle, you must decide what the word "sound" means. If sound is something that a person must hear, then the tree makes no sound. If sound can happen whether a person hears it or not, then the tree makes a sound.

Sound Waves

To a scientist, a falling tree makes a sound whether someone hears it or not. When a tree crashes down, the energy with which it strikes the ground causes a disturbance. Particles in the ground and the air begin to vibrate, or move back and forth. The vibrations create a sound wave as the energy travels through the two mediums. **Sound is a disturbance that travels through a medium as a longitudinal wave.**

A falling tree ▶

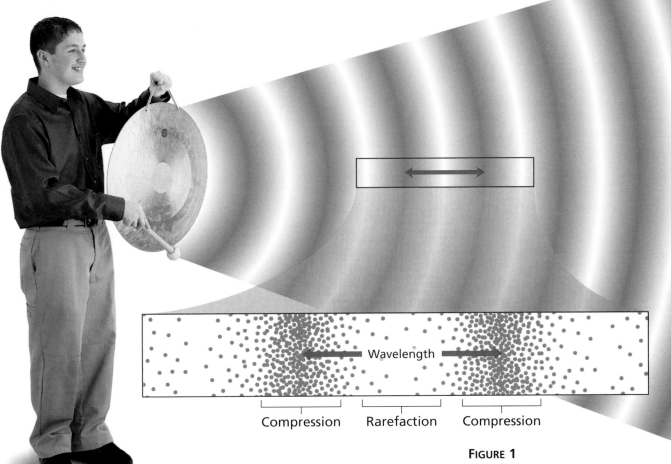

Wavelength

Compression   Rarefaction   Compression

FIGURE 1
Sound Waves
As a gong vibrates, it creates sound waves that travel through the air. **Observing** *What do you observe about the spacing of particles in a compression?*

Making Sound Waves A sound wave begins with a vibration. Look at the metal gong shown in Figure 1. When the gong is struck, it vibrates rapidly. The vibrations disturb nearby air particles. Each time the gong moves to the right, it pushes air particles together, creating a compression. When the gong moves to the left, the air particles bounce back and spread out, creating a rarefaction. These compressions and rarefactions travel through the air as longitudinal waves.

How Sound Travels Like other mechanical waves, sound waves carry energy through a medium without moving the particles of the medium along. Each particle of the medium vibrates as the disturbance passes. When the disturbance reaches your ears, you hear the sound.

A common medium for sound is air. But sound can travel through solids and liquids, too. For example, when you knock on a solid wood door, the particles in the wood vibrate. The vibrations make sound waves that travel through the door. When the waves reach the other side of the door, they make sound waves in the air on the far side.

 **Reading Checkpoint** **What are three types of mediums that sound can travel through?**

For: Links on sound
Visit: www.SciLinks.org
Web Code: scn-1521

FIGURE 2
Reflection of Sound
Clapping your hands in a gym produces an echo when sound waves reflect off the wall.
Drawing Conclusions *What kind of material is the wall made of?*

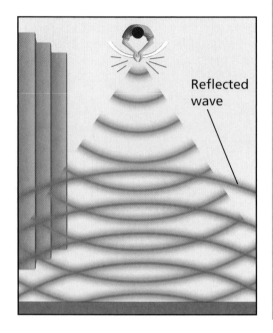

Reflected wave

Interactions of Sound Waves

Sound waves interact with the surfaces they contact and with each other. **Sound waves reflect off objects, diffract through narrow openings and around barriers, and interfere with each other.**

Reflection Sound waves may reflect when they hit a surface. A reflected sound wave is called an **echo.** In general, the harder and smoother the surface, the stronger the reflection. Look at Figure 2. When you clap your hands in a gym, you hear an echo because the hard surfaces—wood, brick, and metal—reflect sound directly back at you. But you don't always hear an echo in a room. In many rooms, there are soft materials that absorb most of the sound that strikes them.

Diffraction Have you ever wondered why you can hear your friends talking in a classroom before you walk through the doorway? You hear them because sound waves do not always travel in a straight line. Figure 3 shows how sound waves can diffract through openings such as doorways.

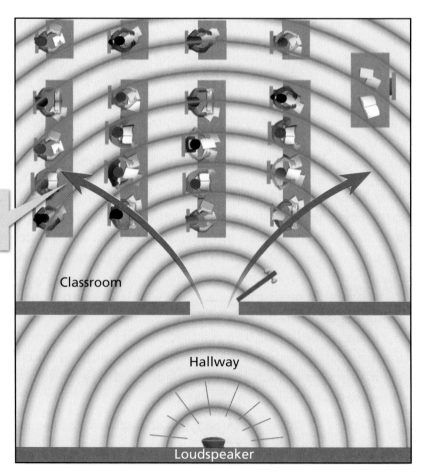

Sound waves spread out after passing through a doorway.

Classroom

Hallway

Loudspeaker

FIGURE 3
Diffraction of Sound
Sound waves can spread out after passing through a doorway, and can bend around a corner.

Sound waves can also diffract, or bend, around corners. This is why you can hear someone who is talking in the hallway before you come around the corner. The person's sound waves bend around the corner. Then they spread out so you can hear them even though you cannot see who is talking. Remember this the next time you want to tell a secret!

Interference Sound waves may meet and interact with each other. You may recall that this interaction is called interference. The interference that occurs when sound waves meet can be constructive or destructive. In Section 3, you will learn how interference affects the sound of musical instruments.

✓ Reading Checkpoint What are two ways that sound waves diffract?

The Speed of Sound

Have you ever wondered why the different sounds from musicians and singers at a concert all reach your ears at the same time? It happens because the sounds travel through air at the same speed. At room temperature, about 20°C, sound travels through air at about 343 m/s. This speed is much faster than most jet planes travel through the air!

The speed of sound is not always 343 m/s. Sound waves travel at different speeds in different mediums. Figure 4 shows the speed of sound in different mediums. **The speed of sound depends on the elasticity, density, and temperature of the medium the sound travels through.**

Speed of Sound	
Medium	**Speed (m/s)**
Gases	
Air (0°C)	331
Air (20°C)	343
Liquids (30°C)	
Fresh water	1,509
Salt water	1,546
Solids (25°C)	
Lead	1,210
Cast iron	4,480
Aluminum	5,000
Glass	5,170

FIGURE 4
The speed of sound depends on the medium it travels through.

Math Analyzing Data

Temperature and the Speed of Sound

The speed of sound in dry air changes as the temperature changes. The graph shows data for the speed of sound in air at temperatures from −20°C to 30°C.

1. **Reading Graphs** What is the speed of sound in air at −10°C?

2. **Interpreting Data** Does the speed of sound increase or decrease as temperature increases?

3. **Predicting** What might be the speed of sound at 30°C?

Speed of Sound in Dry Air

FIGURE 5

Modeling Elasticity
You can model elasticity by representing the particles in a medium as being held together by springs.

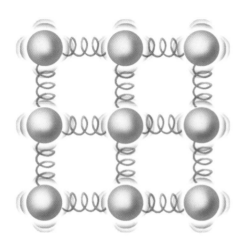

Elasticity If you stretch a rubber band and then let it go, it returns to its original shape. However, when you stretch modeling clay and then let it go, it stays stretched. Rubber bands are more elastic than modeling clay. **Elasticity** is the ability of a material to bounce back after being disturbed.

The elasticity of a medium depends on how well the medium's particles bounce back after being disturbed. To understand this idea, look at Figure 5. In this model, the particles of a medium are linked by springs. If one particle is disturbed, it is pulled back to its original position. In an elastic medium, such as a rubber band, the particles bounce back quickly. But in a less elastic medium, the particles bounce back slowly.

The more elastic a medium, the faster sound travels in it. Sounds can travel well in solids, which are usually more elastic than liquids or gases. The particles of a solid do not move very far, so they bounce back and forth quickly as the compressions and rarefactions of the sound waves pass by. Most liquids are not very elastic. Sound does not travel as well in liquids as it does in solids. Gases generally are not very elastic. Sound travels slowly in gases.

Density The speed of sound also depends on the density of a medium. **Density** is how much matter, or mass, there is in a given amount of space, or volume. The denser the medium, the more mass it has in a given volume. Figure 6 shows two cubes that have the same volume. The brass cube is denser because it has more mass in a given volume.

In materials in the same state of matter—solid, liquid, or gas—sound travels more slowly in denser mediums. The particles of a dense material do not move as quickly as those of a less dense material. Sound travels more slowly in dense metals, such as lead or silver, than in iron or steel.

FIGURE 6

Comparing Density
The volumes of these cubes are the same, but the brass cube has more mass.
Interpreting Photographs *Which cube has a greater density: brass or aluminum?*

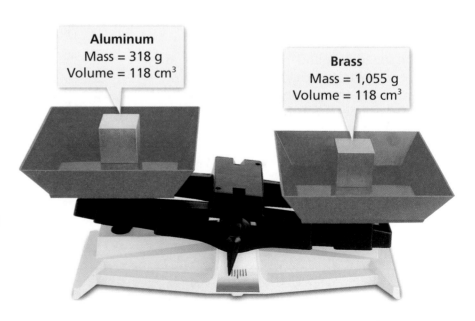

Aluminum
Mass = 318 g
Volume = 118 cm³

Brass
Mass = 1,055 g
Volume = 118 cm³

Temperature In a given medium, sound travels more slowly at lower temperatures than at higher temperatures. Why? At a low temperature, the particles of a medium move more slowly than at a high temperature. So, they are more difficult to move, and return to their original positions more slowly. For example, at 20°C, the speed of sound in air is about 343 m/s. But at 0°C, the speed of sound is about 330 m/s.

At higher altitudes, the air is colder than at lower altitudes, so sound travels more slowly at higher altitudes. On October 14, 1947, Captain Charles E. "Chuck" Yeager of the United States Air Force used this knowledge to fly faster than the speed of sound.

To fly faster than the speed of sound, Captain Yeager flew his plane to an altitude of more than 12,000 meters. Here, the air temperature was −59°C. The speed of sound at this temperature is only about 293 m/s. At 12,000 meters, Captain Yeager accelerated his plane to a record-breaking 312 m/s. By doing this, he became the first person to "break the sound barrier."

FIGURE 7
Breaking the Sound Barrier
On October 14, 1947, Captain Chuck Yeager became the first person to fly a plane faster than the speed of sound.

 **Reading Checkpoint** How does temperature affect the speed of sound?

Section 1 Assessment

Target Reading Skill Identifying Main Ideas Use your graphic organizer to help you answer Question 2 below.

Reviewing Key Concepts

1. **a. Reviewing** What is sound?
   b. Explaining How is a sound wave produced?
   c. Sequencing Explain how a ringing telephone can be heard through a closed door.
2. **a. Listing** What are three ways that sound waves can interact?
   b. Applying Concepts Explain why you can hear a teacher through the closed door of a classroom.
   c. Inferring At a scenic overlook, you can hear an echo only if you shout in one particular direction. Explain why.

3. **a. Identifying** What property describes how a material bounces back after being disturbed?
   b. Summarizing What three properties of a medium affect the speed of sound?
   c. Developing Hypotheses Steel is denser than plastic, yet sound travels faster in steel than in plastic. Develop a hypothesis to explain why.

Lab zone At-Home **Activity**

Ear to the Sound Find a long metal fence or water pipe. **CAUTION:** *Beware of sharp edges and rust.* Put one ear to one end of the pipe while a family member taps on the other end. In which ear do you hear the sound first? Explain your answer to your family members. What accounts for the difference?

Properties of Sound

Reading Preview

Key Concepts
- What factors affect the loudness of a sound?
- What does the pitch of a sound depend on?
- What causes the Doppler effect?

Key Terms
- loudness • intensity
- decibel (dB) • pitch
- ultrasound • infrasound
- larynx • Doppler effect

🎯 Target Reading Skill

Outlining An outline shows the relationship between main ideas and supporting ideas. As you read, make an outline about the properties of sound. Use the red headings for the main ideas and the blue headings for the supporting ideas.

Properties of Sound
I. Loudness
A. Energy of a sound source
B.
C.
II. Pitch
A.

Lab zone Discover Activity

How Does Amplitude Affect Loudness?

1. Your teacher will give you a wooden board with two nails in it. Attach a guitar string to the nails by wrapping each end tightly around a nail and tying a knot.

2. Hold the string near the middle. Pull it about 1 cm to one side. This distance is the amplitude of vibration. Let it go. How far does the string move to the other side? Describe the sound you hear.

3. Repeat Step 2 four more times. Each time, pull the string back a greater distance. Describe how the sound changes each time.

Think It Over

Forming Operational Definitions How would you define the amplitude of the vibration? What effect did changing the amplitude have on the sound?

Suppose that you and a friend are talking on a sidewalk and a noisy truck pulls up next to you and stops, leaving its motor running. What would you do? You might talk louder, almost shout, so your friend can hear you. You might lean closer and speak into your friend's ear so you don't have to raise your voice. Or you might walk away from the noisy truck so it's not as loud.

Loudness

Loudness is an important property of sound. **Loudness** describes your perception of the energy of a sound. In other words, loudness describes what you hear. You probably already know a lot about loudness. For example, you know that your voice is much louder when you shout than when you speak softly. The closer you are to a sound, the louder it is. Also, a whisper in your ear can be just as loud as a shout from a block away. **The loudness of a sound depends on two factors: the amount of energy it takes to make the sound and the distance from the source of the sound.**

Energy of a Sound Source In general, the greater the energy used to make a sound, the louder the sound. If you did the Discover activity, you may have noticed this. The more energy you used to pull the guitar string back, the louder the sound when you let the string go. This happened because the more energy you used to pull the string, the greater the amplitude of the string's vibration. A string vibrating with a large amplitude produces a sound wave with a large amplitude. Recall that the greater the amplitude of a wave, the more energy the wave has. So, the larger the amplitude of the sound wave, the more energy it has and the louder it sounds.

Distance From a Sound Source If your friend is speaking in a normal voice and you lean in closer, your friend's voice sounds louder. Loudness increases the closer you are to a sound source. But why?

Imagine ripples spreading out in circles after you toss a pebble into a pond. In a similar way, a sound wave spreads out from its source. Close to the sound source, the sound wave covers a small area, as you can see in Figure 8. As the wave travels away from its source, it covers more area. The total energy of the wave, however, stays the same whether it is close to the source or far from it. Therefore, the closer the sound wave is to its source, the more energy it has in a given area. The amount of energy a sound wave carries per second through a unit area is its **intensity.** A sound wave of greater intensity sounds louder. As you move away from a sound source, loudness decreases because the intensity decreases.

Go Online
PHSchool.com

For: More on the properties of sound
Visit: PHSchool.com
Web Code: cgd-5022

FIGURE 8
Intensity and Distance
Because sound waves spread out, intensity decreases with distance from the source.
Interpreting Diagrams How does the intensity at 3 meters compare to the intensity at 2 meters?

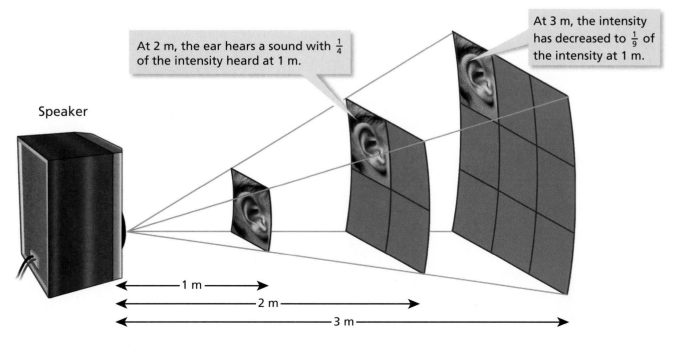

At 2 m, the ear hears a sound with $\frac{1}{4}$ of the intensity heard at 1 m.

At 3 m, the intensity has decreased to $\frac{1}{9}$ of the intensity at 1 m.

Speaker

1 m

2 m

3 m

Measuring Loudness

Sound	Loudness (dB)
Rustling leaves	10
Whisper	15–20
Very soft music	20–30
Normal conversation	40–50
Heavy street traffic	60–70
Loud music	90–100
Rock concert	110–120
Jackhammer	120
Jet plane at takeoff	120–160

FIGURE 9
Some sounds are so soft that you can barely hear them. Others are so loud that they can damage your ears. **Interpreting Data** *Which sounds louder, a rock concert or a jet plane at takeoff?*

Measuring Loudness The loudness of different sounds is compared using a unit called the **decibel (dB).** Figure 9 shows the loudness of some familiar sounds. The loudness of a sound you can barely hear is about 0 dB. Each 10-dB increase in loudness represents a tenfold increase in the intensity of the sound. For example, soft music at 30 dB sounds ten times louder than a 20-dB whisper. The 30-dB music is 100 times louder than the 10-dB sound of rustling leaves. Sounds louder than 100 dB can cause damage to your ears, especially if you listen to those sounds for long periods of time.

 **Reading Checkpoint** What is a decibel?

Pitch

Pitch is another property of sound you may already know a lot about. Have you ever described someone's voice as "high-pitched" or "low-pitched?" The **pitch** of a sound is a description of how high or low the sound seems to a person. **The pitch of a sound that you hear depends on the frequency of the sound wave.**

Pitch and Frequency Sound waves with a high frequency have a high pitch. Sound waves with a low frequency have a low pitch. Frequency is measured in hertz (Hz). For example, a frequency of 50 Hz means 50 vibrations per second. Look at Figure 10. A bass singer can produce frequencies lower than 80 Hz. A trained soprano voice can produce frequencies higher than 1,000 Hz.

FIGURE 10
Pitch Depends on Frequency
The bass singer below sings low notes, and the soprano singer on the right sings high notes.

Frequency of high note

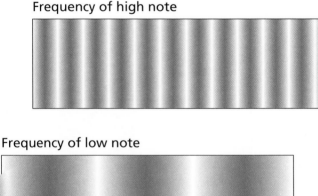

Frequency of low note

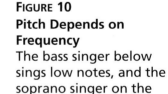

44 ◆ O

Most people can hear sounds with frequencies between 20 Hz and 20,000 Hz. Sound waves with frequencies above the normal human range of hearing are called **ultrasound.** The prefix *ultra-* means "beyond." Sounds with frequencies below the human range of hearing are called **infrasound.** The prefix *infra-* means "below." People cannot hear either ultrasound waves or infrasound waves.

Changing Pitch Pitch is an important property of music because music usually uses specific pitches called notes. To sing or play a musical instrument, you must change pitch often.

When you sing, you change pitch using your vocal cords. Your vocal cords are located in your voice box, or **larynx,** as shown in Figure 11. When you speak or sing, air from your lungs is forced up the trachea, or windpipe. Air then rushes past your vocal cords, making them vibrate. This produces sound waves. Your vocal cords are able to vibrate more than 1,000 times per second!

To sing different notes, you use muscles in your throat to stretch and relax your vocal cords. When your vocal cords stretch, they vibrate more quickly as the air rushes by them. This creates higher-frequency sound waves that have higher pitches. When your vocal cords relax, lower-frequency sound waves with lower pitches are produced.

With musical instruments, you change pitch in different ways depending on the instrument. For example, you can change the pitch of a guitar string by turning a knob to loosen or tighten the string. A tighter guitar string produces a higher frequency, which you hear as a note with higher pitch.

Reading Checkpoint Where are your vocal cords located?

Lab zone Skills Activity

Predicting

1. Flatten one end of a drinking straw and cut the end to form a point.
2. Blow through the straw. Describe what you hear.
3. Predict what changes you would hear if you shortened the straw by cutting off some of the straight end. Test your prediction by making two new straws of different lengths.

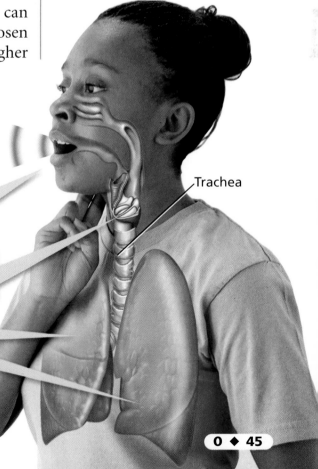

FIGURE 11
The Human Voice
When a person speaks or sings, the vocal cords vibrate. The vibrations produce sound waves in the air.

Sound Sound waves produced by the vibrating vocal cords come out through the mouth.

Vocal Cords The vocal cords inside the larynx vibrate as air rushes past them.

Lungs Air from the lungs rushes up the trachea.

Trachea

The Doppler Effect

If you listen carefully to the siren of a firetruck on its way to a fire, you will notice something surprising. As the truck goes by you, the pitch of the siren drops. But the pitch of the siren stays constant for the firefighters in the truck. The siren's pitch changes only if it is moving toward or away from a listener.

The change in frequency of a wave as its source moves in relation to an observer is called the **Doppler effect.** If the waves are sound waves, the change in frequency is heard as a change in pitch. The Doppler effect is named after the Austrian scientist Christian Doppler (1803–1853).

What Causes the Doppler Effect? Figure 12 shows how sound waves from a moving source behave. When the source moves toward a listener, the frequency of the waves is higher than it would be if the source were stationary. **When a sound source moves, the frequency of the waves changes because the motion of the source adds to the motion of the waves.**

To understand why the frequency changes, imagine that you are standing still and throwing tennis balls at a wall in front of you. If you throw one ball each second the balls hit the wall at a rate of one per second. Now suppose you walk toward the wall while still throwing one ball per second. Because each ball has a shorter distance to travel than the one before, each takes less time to get there. The balls hit the wall more often than one per second, so the frequency is higher. On the other hand, if you throw balls at the wall as you back away, each ball has farther to travel and the frequency is lower.

FIGURE 12

The Doppler Effect
As the firetruck speeds by, the observers hear a change in the pitch of the siren.
Applying Concepts *How could you describe the pitch heard by the firefighter?*

People behind the firetruck hear a lower pitch than the firefighters in the truck hear.

People standing in front of the firetruck hear a higher pitch than the firefighters in the truck hear.

FIRE DEPARTMENT

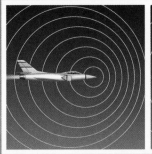

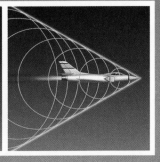

1 Slower than the speed of sound

2 Aproaching the speed of sound

3 Faster than the speed of sound

What Causes Shock Waves? At high speed, the Doppler effect can be spectacular. Look at Figure 13. When the plane travels almost as fast as the speed of sound, the sound waves pile up in front of the plane. This pile-up is the "sound barrier." As the plane flies faster than the speed of sound, it moves through the barrier. A shock wave forms as the sound waves overlap. The shock wave releases a huge amount of energy. People nearby hear a loud noise called a sonic boom when the shock wave passes by them.

FIGURE 13
Breaking the Sound Barrier
When a plane goes faster than the speed of sound, a shock wave is produced. The photo on the right shows how sudden changes in pressure at this speed can cause a small cloud to form.

 **Reading Checkpoint** What is a shock wave?

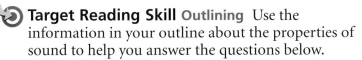

Section 2 Assessment

Target Reading Skill **Outlining** Use the information in your outline about the properties of sound to help you answer the questions below.

Reviewing Key Concepts

1. **a. Identifying** What two factors affect the loudness of a sound?
   b. Applying Concepts Why does moving away from a radio affect the loudness you hear?
   c. Calculating A band plays music at 60 dB and then changes to a rock song at 80 dB. How many times louder is the rock song?
2. **a. Reviewing** What determines the pitch of a sound?
   b. Comparing and Contrasting How are high-pitch sounds different from low-pitch sounds?
   c. Explaining How do your vocal cords produce different pitches?

3. **a. Summarizing** What is the Doppler effect?
   b. Relating Cause and Effect What causes the Doppler effect?
   c. Predicting Would you hear a change in pitch if you are on a moving train and the train's whistle blows? Explain.

Lab zone **At-Home Activity**

Hum Stopper When listening to a cat's heart, a veterinarian will cover the cat's nostrils to keep the cat from purring. At home, ask family members to hum with their lips closed. Then ask them to cover both of their nostrils while humming. Use Figure 11 to explain what happened.

Music

Reading Preview

Key Concepts
- What determines the sound quality of a musical instrument?
- What are the basic groups of musical instruments?
- How is acoustics used in concert hall design?

Key Terms
- music • fundamental tone
- overtone • acoustics
- reverberation

 Target Reading Skill

Previewing Visuals When you preview, you look ahead at the material to be read. Preview Figure 15. Then write two questions that you have about the diagrams in a graphic organizer like the one below. As you read, answer your questions.

Musical Instruments

Q.	How is pitch changed in each type of instrument?
A.	
Q.	

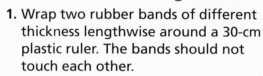 **Discover Activity**

How Can You Change Pitch?
1. Wrap two rubber bands of different thickness lengthwise around a 30-cm plastic ruler. The bands should not touch each other.
2. Place a pencil under the bands at the 10-cm mark.
3. Pluck each band. How are the sounds different?
4. Move the pencil to the 15-cm mark and repeat Step 3.

Think It Over
Drawing Conclusions Why are the sounds you made in Step 4 different from the sounds in Step 3?

You are late. When you arrive at your orchestra rehearsal, your friends are already tuning up. With all the instruments playing different notes, it sounds like noise! You quickly pull out your instrument and take your seat. Then the music starts, and everything changes. What makes noise and music different? The answer is in the way sound waves combine.

◄ Orchestra rehearsal

Sound Quality

Most people agree on what is or is not music. **Music** is a set of notes that combine in patterns that are pleasing. Noise, on the other hand, has no pleasing patterns. When you describe a sound as pleasant or unpleasant, you are describing sound quality. The sound quality of music depends on the instruments making the music. **The sound quality of musical instruments results from blending a fundamental tone with its overtones. Resonance also plays a role in the sound quality.**

Fundamental Tones and Overtones You may recall that standing waves occur when waves with just the right frequency interfere as they reflect back and forth. Standing waves occur in musical instruments when they are played. In a guitar, for example, standing waves occur in a vibrating string. In a trumpet, standing waves occur in a column of vibrating air.

A standing wave can occur only at specific frequencies that are called natural frequencies. Every object has its own natural frequencies. The lowest natural frequency of an object is called the **fundamental tone.** The object's higher natural frequencies are called **overtones.** Overtones have frequencies that are two, three, or more times the frequency of the fundamental tone. Look at Figure 14 to see how the natural frequencies of a guitar string add together to produce a unique sound.

The fundamental tone determines what note you hear. For example, when a guitar and a trumpet play middle C, they both produce waves with a frequency of 262 Hz. But each instrument produces different overtones, so the blending of the fundamental tones and overtones produces different sound qualities.

Resonance Resonance affects the sound quality of a musical instrument by increasing the loudness of certain overtones. Recall that resonance occurs when one object causes a nearby object to vibrate at a natural frequency. A musical instrument is designed so that a part of it will resonate with the overtones it produces. In a guitar, for example, the vibrating strings cause the guitar's hollow body to resonate. The shape and material of the guitar determine which overtones are loudest.

 **Reading Checkpoint** What are overtones?

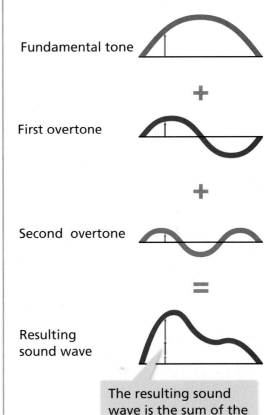

FIGURE 14
Sound Quality
A guitar string can resonate at several frequencies that combine to produce a unique sound quality.
Interpreting Diagrams *What determines the resulting wave?*

Fundamental tone

+

First overtone

+

Second overtone

=

Resulting sound wave

The resulting sound wave is the sum of the fundamental tone and the overtones.

FIGURE 15
Musical Instruments
A musician controls the vibrations of a musical instrument to change pitch and loudness. **Classifying** *How would you classify a tuba, a tambourine, and a banjo?*

Wind Instrument: Clarinet
Loudness is controlled by how hard the musician blows.

Stringed Instrument: Violin
Loudness is increased by the musician pressing the bow harder against the strings.

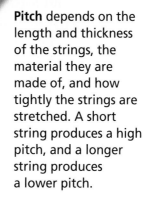

Pitch depends on the length and thickness of the strings, the material they are made of, and how tightly the strings are stretched. A short string produces a high pitch, and a longer string produces a lower pitch.

Groups of Musical Instruments
How does a musician control the sounds produced by a musical instrument? To control pitch, the musician changes the fundamental tones produced by the instrument. To control loudness, the musician changes the energy of the vibrations. The way that pitch and loudness are controlled varies among the groups of instruments, as shown in Figure 15. **There are three basic groups of musical instruments: stringed instruments, wind instruments, and percussion instruments.**

Stringed Instruments The guitar and the violin are stringed instruments. The strings of these instruments produce sound by vibrating when they are strummed or rubbed with a bow. Their loudness is increased by resonance when the instrument's hollow body vibrates as the strings vibrate. The pitch of each string depends on four factors: its length and thickness, the material it is made from, and how tightly it is stretched. An instrument with long strings, such as a cello, produces lower notes than an instrument with short strings, such as a violin.

Percussion Instrument: Drum

Loudness is controlled by how hard the musician strikes the drum.

Pitch depends on the length of the air column, which can be changed by covering different holes. A short air column produces a high pitch, and a longer column produces a lower pitch.

Pitch depends on the size of the drum head, the material, and the tension in the drum head. A smaller drum produces a higher pitch.

Wind Instruments Wind instruments include brass instruments, such as trumpets, and woodwind instruments, such as clarinets. Brass instruments produce sound when a musician's lips vibrate against the mouthpiece, causing the air column in the instrument to vibrate. Woodwinds usually contain a thin, flexible strip of material called a reed. A woodwind produces sound when the reed vibrates, causing the instrument's air column to vibrate. In wind instruments, the length of the vibrating air column determines the note that you hear. A tuba, which has a long air column, produces lower notes than a flute, which has a short air column.

Percussion Instruments Percussion instruments include drums, bells, cymbals, and xylophones. These instruments vibrate when struck. The pitch of a drum depends on its size, the material it is made of, and the tension in the drumhead. A large drum produces lower pitches than a small drum.

 **Reading Checkpoint** What are four examples of percussion instruments?

FIGURE 16
Concert Hall Acoustics
Surfaces in concert halls are designed with a variety of materials and shapes.
Inferring What might be the purpose of the curved panels near the ceiling?

Acoustics

Your surroundings affect the musical sounds that you hear at a concert. To understand this, compare the sound of your voice in different places—in class, outdoors, or in a gym. The differences you hear are due to the different ways that sounds interact. **Acoustics** is the study of how sounds interact with each other and the environment.

Sound waves can interfere with each other. Constructive interference may distort sound, while destructive interference can produce "dead spots" where loudness is reduced. Sound waves interact with the environment, also. For example, if you clap your hands in a gym, you hear echoes after you clap because sound waves reflect back and forth off the hard surfaces. This is **reverberation,** in which the echoes of a sound are heard after the sound source stops producing sound waves. The sound from a handclap can take more than a second to die out in a gym.

Acoustics is used in the design of concert halls to control reverberation and interference. Curved hard surfaces are used to direct sound waves to different parts of the concert hall. Soft surfaces absorb sound waves, reducing reverberation. But some reverberation is desirable. With too little reverberation, instruments would sound thin and distant. With too much reverberation, reflected waves interfere and individual notes become hard to pick out.

Section 3 Assessment

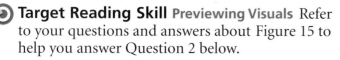

Target Reading Skill Previewing Visuals Refer to your questions and answers about Figure 15 to help you answer Question 2 below.

Reviewing Key Concepts

1. **a. Describing** How do overtones affect the sound quality of a musical instrument?
   b. Explaining How does resonance affect the sound quality of a musical instrument?
2. **a. Listing** What are the three groups of musical instruments?
   b. Summarizing How is pitch controlled in each group of musical instruments?
   c. Comparing and Contrasting How is loudness increased in a drum and in a guitar?

3. **a. Defining** What is acoustics?
   b. Relating Cause and Effect How is acoustics used in the design of concert halls?
   c. Making Judgments Why is some reverberation desirable in a concert hall?

Writing in Science

Explanation A friend e-mails you and asks how your new guitar produces music. Write an e-mail that answers your friend's question. Be sure to explain how you can change pitch, and why the guitar has a hollow body.

Changing Pitch

Problem

When you blow across the mouth of a bottle, you can play a "note." What determines the pitch you hear?

Skills Focus

controlling variables, designing experiments

Suggested Materials

- 1-L soda bottle • 2-L soda bottle
- 250-mL graduated cylinder • metric ruler
- straw • water

Design a Plan

1. Practice making a sound by using a straw to blow across the mouth of a 1-L bottle. Then blow across the mouth of a 2-L bottle in the same way. Compare the pitches. Record your observations in your notebook.

2. Add 250 mL of water to both the 1-L bottle and the 2-L bottle. Blow across the mouth of each bottle and compare the pitches. Record your observations in your notebook.

3. Analyze your observations from Steps 1 and 2 to predict what may have affected the pitches. For example, measure the height of the air column, and calculate the volume of air in each bottle. (*Hint:* Subtract the volume of water in the bottle from the total volume of the bottle.)

4. Develop a hypothesis about what determines the pitch of the sound produced by blowing across the mouth of a bottle. Record your hypothesis in your notebook.

5. Design an experiment to test your hypothesis. Create a data table to record information about the variables. Write your plan. (*Hint:* You can change the height of the air column in a bottle by changing the amount of water in the bottle.)

6. After receiving your teacher's approval of your plan, conduct your experiment and record the results in your notebook.

Analyze and Conclude

1. **Observing** Describe the pitch of the sound produced by each bottle in Steps 1 and 2.

2. **Designing Experiments** Did your experiment support your hypothesis? Explain.

3. **Controlling Variables** Identify the manipulated and responding variables in your experiment.

4. **Inferring** If you had a 1-L bottle that contained 250 mL of water, what would you do to produce a higher-pitched sound?

5. **Drawing Conclusions** What is the relationship between the height of the air column and the pitch of the sound produced by blowing across the mouth of a bottle?

6. **Communicating** Based on your results, describe how you could use a set of bottles as a musical instrument.

More to Explore

Use a set of tuning forks or a pitch pipe to "tune" five bottles to match the notes C, D, E, F, and G. What can you conclude about the pitches of the five notes from the height of the air column in each bottle? Use the bottles to play the following notes: E D C D E E E D D D E G G E D C D E E E E D D E D C.

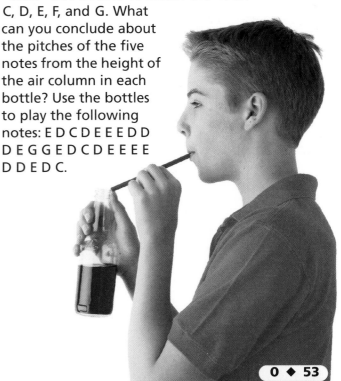

How You Hear Sound

Reading Preview

Key Concepts
- What is the function of each section of the ear?
- What causes hearing loss?

Key Terms
- ear canal
- eardrum
- cochlea

Target Reading Skill

Sequencing A sequence is the order in which the steps in a process occur. As you read, make a flowchart that shows how you hear sound. Put the steps of the process in separate boxes in the order in which they occur.

How You Hear Sound

The outer ear funnels sound waves into the ear canal.

↓

Sound waves make the eardrum vibrate.

↓

Discover Activity

Where Is the Sound Coming From?

1. Ask your partner to sit on a chair, with eyes closed.
2. Clap your hands near your partner's left ear. Ask your partner what direction the sound came from. Record the answer.
3. Now clap near your partner's right ear. Again, ask your partner what direction the sound came from and record the answer. Continue clapping in different locations around your partner's head and face. How well did your partner identify the directions the sounds came from?
4. Switch places with your partner and repeat Steps 1–3.

Think It Over
Observing From which locations are claps easily identified? For which locations are claps impossible to identify? Is there a pattern? If so, suggest an explanation for the pattern.

The house is quiet. You are sound asleep. All of a sudden, your alarm clock goes off. Startled, you jump up out of bed. Your ears detected the sound waves produced by the alarm clock. But how exactly did your brain receive the information?

The Human Ear

The function of your ear is to gather sound waves and send, or transmit, information about sound to your brain. Your ear has three main sections: the outer ear, the middle ear, and the inner ear. Each section has a different function. **The outer ear funnels sound waves, the middle ear transmits the waves inward, and the inner ear converts sound waves into a form that travels to your brain.**

Outer Ear Look at Figure 17. The first section of your ear is the outer ear. The outermost part of your outer ear looks and acts like a funnel. It collects sound waves and directs them into a narrow region called the **ear canal.** Your ear canal is a few centimeters long and ends at the eardrum. The **eardrum** is a small, tightly stretched, drumlike membrane. The sound waves make your eardrum vibrate, just as a drum vibrates when you strike it.

FIGURE 17
The Human Ear

The ear is a complex structure that allows you to hear. **Interpreting Diagrams** *What three bones make up the middle ear?*

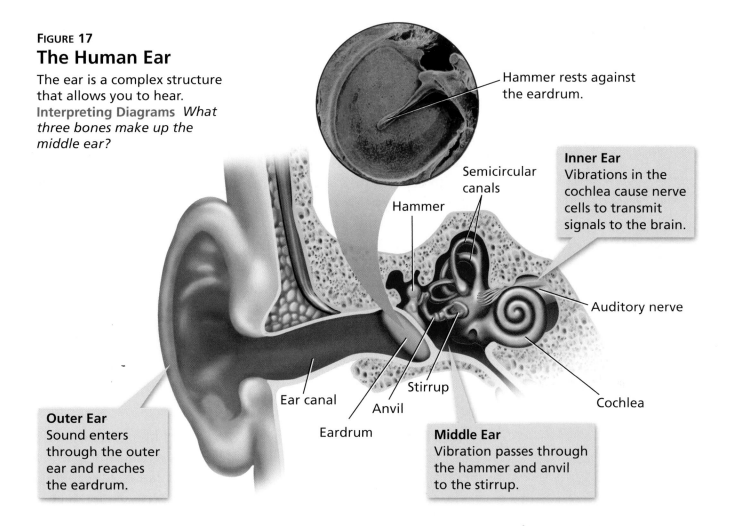

Hammer rests against the eardrum.

Semicircular canals

Hammer

Inner Ear Vibrations in the cochlea cause nerve cells to transmit signals to the brain.

Auditory nerve

Stirrup

Cochlea

Ear canal

Anvil

Eardrum

Outer Ear Sound enters through the outer ear and reaches the eardrum.

Middle Ear Vibration passes through the hammer and anvil to the stirrup.

Middle Ear Behind the eardrum is the middle ear. The middle ear contains the three smallest bones in your body—the hammer, the anvil, and the stirrup. The hammer is attached to the eardrum, so when the eardrum vibrates, the hammer does too. The hammer then transmits vibrations first to the anvil and then to the stirrup.

Inner Ear A membrane separates the middle ear from the inner ear, the third section of the ear. When the stirrup vibrates against this membrane, the vibrations pass into the cochlea. The **cochlea** (KAHK lee uh) is a fluid-filled cavity shaped like a snail shell. The cochlea contains more than 10,000 tiny structures called hair cells. These hair cells have hairlike projections that float in the fluid of the cochlea. When vibrations move through the fluid, the hair cells move, causing messages to be sent to the brain through the auditory nerve. The brain processes these messages and tells you that you've heard sound.

 **Reading Checkpoint** **What are the three main sections of the ear?**

Lab zone Try This **Activity**

Listen to This

1. Tie two strings to the handle of a metal spoon. Each string should be about 40 cm long.

2. Hold the loose end of each string in each hand. Bump the spoon against a desk or other hard solid object. Listen to the sound.

3. Now wrap the ends of the string around your fingers. Put your index fingers against your ears and bump the spoon again. How is the sound different?

Inferring What can you infer about how sound travels to your ears?

FIGURE 18
A Modern Hearing Aid
Some hearing aids are about the size of a dime. **Inferring** *What are some benefits and drawbacks of tiny hearing aids?*

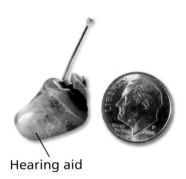

Hearing aid

Hearing Loss

When hearing loss occurs, a person may have difficulty hearing soft sounds or high-pitched sounds. **There are many causes of hearing loss, including injury, infection, exposure to loud sounds, and aging.**

Causes of Hearing Loss Hearing loss can occur suddenly if the eardrum is damaged or punctured. (Imagine trying to play a torn drum!) For this reason, it is dangerous to put objects into your ear, even to clean it. Infections also can damage the delicate inner ear, causing permanent hearing loss.

Extended exposure to loud sounds can damage hair cells in the ear. The damaged cells will no longer send signals to the brain. You can prevent this type of hearing loss by wearing hearing protection when you are around loud sounds.

The most common type of hearing loss occurs gradually. As a person gets older, some hair cells in the cochlea die and are not replaced. People with this kind of hearing loss often have difficulty hearing high-frequency sounds.

Hearing Aids For some types of hearing loss, hearing aids can restore some ability to hear. Hearing aids amplify sounds entering the ear. Some are so tiny that they can fit invisibly in the ear canal. Others can amplify specific frequencies that a person has lost the ability to hear.

Reading Checkpoint **What happens when a hearing loss occurs?**

Section 4 Assessment

Target Reading Skill Sequencing Refer to your flowchart about hearing as you answer Question 1.

Reviewing Key Concepts

1. a. **Identifying** What is the function of each section of your ear?
   b. **Interpreting Diagrams** Look at Figure 17. What happens to a sound wave as it enters your ear canal?
   c. **Relating Cause and Effect** How are sound waves transmitted through the middle ear?

2. a. **Listing** What are four causes of hearing loss?
   b. **Explaining** How can loud sounds lead to hearing loss?

c. **Making Judgments** Should people at a rock concert wear earplugs? Why or why not?

 Lab zone At-Home **Activity**

Sound Survey Ask family members to survey the sounds they hear in a day. Ask them to rate the sounds as quiet, normal, loud, or painful. Then rate each sound as pleasant, neutral, or annoying. For each sound record the source, location, time of day, and time exposed to the sound. How are the ratings similar? How are they different?

Technology Lab
• Tech & Design •

Design and Build Hearing Protectors

Problem

Can you design and build hearing protectors that block some sound from reaching your ears?

Design Skills

designing a solution, evaluating the design

Suggested Materials

- sound source (radio, tape player, or CD player)
- soundproofing materials
- tape measure
- scissors
- string
- pencil
- different types of headgear
- glue

Procedure

PART 1 Research and Investigate

1. Copy the data table on a separate sheet of paper.

2. Select a soundproofing material.

3. Stand quietly at the back of the room. Your teacher will adjust the loudness of a sound source until you are just able to hear it. Ask your partner to measure and record your distance from the sound source. Record the measurement in your data table.

4. Cover both ears with the soundproofing material. **CAUTION:** *Do not insert any material into your ears.* Move slowly forward until you can just hear the sound source again. Stop. Then have your partner measure your distance from the sound source. Record the measurement in your data table.

5. Repeat Steps 2–4 using three other materials.

Data Table	
Soundproofing Material	Distance From Sound Source (m)
No material	
Material 1	
Material 2	
Material 3	
Material 4	

PART 2 Design and Build

6. Based on what you learned in Part 1, design and build hearing protectors. Your device should
   - keep you from hearing a pencil dropped on a table at a distance of 5 meters
   - fit comfortably on your head without needing to be held in place
   - be made of materials approved by your teacher

7. Sketch your design and list the materials you will use. After your teacher approves your design, build your hearing protectors.

Analyze and Conclude

1. **Designing a Solution** What did you learn about soundproofing materials in Part 1 that helped you design your device?

2. **Evaluating the Design** Test your hearing protectors. Did your device meet all of the goals stated in Step 6? Explain.

3. **Troubleshooting** As you designed, built, and tested your hearing protectors, what problems did you encounter? How did you solve them?

Communicate

A construction company is considering buying your hearing protectors. Write a summary of your test results to convince the company that the device meets the design goals stated in Step 6.

Science and Society

Keeping It Quiet…

A construction worker uses a jackhammer; a woman waits in a noisy airport; a spectator watches a car race. All three experience noise pollution. In the United States alone, 40 million people face danger to their health from noise pollution.

People start to feel pain at about 120 decibels. But noise that "doesn't hurt" can still damage your hearing. Exposure to 85 decibels (a kitchen blender) can slowly damage the hair cells in your cochlea. As many as 9 million Americans have hearing loss caused by noise. What can be done about noise pollution?

The Issues

What Can Individuals Do?

Some work conditions are noisier than others. Construction workers, airport employees, and truck drivers are all at risk. Workers in noisy environments can help themselves by using ear protectors, which can reduce noise levels by 35 decibels.

Many leisure activities also pose a risk. A listener at a rock concert or someone riding a motorbike can prevent damage by using ear protectors. People can also reduce noise at the source. They can buy quieter machines and avoid using lawnmowers or power tools at quiet times of the day. Simply turning down the volume on headphones for radios and CD players can help prevent hearing loss in young people.

What Can Communities Do?

Transportation—planes, trains, trucks, and cars—is the largest source of noise pollution. About 15 million Americans live near airports or under airplane flight paths. Careful planning to locate airports away from dense populations can reduce noise. Cities can also prohibit late-night flights.

Many communities have laws against noise that exceeds a certain decibel level, but these laws are hard to enforce. In some cities, "noise police" can give fines to people who use noisy equipment.

What Can the Government Do?

A National Office of Noise Abatement and Control was set up in the 1970s. It required labels on power tools to tell how much noise they made. But in 1982, this office lost its funding. In 1997, lawmakers proposed The Quiet Communities Act to bring the office back and set limits to many types of noise. But critics say that national laws have little effect. They want the federal government to encourage—and pay for—research into making quieter vehicles and machines.

You Decide

1. Identify the Problem
In your own words, describe the issues of noise pollution.

2. Analyze the Options
List as many methods as you can for dealing with noise. How would each method reduce noise or protect people from noise?

3. Find a Solution
Choose one method for reducing noise in your community. Make a poster to convince people to support your proposal.

Go Online
PHSchool.com

For: More on noise pollution
Visit: PHSchool.com
Web Code: cgh-5020

Using Sound

Reading Preview

Key Concepts
- Why do some animals use echolocation?
- What are ultrasound technologies used for?

Key Terms
- echolocation • sonar
- sonogram

Target Reading Skill
Comparing and Contrasting
As you read, compare and contrast echolocation and sonar by completing a table like the one below.

Using Sound

Feature	Echolocation	Sonar
Type of wave	Ultrasound	
Medium(s)		Water
Purposes		

Discover Activity

How Can You Use Time to Measure Distance?

1. Measure a distance 3 meters from a wall and mark the spot with a piece of masking tape.
2. Roll a soft ball in a straight line from that spot toward the wall. What happens to the ball?
3. Roll the ball again. Try to roll the ball at the same speed each time. Have a classmate use a stopwatch to record the time it takes for the ball to leave your hand, reflect off the wall, and then return to you.
4. Now move 6 meters away from the wall. Mark the spot with tape. Repeat Steps 2 and 3.
5. Compare the time for both distances.

Think It Over
Inferring What does the difference in time tell you about the distance the ball has traveled?

A dog trainer stands quietly, watching the dog a short distance away. To get the dog's attention, the trainer blows into a small whistle. You don't hear a thing. But the dog stops, cocks an ear, and then comes running toward the trainer. Dogs can hear ultrasound frequencies up to about 45,000 Hz, well above the upper limit for humans. Other animals, such as cats and mice, can also hear ultrasound frequencies.

Some types of animals not only hear ultrasound, but also produce ultrasound waves. They use ultrasound waves to "see in the dark."

◄ **Dog hearing an ultrasound whistle**

Echolocation

Imagine trying to walk around in a totally dark room. You would probably bump into objects every few steps. Unlike you, bats find it easy to move around in dark places. This is because they use echolocation. **Echolocation** (ek oh loh KAY shun) is the use of reflected sound waves to determine distances or to locate objects. **Some animals, including bats and dolphins, use echolocation to navigate and to find food.**

Bats Bats use ultrasound waves with frequencies up to 100,000 Hz to move around and hunt. As a bat flies, it sends out short pulses of ultrasound waves—as many as 200 pulses per second! The waves reflect off objects and return to the bat's ears. The time it takes for the sound waves to return tells the bat how far it is from obstacles or prey. The bat uses the reflected sound waves to build up a "picture" of what lies ahead.

Dolphins, Porpoises, and Whales Dolphins, porpoises, and some whales must often hunt in darkness. Like bats, these animals use echolocation. For example, dolphins send out ultrasound waves with frequencies up to 150,000 Hz. The sound waves travel through the water and bounce off fish or other prey, as shown in Figure 19. Dolphins sense the reflected sound waves through their jawbones. They use echolocation to hunt at night or in murky or deep water.

Sound

Video Preview
▶ Video Field Trip
Video Assessment

Reading Checkpoint **What animals use echolocation?**

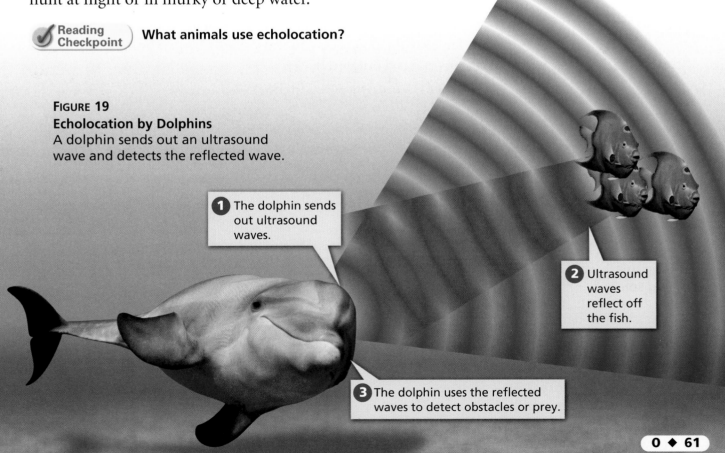

FIGURE 19
Echolocation by Dolphins
A dolphin sends out an ultrasound wave and detects the reflected wave.

1 The dolphin sends out ultrasound waves.

2 Ultrasound waves reflect off the fish.

3 The dolphin uses the reflected waves to detect obstacles or prey.

Ultrasound Technologies

People cannot send out pulses of ultrasound to help them move around in the dark. But people sometimes need to explore places they cannot easily reach, such as deep underwater or inside the human body. **Ultrasound technologies such as sonar and ultrasound imaging are used to observe things that cannot be seen directly.**

Sonar A system that uses reflected sound waves to detect and locate objects underwater is called **sonar**. The word *sonar* comes from the initial letters of **so**und **n**avigation **a**nd **r**anging. *Navigation* means finding your way around on the ocean (or in the air), and *ranging* means finding the distance between objects. Today, sonar is used to determine the depth of water, to map the ocean floor, and to locate sunken ships, schools of fish, and other objects in the ocean.

A sonar device sends a burst of ultrasound waves that travel through the water. When the sound waves strike an object or the ocean floor, they reflect as shown in Figure 20. The sonar device detects the reflected waves.

The farther a sound wave travels before bouncing off an object, the longer it takes to return to the sonar device. A computer in the sonar device measures the time it takes for the sound waves to go out and return. Then, it multiplies this time by the speed of sound in water. The result is the total distance the sound waves traveled. The total distance is divided by two to find how far away the object is. You must divide by two because the sound waves travel out and back.

FIGURE 20
Using Sonar
A sonar device sends out ultrasound waves and then detects the reflected waves. **Interpreting Diagrams** *What happens to the reflected sound waves?*

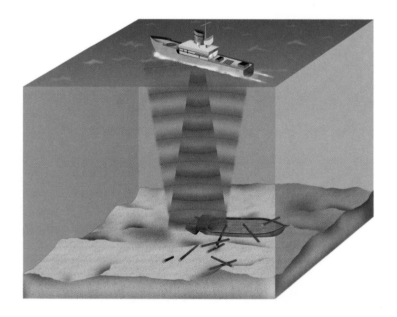

Ultrasound Imaging Doctors use ultrasound imaging to look inside the human body. Ultrasound imaging devices send ultrasound waves into the body and detect the reflected sound waves. Different parts of the body, such as bones, muscles, the liver, or the heart, reflect sound differently. The device uses the reflected ultrasound waves to create a picture called a **sonogram**. A doctor can use sonograms to diagnose and treat many medical conditions.

Ultrasound imaging is used to examine developing babies before they are born. A technician or doctor holds a small probe on a pregnant woman's abdomen. The probe sends out very high frequency ultrasound waves (about 4 million Hz). By analyzing the reflected sound waves, the device builds up a sonogram. The sonogram can show the position of the baby. Sonograms can also show if more than one baby will be born. In addition to a still picture, ultrasound imaging can produce a video of a developing baby.

 **Reading Checkpoint** What is a sonogram?

FIGURE 21
Ultrasound in Medicine
An ultrasound imaging device uses reflected ultrasound waves to build up a picture of a developing baby.

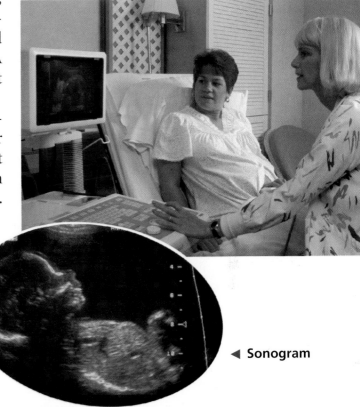

◄ Sonogram

Section 5 Assessment

Target Reading Skill

Comparing and Contrasting Use your table about echolocation and sonar to help you answer the questions below.

Reviewing Key Concepts

1. a. **Defining** What is echolocation?
   b. **Summarizing** Why do bats and dolphins use echolocation?
   c. **Interpreting Diagrams** Look at Figure 19. Why would a dolphin need to continue sending out sound waves as it nears its prey?
2. a. **Reviewing** Why do people use ultrasound technologies?
   b. **Drawing Conclusions** A sonar device can show the size of a fish but not the type of fish. Explain why.

c. **Comparing and Contrasting** How is sonar similar to ultrasound imaging used in medicine? How is it different?

Writing in Science

Advertisement Write a short advertisement for a depth finder used on fishing boats. Describe how the depth finder can determine the depth and direction of fish in the area. Include a diagram to show how the depth finder works.

Chapter 2

Study Guide

1 The Nature of Sound

Key Concepts

- Sound is a disturbance that travels through a medium as a longitudinal wave.
- Sound waves reflect off objects, diffract through narrow openings and around barriers, and interfere with each other.
- The speed of sound depends on the elasticity, density, and temperature of the medium the sound travels through.

Key Terms
echo
elasticity
density

2 Properties of Sound

Key Concepts

- The loudness of a sound depends on two factors: the amount of energy it takes to make the sound and the distance from the source of the sound.
- The pitch of a sound that you hear depends on the frequency of the sound wave.
- When a sound source moves, the frequency of the waves changes because the motion of the source adds to the motion of the waves.

Key Terms

loudness	ultrasound
intensity	infrasound
decibel (dB)	larynx
pitch	Doppler effect

3 Music

Key Concepts

- Sound quality results from the blending of a fundamental tone with its overtones. Resonance also plays a role in sound quality.
- There are three basic groups of musical instruments: stringed instruments, wind instruments, and percussion instruments.
- Acoustics is used in the design of concert halls to control reverberation and interference.

Key Terms
music
fundamental tone
overtone
acoustics
reverberation

4 How You Hear Sound

Key Concepts

- The outer ear funnels sound waves, the middle ear transmits the waves inward, and the inner ear converts sound waves into a form that travels to your brain.
- There are many causes of hearing loss, including injury, infection, exposure to loud sounds, and aging.

Key Terms
ear canal
eardrum
cochlea

5 Using Sound

Key Concepts

- Some animals, including bats and dolphins, use echolocation to navigate and to find food.
- Ultrasound technologies such as sonar and ultrasound imaging are used to observe things that cannot be seen directly.

Key Terms
echolocation
sonar
sonogram

Review and Assessment

Organizing Information

Concept Mapping Copy the concept map about sound onto a separate sheet of paper. Then complete it and add a title. (For more on Concept Mapping, see the Skills Handbook.)

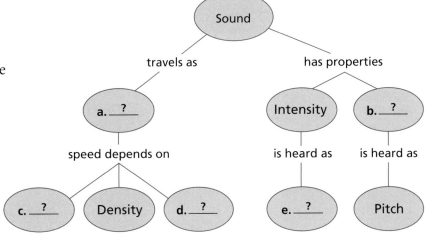

Reviewing Key Terms

Choose the letter of the best answer.

1. The ability of a medium to bounce back after being disturbed is called
   a. echolocation.   **b.** elasticity.
   c. density.   **d.** interference.

2. Which property of sound describes your perception of the energy of a sound?
   a. loudness
   b. intensity
   c. pitch
   d. wave speed

3. The lowest natural frequency of a sound is
   a. a standing wave.
   b. an overtone.
   c. an echo.
   d. the fundamental tone.

4. In the ear, a fluid-filled cavity that is shaped like a snail shell is the
   a. ear canal.   **b.** eardrum.
   c. cochlea.   **d.** larynx.

5. A system of using reflected sound waves to detect and locate objects underwater is called
   a. sonar.   **b.** acoustics.
   c. echolocation.   **d.** reverberation.

If the statement is true, write *true*. If it is false, change the underlined word or words to make the statement true.

6. <u>Intensity</u> is mass per unit volume.

7. <u>Loudness</u> is how the ear perceives frequency.

8. <u>Music</u> is a set of notes that are pleasing.

9. The <u>ear canal</u> is a small, drumlike membrane.

10. A <u>sonogram</u> is a picture made using reflected ultrasound waves.

Writing in Science

Firsthand Account Imagine that you are a dolphin researcher. Write a letter to a friend describing your latest research. Be sure to include information about how dolphins use their sonar.

DISCOVERY CHANNEL SCHOOL

Sound
Video Preview
Video Field Trip
▶ Video Assessment

Review and Assessment

Checking Concepts

11. When a gong vibrates, the air particles next to the gong do not reach your ears, yet you hear the sound of the gong. Explain.

12. Explain when a whisper would sound louder than a shout.

13. Why do you hear friends talking in the hallway even though you cannot see them around a corner?

14. As a car drives past you, the driver keeps a hand pressing on the horn. Describe what you hear as the car approaches and after it has passed by.

15. The same note is played on a flute and a cello. Why is there a difference in the sound?

16. How can a sound continue to be heard after a sound source stops making the sound?

17. How can loud noises damage your hearing?

18. How are ultrasound waves used in medicine?

Thinking Critically

19. **Comparing and Contrasting** How do sound waves behave like waves in a spring toy? How are they different?

20. **Inferring** Thunder and lightning happen at the same time. Explain why you see the lightning before you hear the thunder.

21. **Predicting** Look at the table below. Which material would you use in hearing protectors to reduce the transmission of sound waves? Explain your answer.

Substance	Speed (m/s)
Rubber	60
Plastic	1,800
Gold	3,240
Brick	3,650
Steel	5,200

22. **Classifying** Classify the following instruments into three groups: a guitar, a tuba, a bell, a clarinet, a drum, and a harp.

Applying Skills

Use the data in the table below to answer Questions 23–25.

The table shows the range of frequencies produced and heard by various animals.

Animal	Highest Frequency Heard (Hz)	Highest Frequency Produced (Hz)
Human	20,000	1,100
Dog	50,000	1,800
Cat	65,000	1,500
Bat	120,000	120,000
Porpoise	150,000	120,000

23. **Interpreting Data** Can you hear the ultrasound waves that a bat uses for echolocation? Why or why not?

24. **Graphing** Draw a bar graph to compare the highest frequencies heard and the highest frequencies produced by the animals.

25. **Calculating** If the speed of sound in air is 343 m/s, what is the shortest wavelength of sound that humans can hear? (*Hint:* Wavelength = Speed ÷ Frequency)

Lab zone Chapter Project

Performance Assessment Present your musical instrument to your class. Explain how it was built and how you solved any design problems. Then demonstrate how you can change the pitch or loudness of your instrument. Brainstorm with the class methods for improving the design of the instrument. How is your instrument similar to or different from instruments your classmates built?

Standardized Test Prep

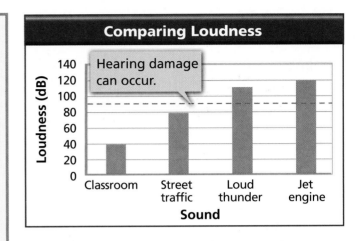

Choose the letter of the best answer.

1. Bats and dolphins use echolocation to determine distances and find prey. What characteristic of sound waves is most important for echolocation?

  A Sound waves reflect when they hit a surface.

  B Sound waves spread out from a source.

  C Sound waves diffract around a corner.

  D Sound waves interfere when they overlap.

2. A scientist is doing research with 110-dB sound waves. What piece of safety equipment must she wear in the lab?

  F goggles

  G gloves

  H lab apron

  J hearing protectors

3. Use the graph above to determine how much more intense the sound of a jet engine is than the sound of loud thunder.

  A ten times more intense

  B two times more intense

  C four times more intense

  D Both sounds are about the same intensity.

4. An experiment was conducted in which two containers held solids *A* and *B* at the same temperature. The speed of a sound wave traveling through solid *A* was greater than its speed through solid *B*. What can you conclude from this experiment?

  F Solid *A* is denser than solid *B*.

  G Solid *A* is less dense than solid *B*.

  H Solid *A* is more elastic than solid *B*.

  J Solid *A* is less dense than solid *B* or solid *A* is more elastic than solid *B*.

5. After a new concert hall is built, it is found that the acoustics are poor because of reverberation. How can the acoustics be improved?

  A Add metal seats to the hall.

  B Remove the drapes covering the windows.

  C Cover the wooden floor with carpeting.

  D Install a wooden backdrop behind the stage.

Constructed Response

6. You drop a book onto the floor in the bedroom of your apartment. Your neighbor downstairs hears the sound. Describe how the sound travels to your neighbor's ears. What mediums do the sound waves have to travel through?

Chapter

3

The Electromagnetic Spectrum

Astronomers use these telescopes to map radio waves given off by objects in space. ▶

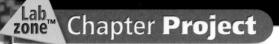

Chapter **Project**

You're on the Air

How do people communicate? Look around you! Radios, televisions, and cellular phones are part of everyday life. Wireless communication has made it convenient for people to communicate anytime and anywhere. In this Chapter Project, you will conduct a survey to find out how people use wireless communication devices.

Your Goal To collect and analyze data about when, where, and why people use different wireless communication devices

To complete this project you must

- develop a survey sheet about communication devices
- distribute your survey sheet to other students, family members, and neighbors
- compile and analyze your data
- create tables and graphs to display your findings

Plan It! To get started, think about the format and content of your survey sheet. Brainstorm what kinds of questions you will ask. Develop a plan for involving students in other classes so you can gather more data.

The Nature of Electromagnetic Waves

Reading Preview

Key Concepts
- What does an electromagnetic wave consist of?
- What models explain the behavior of electromagnetic waves?

Key Terms
- electromagnetic wave
- electromagnetic radiation
- polarized light
- photoelectric effect
- photon

Target Reading Skill

Outlining An outline shows the relationship between major ideas and supporting ideas. As you read, make an outline about electromagnetic waves. Use the red headings for the main topics and the blue headings for the subtopics.

The Nature of Electromagnetic Waves
I. What is an electromagnetic wave?
A. Producing electromagnetic waves
B.
C.
II. Models of electromagnetic waves
A.
B.

Discover **Activity**

How Does a Beam of Light Travel?

1. Punch a hole (about 0.5 cm in diameter) through four large index cards.
2. Use binder clips or modeling clay to stand each card upright so that the long side of the index card is on the tabletop. Space the cards about 10 cm apart, as shown in the photo. To line the holes up in a straight line, run a piece of string through them and pull it tight.
3. Place a flashlight in front of the card nearest you. Shut off all light except the flashlight. What do you see on the wall?
4. Move one of the cards sideways about 3 cm and repeat Step 3. Now what do you see on the wall?

Think It Over
Inferring Explain what happened in Step 4. What does this activity tell you about the path of light?

Have you ever been caught in a rain shower? You run for cover until it passes, so you don't get wet. Believe it or not, you are being "showered" all the time, not by rain but by waves. You cannot see, feel, or hear most of these waves. But as you read this, you are surrounded by radio waves, infrared rays, visible light, ultraviolet rays, and maybe even tiny amounts of X-rays and gamma rays. They are all electromagnetic waves.

Electromagnetic waves ▶

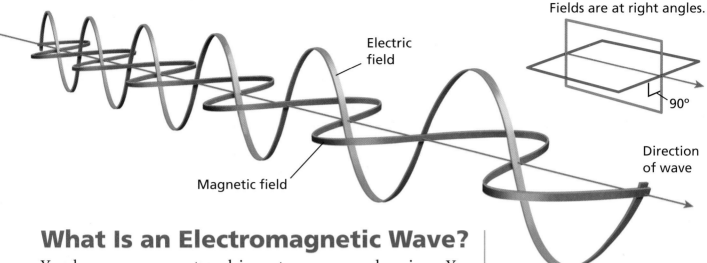

Fields are at right angles.

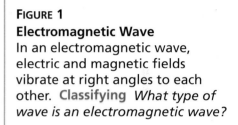

90°

Electric field

Magnetic field

Direction of wave

What Is an Electromagnetic Wave?

You have seen waves travel in water, ropes, and springs. You have heard sound waves that travel through air and water. All these waves have two things in common—they transfer energy and they also require a medium through which to travel. But electromagnetic waves can transfer energy without a medium. An **electromagnetic wave** is a transverse wave that transfers electrical and magnetic energy. **An electromagnetic wave consists of vibrating electric and magnetic fields that move through space at the speed of light.**

Producing Electromagnetic Waves Light and all other electromagnetic waves are produced by charged particles. Every charged particle has an electric field surrounding it. The electric field produces electric forces that can push or pull on other charged particles.

When a charged particle moves, it produces a magnetic field. A magnetic field exerts magnetic forces that can act on certain materials. If you place a paper clip near a magnet, for example, the paper clip moves toward the magnet because of the magnetic field surrounding the magnet.

When a charged particle changes its motion, its magnetic field changes. The changing magnetic field causes the electric field to change. When one field vibrates, so does the other. In this way, the two fields constantly cause each other to change. The result is an electromagnetic wave, as shown in Figure 1. Notice that the two fields vibrate at right angles to each other.

Energy The energy that is transferred through space by electromagnetic waves is called **electromagnetic radiation.** Electromagnetic waves do not require a medium, so they can transfer energy through a vacuum, or empty space. This is why you can see the sun and stars—their light reaches Earth through the vacuum of space.

FIGURE 1
Electromagnetic Wave
In an electromagnetic wave, electric and magnetic fields vibrate at right angles to each other. Classifying *What type of wave is an electromagnetic wave?*

Go Online
SciLINKS NSTA

For: Links on the nature of waves
Visit: www.SciLinks.org
Web Code: scn-1531

Speed All electromagnetic waves travel at the same speed in a vacuum—about 300,000 kilometers per second. This speed is called the speed of light. At this speed, light from the sun takes about 8 minutes to travel the 150 million kilometers to Earth. When light waves travel through a medium such as air, they travel more slowly. But the speed of light waves in air is still about a million times faster than the speed of sound waves in air.

 **What is the speed of light in a vacuum?**

Models of Electromagnetic Waves

Many properties of electromagnetic waves can be explained by a wave model. However, some properties are best explained by a particle model. As you have learned, light is an electromagnetic wave. Both a wave model and a particle model are needed to explain all of the properties of light.

Wave Model of Light The lenses of many sunglasses, like the ones shown in Figure 2, are polarizing filters. Light acts as a wave when it passes through a polarizing filter. Ordinary light has waves that vibrate in all directions—up and down, left and right, and at all other angles. A polarizing filter acts as though it has tiny slits that are aligned in one direction.

Only some light waves pass through a polarizing filter. The light that passes through vibrates in only one direction and is called **polarized light.** No light passes through two polarizing filters that are placed at right angles to each other.

FIGURE 2
Light as a Wave
The lenses of some sunglasses are polarizing filters. Light behaves like a wave when it passes through polarizing filters.
Observing What is the angle between the polarizing filters?

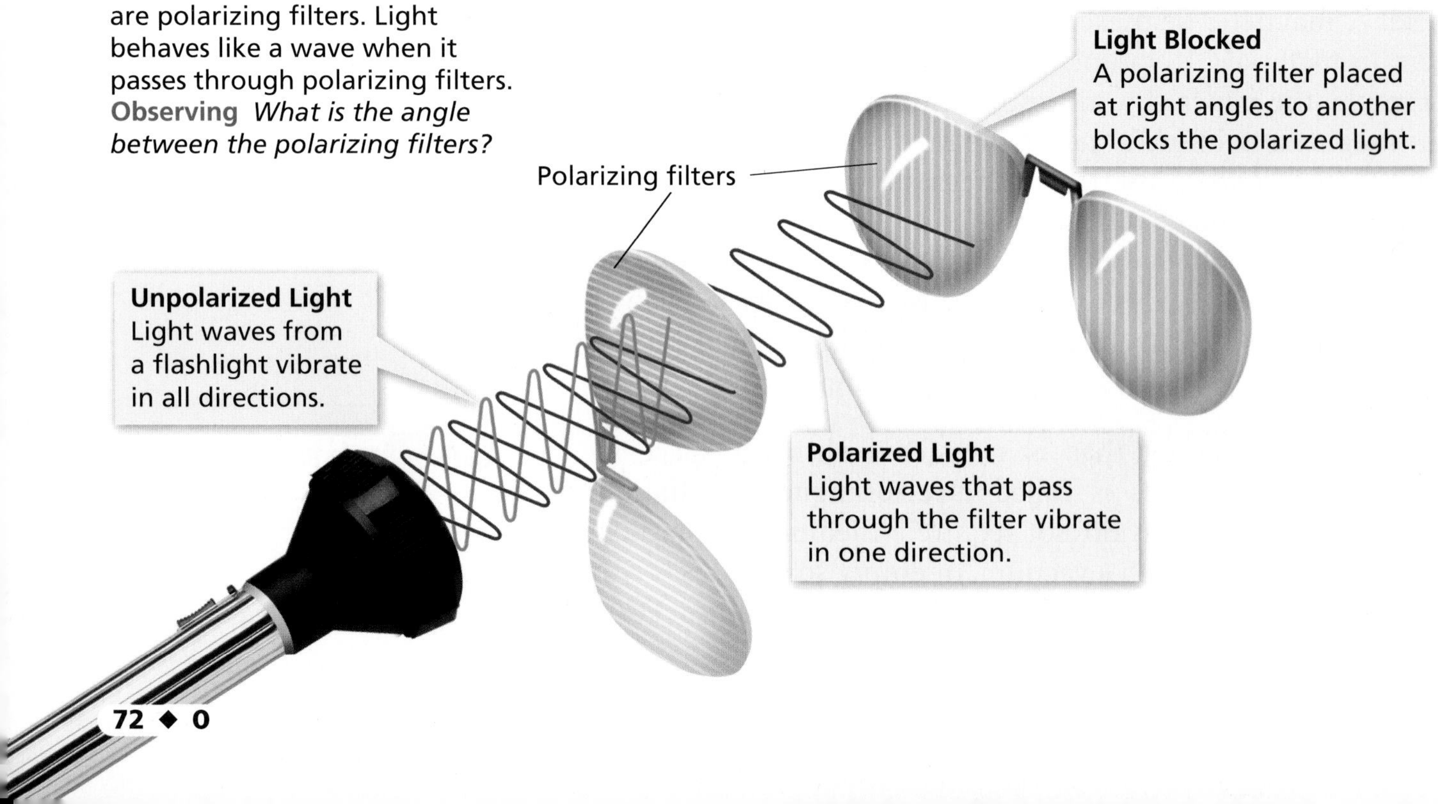

Polarizing filters

Light Blocked
A polarizing filter placed at right angles to another blocks the polarized light.

Unpolarized Light
Light waves from a flashlight vibrate in all directions.

Polarized Light
Light waves that pass through the filter vibrate in one direction.

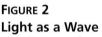

To help you understand the wave model of light, think of waves of light as being like transverse waves on a rope. If you shake a rope through a fence with vertical slats, only waves that vibrate up and down will pass through. If you shake the rope side to side, the waves will be blocked. A polarizing filter acts like the slats in a fence. It allows only waves that vibrate in one direction to pass through.

Particle Model of Light Sometimes light behaves like a stream of particles. When a beam of light shines on some substances, it causes tiny particles called electrons to move. The movement of electrons causes an electric current to flow. Sometimes light can even cause an electron to move so much that it is knocked out of the substance. This is called the **photoelectric effect.** The photoelectric effect can be explained only by thinking of light as a stream of tiny packets, or particles, of energy. Each packet of light energy is called a **photon.** Albert Einstein first explained the science behind the photoelectric effect in 1905.

It may be difficult for you to picture light as being particles and waves at the same time. But both models are necessary to explain all the properties of light.

 **Reading Checkpoint** **What is a photon?**

Lab zone Try This **Activity**

Waves or Particles?

1. Fill two plastic cups with water. Slowly pour the water from both cups into a sink so the streams of water cross. How do the two streams interfere with each other?

2. Darken a room. Use a slide projector to project a slide on a wall. Shine a flashlight beam across the projector's beam. What is the effect on the projected picture?

Drawing Conclusions
Compare the interference of light beams with the interference of water streams. Does this activity support a wave model or a particle model of light? Explain.

Section 1 Assessment

Target Reading Skill Outlining Use the information in your outline about electromagnetic waves to help you answer the questions below.

Reviewing Key Concepts

1. a. **Defining** What is an electromagnetic wave?
   b. **Explaining** How do electromagnetic waves travel?
   c. **Comparing and Contrasting** What is an electric field? What is a magnetic field?
2. a. **Reviewing** What two models explain the properties of electromagnetic waves?
   b. **Describing** Use one of the models of light to describe what happens when light passes through a polarizing filter.

c. **Relating Cause and Effect** Use one of the models of light to explain what causes the photoelectric effect.

Lab zone At-Home **Activity**

Polarized Sunglasses On a sunny day, go outside with your family members and compare your sunglasses. Do any have polarizing lenses? If so, which ones? Try rotating sunglasses as you look through them at surfaces that create glare, such as water or glass. Which sunglasses are best designed to reduce glare? **CAUTION:** *Do not look directly at the sun.*

Waves of the Electromagnetic Spectrum

Reading Preview

Key Concepts
- How are electromagnetic waves alike, and how are they different?
- What waves make up the electromagnetic spectrum?

Key Terms
- electromagnetic spectrum
- radio waves • microwaves
- radar • infrared rays
- thermogram • visible light
- ultraviolet rays • X-rays
- gamma rays

Target Reading Skill

Previewing Visuals Before you read, preview Figure 3. Then write two questions that you have about the diagram in a graphic organizer like the one below. As you read, answer your questions.

The Electromagnetic Spectrum

Q.	Which electromagnetic waves have the shortest wavelength?
A.	
Q.	

What Is White Light?

1. Line a cardboard box with white paper. Hold a small triangular prism up to direct sunlight. **CAUTION:** *Do not look directly at the sun.*

2. Rotate the prism until the light coming out of the prism appears on the inside of the box as a wide band of colors. Describe the colors and their order.

3. Using colored pencils, draw a picture of what you see inside the box.

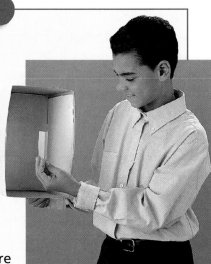

Think It Over

Forming Operational Definitions The term *spectrum* describes a range. How is this term related to what you just observed?

Can you imagine trying to take a photo with a radio? How about trying to tune in a radio station on your flashlight or heat your food with X-rays? Light, radio waves, and X-rays are all electromagnetic waves. But each has properties that make it more useful for some purposes and less useful for others. What makes light different from radio waves and X-rays?

Radio waves

Microwaves

Long wavelength
Low frequency

What Is the Electromagnetic Spectrum?

All electromagnetic waves travel at the same speed in a vacuum, but they have different wavelengths and different frequencies. Radiation in the wavelengths that your eyes can see is called visible light. But only a small portion of electromagnetic radiation is visible light. The rest of the wavelengths are invisible. Your radio detects radio waves, which have much longer wavelengths than visible light. X-rays, on the other hand, are waves with much shorter wavelengths than visible light.

Recall how speed, wavelength, and frequency are related:

$$\text{Speed} = \text{Wavelength} \times \text{Frequency}$$

Because the speed of all electromagnetic waves is the same, as the wavelength decreases, the frequency increases. Waves with the longest wavelengths have the lowest frequencies. Waves with the shortest wavelengths have the highest frequencies. The amount of energy carried by an electromagnetic wave increases with frequency. The higher the frequency of a wave, the higher its energy is.

The **electromagnetic spectrum** is the complete range of electromagnetic waves placed in order of increasing frequency. The full spectrum is shown in Figure 3. **The electromagnetic spectrum is made up of radio waves, infrared rays, visible light, ultraviolet rays, X-rays, and gamma rays.**

Reading Checkpoint What is the electromagnetic spectrum?

FIGURE 3
The Electromagnetic Spectrum
The electromagnetic spectrum shows the range of different electromagnetic waves in order of increasing frequency and decreasing wavelength.
Interpreting Diagrams *Which electromagnetic waves have the longest wavelengths?*

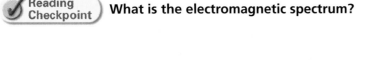

Red   Orange   Yellow   Green   Blue   Violet

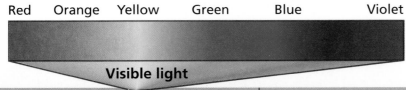

Visible light

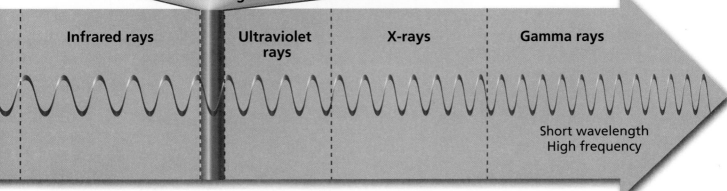

Infrared rays   Ultraviolet rays   X-rays   Gamma rays

Short wavelength
High frequency

Lab zone Try This **Activity**

Microwave Test

In this activity, you will compare how water, corn oil, and sugar absorb microwaves.

1. Add 25 mL of water to a glass beaker. Record the temperature of the water.
2. Microwave the beaker for 10 seconds and record the water temperature again.
3. Repeat Steps 1 and 2 two more times, using 25 mL of corn oil and 25 mL of sugar.

Drawing Conclusions
Compare the temperature change of the three materials. Which material absorbed the most energy from the microwaves?

Radio Waves

Radio waves are the electromagnetic waves with the longest wavelengths and lowest frequencies. They include broadcast waves (for radio and television) and microwaves.

Broadcast Waves Radio waves with longer wavelengths are used in broadcasting. They carry signals for both radio and television programs. A broadcast station sends out radio waves at certain frequencies. Your radio or TV antenna picks up the waves and converts the radio signal into an electrical signal. Inside your radio, the electrical signal is converted to sound. Inside your TV, the signal is converted to sound and pictures.

Microwaves The radio waves with the shortest wavelengths and the highest frequencies are **microwaves.** When you think of microwaves, you probably think of microwave ovens that cook and heat your food. But microwaves have many uses, including cellular phone communication and radar.

Radar stands for **ra**dio **d**etection **a**nd **r**anging. **Radar** is a system that uses reflected radio waves to detect objects and measure their distance and speed. To measure distance, a radar device sends out radio waves that reflect off an object. The time it takes for the reflected waves to return is used to calculate the object's distance. To measure speed, a radar device uses the Doppler effect, which you learned about in an earlier chapter. For example, a police radar gun like the one in Figure 4 sends out radio waves that reflect off a car. Because the car is moving, the frequency of the reflected waves is different from the frequency of the original waves. The difference in frequency is used to calculate the car's speed.

 **What does** *radar* **stand for?**

FIGURE 4
Radar Gun
Radio waves and the Doppler effect are used to find the speeds of moving vehicles.

Infrared Rays

If you turn on a burner on an electric stove, you can feel it warm up before the heating element starts to glow. The invisible heat you feel is infrared radiation, or infrared rays. **Infrared rays** are electromagnetic waves with wavelengths shorter than those of radio waves.

Heat Lamps Infrared rays have a higher frequency than radio waves, so they have more energy than radio waves. Because you can feel the energy of infrared rays as heat, these rays are often called heat rays. Heat lamps have bulbs that give off mostly infrared rays and very little visible light. These lamps are used to keep food warm at a cafeteria counter. Some people use heat lamps to warm up their bathrooms quickly.

Infrared Cameras Most objects give off some infrared rays. Warmer objects give off infrared waves with more energy and higher frequencies than cooler objects. An infrared camera takes pictures using infrared rays instead of light. These pictures are called thermograms. A **thermogram** is an image that shows regions of different temperatures in different colors. Figure 5 shows a thermogram of a house. You can use an infrared camera to see objects in the dark. Firefighters use infrared cameras to locate fire victims inside a dark or smoky building. Satellites in space use infrared cameras to study the growth of plants and the motions of clouds.

 **Reading Checkpoint** What does an infrared camera use to take pictures?

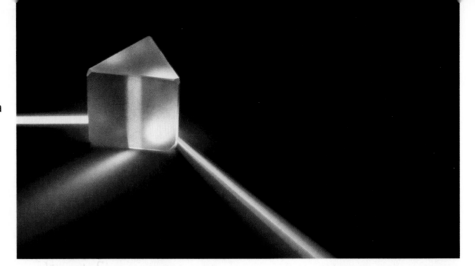

FIGURE 6
Refraction in a Prism
When white light passes through a prism, refraction causes the light to separate into its wavelengths.
Observing *Which color of light is refracted the least?*

Visible Light

Electromagnetic waves that you can see are called **visible light.** They make up only a small part of the electromagnetic spectrum. Visible light waves have shorter wavelengths and higher frequencies than infrared rays. Visible light waves with the longest wavelengths appear red in color. As the wavelengths decrease, you can see other colors of light. The shortest wavelengths of visible light appear violet in color.

Visible light that appears white is actually a mixture of many colors. White light from the sun can be separated by a prism into the colors of the visible spectrum—red, orange, yellow, green, blue, and violet. Recall that when waves enter a new medium, the waves bend, or refract. The prism refracts different wavelengths of visible light by different amounts and thereby separates the colors. Red light waves refract the least. Violet light waves refract the most.

Ultraviolet Rays

Electromagnetic waves with wavelengths just shorter than those of visible light are called **ultraviolet rays.** Ultraviolet rays have higher frequencies than visible light, so they carry more energy. The energy of ultraviolet rays is great enough to damage or kill living cells. In fact, ultraviolet lamps are often used to kill bacteria on hospital equipment.

Small doses of ultraviolet rays are useful. For example, ultraviolet rays cause skin cells to produce vitamin D, which is needed for healthy bones and teeth. However, too much exposure to ultraviolet rays is dangerous. Ultraviolet rays can burn your skin, cause skin cancer, and damage your eyes. If you apply sunblock and wear sunglasses that block ultraviolet rays, you can limit the damage caused by ultraviolet rays.

Reading Checkpoint How can ultraviolet rays be useful?

Math Skills

Scientific Notation

Frequencies of waves often are written in scientific notation. A number in scientific notation consists of a number between 1 and 10 that is multiplied by a power of 10. To write 150,000 Hz in scientific notation, move the decimal point left to make a number between 1 and 10:

150,000 Hz

In this case, the number is 1.5. The power of 10 is the number of spaces you moved the decimal point. In this case, it moved 5 places, so

150,000 Hz = 1.5×10^5 Hz

Practice Problem A radio wave has a frequency of 5,000,000 Hz. Write this number in scientific notation.

X-Rays

X-rays are electromagnetic waves with wavelengths just shorter than those of ultraviolet rays. Their frequencies are just a little higher than ultraviolet rays. Because of their high frequencies, X-rays carry more energy than ultraviolet rays and can penetrate most matter. But dense matter, such as bone or lead, absorbs X-rays and does not allow them to pass through. Therefore, X-rays are used to make images of bones inside the body or of teeth, as shown in Figure 7. X-rays pass through skin and soft tissues, causing the photographic film in the X-ray machine to darken when it is developed. The bones, which absorb X-rays, appear as the lighter areas on the film.

Too much exposure to X-rays can cause cancer. If you've ever had a dental X-ray, you'll remember that the dentist gave you a lead apron to wear during the procedure. The lead absorbs X-rays and prevents them from reaching your body.

X-rays are sometimes used in industry and engineering. For example, to find out if a steel or concrete structure has tiny cracks, engineers can take an X-ray image of the structure. X-rays will pass through tiny cracks that are invisible to the human eye. Dark areas on the X-ray film show the cracks. This technology is often used to check the quality of joints in oil and gas pipelines.

 Reading Checkpoint **What kind of matter blocks X-rays?**

FIGURE 7
Dental X-Ray
X-rays pass through soft parts of the body but are absorbed by teeth. When the photographic plate is developed, the teeth and fillings show up as lighter areas.

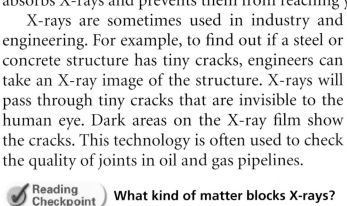

FIGURE 8
Electromagnetic Waves
Electromagnetic waves are all around you—in your home, your neighborhood, and your town.

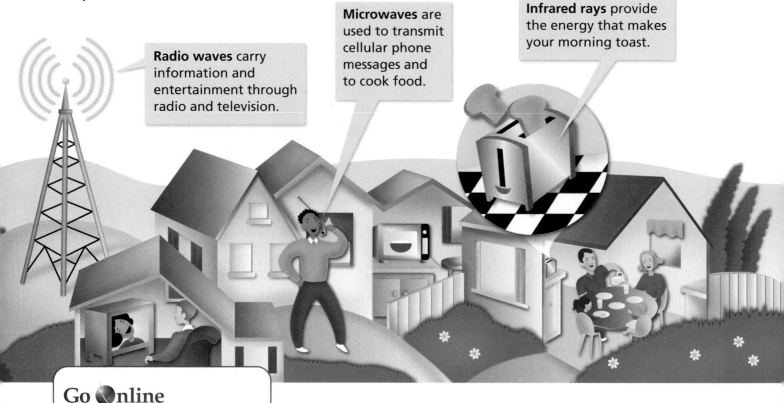

Radio waves carry information and entertainment through radio and television.

Microwaves are used to transmit cellular phone messages and to cook food.

Infrared rays provide the energy that makes your morning toast.

Go Online
active.art

For: Electromagnetic Waves activity
Visit: PHSchool.com
Web Code: cgp-5032

Gamma Rays

Gamma rays are the electromagnetic waves with the shortest wavelengths and highest frequencies. Because they have the greatest amount of energy, gamma rays are the most penetrating of all the electromagnetic waves.

Some radioactive substances and certain nuclear reactions produce gamma rays. Because of their great penetrating ability, gamma rays have some medical uses. For example, gamma rays can be used to kill cancer cells inside the body. To examine the body's internal structures, a patient can be injected with a fluid that emits gamma rays. Then a gamma-ray detector can form an image of the inside of the body.

Some objects in space give off bursts of gamma rays. The gamma rays are blocked by Earth's atmosphere, so gamma-ray telescopes that detect them must orbit above Earth's atmosphere. Astronomers think that explosions of stars in distant galaxies are one way of producing these gamma rays.

Reading Checkpoint How are gamma rays produced?

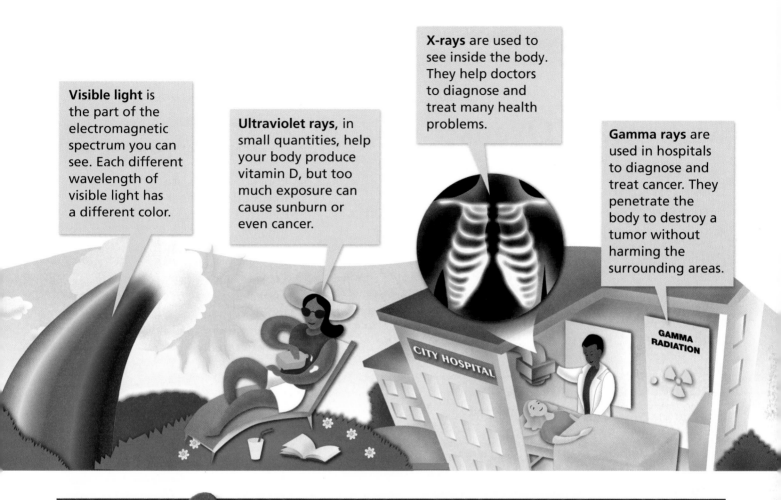

Visible light is the part of the electromagnetic spectrum you can see. Each different wavelength of visible light has a different color.

Ultraviolet rays, in small quantities, help your body produce vitamin D, but too much exposure can cause sunburn or even cancer.

X-rays are used to see inside the body. They help doctors to diagnose and treat many health problems.

Gamma rays are used in hospitals to diagnose and treat cancer. They penetrate the body to destroy a tumor without harming the surrounding areas.

GAMMA RADIATION

CITY HOSPITAL

Section 2 Assessment

Target Reading Skill Previewing Visuals
Refer to your questions and answers about Figure 3 to help you answer Question 2 below.

Reviewing Key Concepts

1. a. Reviewing What is the mathematical relationship among wavelength, frequency, and speed?

b. Summarizing In what way are all electromagnetic waves the same? In what ways are they different?

c. Making Generalizations As the wavelengths of electromagnetic waves decrease, what happens to their frequencies? To their energies?

2. a. Listing List the waves in the electromagnetic spectrum in order from lowest frequency to highest frequency.

b. Explaining Why are some electromagnetic waves harmful to you but others are not?

c. Classifying List one or more types of electromagnetic waves that are useful for each of these purposes: cooking food, communication, seeing inside the body, curing diseases, reading a book, warming your hands.

Math Practice

Scientific Notation

3. An FM radio station broadcasts at a frequency of 9×10^5 Hz. Write the frequency as a number without an exponent.

4. Red light has a frequency of 4×10^{14} Hz. Express the frequency without using an exponent.

Microwave Ovens

In 1946, as Dr. Percy Spencer worked on a radar device that produced microwaves, a candy bar melted in his pocket. Curious, he put some popcorn kernels near the device—they popped within minutes. Then, he put an egg near the device. It cooked so fast that it exploded. Dr. Spencer had discovered a new way of cooking food quickly. The microwave-oven industry was born.

Cooking With Microwaves

How do microwave ovens cook food? The answer lies in the way microwaves are reflected, transmitted, and absorbed when they strike different types of materials, such as food, metal, and plastic. In a microwave oven, microwaves reflect off the inner metal walls, bouncing around in the cooking chamber. They mostly pass right through food-wrapping materials such as plastic, glass, and paper. But foods absorb microwaves. Within seconds, the energy from the absorbed microwaves causes water and fat particles in the foods to start vibrating rapidly. These vibrations produce the heat that cooks the food.

Faster Cooking, But Is It Safe?

Using microwave ovens has made preparing food faster and easier than using conventional ovens. But, using microwave ovens has drawbacks. Overheating liquids in a microwave oven can cause the liquids to boil over or can cause serious burns. Also, microwave ovens can cook foods unevenly. This can result in foods being undercooked. Health risks can result from not cooking some foods, such as meats and poultry, thoroughly.

Making Microwave Popcorn

1. Popcorn kernels are enclosed in a paper bag that microwaves pass through.

   Microwave

2. Microwaves strike water particles in the kernels, causing them to vibrate rapidly and produce heat.

3. The heat turns the water to steam, causing the kernels to explode.

   Water particle

How a Microwave Oven Works

A microwave oven produces microwaves and scatters them throughout the oven to reach the food to be cooked.

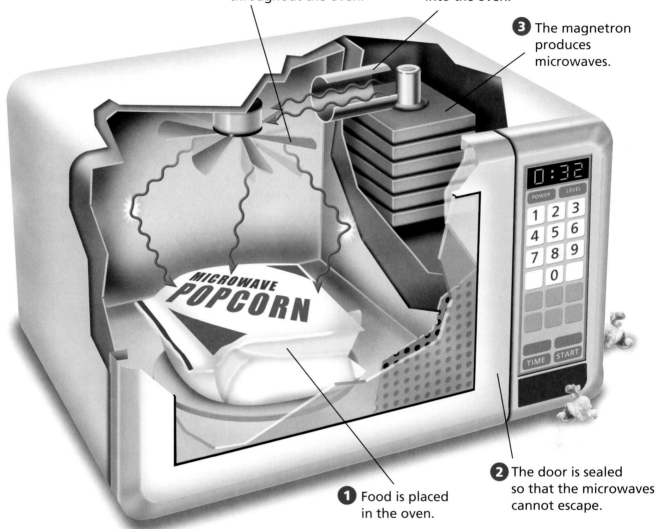

5 A rotating paddle scatters the microwaves throughout the oven.

4 The microwaves travel through a tube into the oven.

3 The magnetron produces microwaves.

2 The door is sealed so that the microwaves cannot escape.

1 Food is placed in the oven.

Weigh the Impact

1. Identify the Need
What advantages do microwave ovens have over conventional ovens?

2. Research
The U.S. Food and Drug Administration (FDA) regulates safety issues for microwave ovens. Research microwave ovens on the Internet to find FDA guidelines about this technology. What safety measures does the FDA recommend?

3. Write
Based on your research, create a poster showing how to use microwave ovens safely. With your teacher's permission, display your poster in the school cafeteria.

Go Online
PHSchool.com

For: More on microwave ovens
Visit: PHSchool.com
Web Code: cgh-5030

Producing Visible Light

Reading Preview

Key Concept
- What are the different types of light bulbs?

Key Terms
- illuminated
- luminous
- spectroscope
- incandescent light
- tungsten-halogen bulb
- fluorescent light
- vapor light
- neon light

Target Reading Skill

Comparing and Contrasting
Compare and contrast the five types of light bulbs by completing a table like the one below.

Light Bulbs

Feature	Ordinary Light Bulb	Tungsten-Halogen
Bulb material	Glass	
Hot/Cool		

Lab zone **Discover Activity**

How Do Light Bulbs Differ?

1. Your teacher will give you one incandescent and one fluorescent light bulb.
2. Examine the bulbs. Record your observations and describe any differences. Draw each type of bulb.
3. How do you think each bulb produces light?

Think It Over

Posing Questions Make a list of five questions you could ask to help you understand how each bulb works.

Look around you. Most of the objects you see are visible because they reflect light from some kind of light source. An object is **illuminated** if you see it by reflected light. The page you are reading, your desk, and the moon are examples of illuminated objects. An object is **luminous** if it gives off its own light. A light bulb, a burning log, and the sun all are examples of luminous objects.

Different types of light bulbs may be used to illuminate the spaces around you. **Common types of light bulbs include incandescent, tungsten-halogen, fluorescent, vapor, and neon lights.** Some light bulbs produce a continuous spectrum of all of the wavelengths of visible light. Others produce only a few wavelengths. You can use an instrument called a **spectroscope** to view the different colors of light produced by a light bulb.

Incandescent Lights

Have you heard the phrase "red hot"? When a glassblower heats glass, it glows and gives off red light. At a higher temperature, it gives off white light and the glass is said to be "white hot." An **incandescent light** (in kun DES unt) is a light bulb that glows when a filament inside it gets white hot. Thomas Edison, the American inventor, patented the first practical incandescent light bulb in 1879.

◄ **Glassblower working with heated glass**

FIGURE 9

Incandescent Lights

A filament glows when electric current passes through it. **Comparing and Contrasting** *How are ordinary light bulbs like tungsten-halogen bulbs? How are they different?*

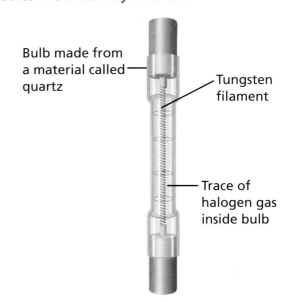

Glass bulb ——

Tungsten filament

—— Nitrogen gas and argon gas inside bulb

Ordinary Light Bulb

Bulb made from a material called quartz

—— Tungsten filament

—— Trace of halogen gas inside bulb

Tungsten-Halogen Bulb

Ordinary Light Bulbs Look closely at the ordinary light bulb shown in Figure 9. Notice the thin wire called the filament. It is made of a metal called tungsten. When an electric current passes through the filament, it quickly heats up and becomes hot, giving off white light. The filament is enclosed in an airtight glass bulb. Most ordinary light bulbs contain small amounts of nitrogen and argon gases.

Ordinary light bulbs are not efficient. Less than 10 percent of their energy is given off as light. Most of their energy is given off as infrared rays. That's why they get so hot.

Tungsten-Halogen Bulbs A bulb that has a tungsten filament and contains a halogen gas such as iodine or bromine is called a **tungsten-halogen bulb.** The filament of this bulb gets much hotter than in an ordinary light bulb, so the bulb looks whiter.

Tungsten-halogen bulbs are more efficient than ordinary bulbs because they give off more light and use less electrical energy. But they also give off more heat. Because tungsten-halogen bulbs get so hot, they must be kept away from materials that could catch fire.

 **Reading Checkpoint** What gases are used in tungsten-halogen bulbs?

Lab zone Skills **Activity**

Observing

Use a spectroscope to view light from two sources. **CAUTION:** *Do not view the sun with the spectroscope.*

1. Look through the spectroscope at an ordinary light bulb. Use colored pencils to draw and label what you see.
2. Now, look at a fluorescent light through the spectroscope. Again, draw and label what you see.

How are the colors you see the same? How are they different?

FIGURE 10
Fluorescent Light
A fluorescent light
is cool because very little
energy is given off as infrared
rays. **Inferring** *Why is a
fluorescent light efficient?*

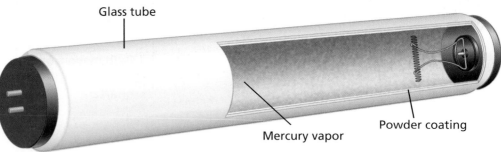

Glass tube

Powder coating

Mercury vapor

Other Light Sources

Incandescent light bulbs are not the only light bulbs you see around you. Some spaces are lit by fluorescent lights. Streets and parking lots may be lit with vapor lights. Neon lights are often used to attract attention to stores and theaters.

Fluorescent Lights Have you ever noticed long, narrow glass tubes that illuminate schools and stores? These are fluorescent light bulbs. A **fluorescent light** (floo RES unt) is a bulb that contains a gas and is coated on the inside with a powder. When an electric current passes through the bulb, it causes the gas inside to give off ultraviolet rays. When the ultraviolet rays hit the powder in the tube, the powder gives off visible light.

Fluorescent lights give off most of their energy as visible light and only a little energy as infrared rays. Therefore, fluorescent lights do not get as hot as incandescent light bulbs. They also usually last longer than incandescent lights and use less electrical energy for the same brightness. So, fluorescent lights are very efficient.

Vapor Lights A bulb that contains neon or argon gas and a small amount of solid sodium or mercury is a **vapor light.** When an electric current passes through the gas, the gas heats up. The hot gas then heats the sodium or mercury. The heating causes the sodium or mercury to change from a solid into a gas. In a sodium vapor light, the particles of sodium gas glow to give off a yellowish light. A mercury vapor light produces a bluish light.

Both sodium and mercury vapor lights are used for street lighting and parking lots. They require very little electrical energy to give off a great deal of light, so they are quite efficient.

FIGURE 11
Sodium Vapor Lights
Sodium vapor lights give off
a yellowish light.

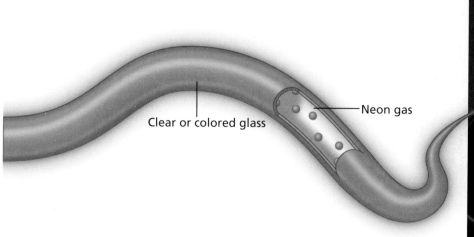

Clear or colored glass

Neon gas

Neon Lights A **neon light** is a sealed glass tube that contains neon gas. When an electric current passes through the neon, particles of the gas absorb energy. However, the gas particles cannot hold the energy for very long. The energy is released in the form of light. This process is called electric discharge through gases.

A true neon light gives off red light, as shown in Figure 12. But often, lights that contain different gases or a mixture of gases are also called neon lights. Different gases produce different colors of light. For example, both argon gas and mercury vapor produce greenish-blue light. Helium gives pink light. Krypton gives a pale violet light. Sometimes colored glass tubes are used to produce other colors. Neon lights are commonly used for bright, flashy signs.

FIGURE 12
Neon Lights
The color of a neon light depends in part on which gas or gases are in the tube.

✓ **Reading Checkpoint** **What color of light does a neon light give off?**

Section 3 Assessment

🎯 **Target Reading Skill** Comparing and Contrasting Use the information in your table about light bulbs to help you answer Question 1 below.

Reviewing Key Concepts

1. **a. Listing** What are five common types of light bulbs?
   b. Explaining How do incandescent light bulbs work?
   c. Inferring Lamps that use ordinary light bulbs often have cloth or paper shades. But tungsten-halogen lamps usually have metal shades. Explain.
   d. Making Generalizations What gives off light in incandescent light bulbs? What gives off light in other types of light bulbs?

Lab zone **At-Home Activity**

Buying Light Bulbs Invite family members to visit a hardware store. Ask a salesperson to describe the different kinds of light bulbs available. Read the information about each bulb on the packages. Look for the cost and the expected life of the bulbs. How does this information help you and your family to choose bulbs for different purposes?

Comparing Light Bulbs

Problem

Which types of light bulbs provide the best illumination?

Skills Focus

inferring, interpreting data, drawing conclusions

Materials

- a variety of incandescent light bulbs that can fit in the same lamp or socket
- medium-sized cardboard box
- light socket or lamp (without shade)
- meter stick
- wax paper
- scissors
- plain paper
- tape

Procedure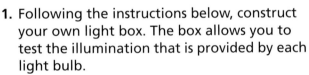

1. Following the instructions below, construct your own light box. The box allows you to test the illumination that is provided by each light bulb.

2. Make a data table like the one shown to record your data.

3. With a partner, examine the different bulbs. What is the power (watts), light output (lumens), and life (hours) for each bulb? Predict which light bulb will be the brightest. Explain your choice.

4. How will you test your prediction? What kinds of incandescent light bulbs will you use? What variables will you keep constant? What variables will you change?

5. Review your plan. Will your procedure help you find an answer to the problem?

6. Ask your teacher to check your procedure.

7. Before you repeat the steps for a second light bulb, look back at your procedure. How could you improve the accuracy of your results?

8. Test the illumination of the rest of your light bulbs.

How to Build and Use a Light Box

A Use a medium-sized cardboard box, such as the kind of box copy paper comes in. If the box has flaps, cut them off.

B Carefully cut a viewing hole (about 2 cm x 4 cm) in the bottom of the box. This will be on top when the box is used. This is hole A.

C Punch another hole (about 1 cm x 1 cm) on one side of the box. This is hole B. It will allow light from the bulb to enter the box.

D To decrease the amount of light that can enter, cover hole B with two layers of wax paper.

E Put one of your light bulbs in the lamp and place it at the side of the box, about 1 m from hole B.

F Have your partner write a secret letter on a piece of plain paper. Put the paper on the table. Place the light box over the paper with the viewing hole facing up.

G Now look through hole A. Turn the lamp on and move the light toward the box until you can read the secret letter. Measure the distance between the light bulb and hole B.

Data Table

Bulb Number	Brand Name	Power (watts)	Light Output (lumens)	Life (h)	Cost (dollars)	Distance From Bulb to Light Box (cm)

Analyze and Conclude

1. **Observing** How does the distance between the bulb and hole B affect how easily you can read the secret letter?

2. **Inferring** Based on your observations, what can you infer about the illumination provided by each bulb? Which bulb gave the most illumination?

3. **Interpreting Data** How did your results compare with your prediction? What did you learn that you did not know when you made your prediction?

4. **Interpreting Data** What factors affect the illumination given by a light bulb?

5. **Drawing Conclusions** Based on your results, do you think that the most expensive bulb is the best?

6. **Communicating** Using what you have learned, write an advertisement for the best light bulb. Explain why it is the best.

Design an Experiment

A lighting company claims that one of their 11-watt fluorescent bulbs gives off as much light as a 75-watt ordinary light bulb. Design an experiment to test this claim. *Obtain your teacher's permission before carrying out your investigation.*

For: Data sharing
Visit: PHSchool.com
Web Code: cgd-5033

Wireless Communication

Reading Preview

Key Concepts
- How do radio waves transmit information?
- How do cellular phones work?
- How do communications satellites relay information?

Key Terms
- amplitude modulation
- frequency modulation

Target Reading Skill

Using Prior Knowledge Your prior knowledge is what you know before you read about a topic. Before you read, write what you know about wireless communication in a graphic organizer. As you read, continue to write in what you learn.

FIGURE 13
Miniature Television
Radio waves transmit the signals for this small portable television.

Lab zone Discover **Activity**

How Can Radio Waves Change?

1. Trace the wave diagram onto a piece of tracing paper. Then transfer the tracing onto a flat piece of latex from a balloon or a glove.
2. Stretch the latex horizontally. How is the stretched wave different from the wave on the tracing paper?
3. Now stretch the latex vertically. How is this wave different from the wave on the tracing paper? How is it different from the wave in Step 2?

Think It Over
Making Models Which stretch changes the wave's amplitude? The wave's frequency?

You race home from school and switch on the TV to catch the final innings of your favorite team's big game. In an instant, you see and hear the game just as if you were sitting in the stands.

Today you can communicate with people far away in just seconds. You can watch a live television broadcast of a soccer game from Europe or listen to a radio report from Africa. How do these radio and television programs reach you?

Radio and Television

Radio waves carry, or transmit, signals for both radio and television programs. The radio waves are produced by charged particles moving back and forth inside transmission antennas. **Transmission antennas send out, or broadcast, radio waves in all directions. Radio waves carry information from the antenna of a broadcasting station to the receiving antenna of your radio or television.** There are two methods of transmitting the signals—amplitude modulation and frequency modulation. Radio stations broadcast using either method. Television stations use both methods—amplitude modulation for pictures and frequency modulation for sound.

Amplitude Modulation AM stands for amplitude modulation. **Amplitude modulation** is a method of transmitting signals by changing the amplitude of a wave. The information that will become sound, such as speech and music, is coded in changes, or modulations, of a wave's amplitude. The frequency of the wave remains constant, as shown in Figure 14. At a radio broadcasting station, sound is converted into electronic signals. The electronic signals are then converted into a pattern of changes in the amplitude of a radio wave. Your radio receives the wave and converts it back into sound.

AM radio waves have relatively long wavelengths and are easily reflected by Earth's ionosphere. The ionosphere is a region of charged particles high in the atmosphere. The reflected waves bounce back to Earth's surface. Therefore, AM radio stations can broadcast over long distances.

Frequency Modulation FM stands for frequency modulation. **Frequency modulation** is a method of transmitting signals by changing the frequency of a wave. FM signals travel as changes, or modulations, in the frequency of the wave. The amplitude of the wave remains constant.

FM waves have higher frequencies and more energy than AM waves. As shown in Figure 14, they pass through the ionosphere instead of being reflected back to Earth. Thus, FM waves do not travel as far as AM waves. So, if you go on a long car trip with an FM radio station tuned in, you may quickly lose reception of the station. But FM waves are usually received clearly and produce better sound quality than AM waves.

FIGURE 14
AM and FM Radio Waves
In AM transmissions, the amplitude of a radio wave is changed. In FM transmissions, the frequency is changed.
Interpreting Diagrams *What property is constant in the AM wave? In the FM wave?*

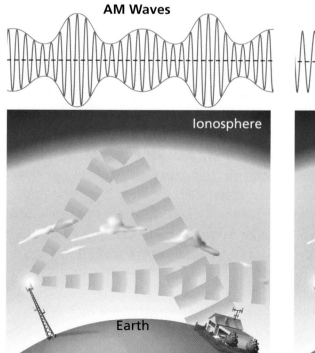

AM Waves

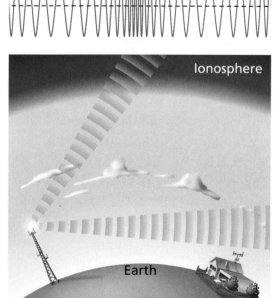

FM Waves

Comparing Frequencies

The table shows the ranges of radio broadcast frequencies used for AM radio, UHF television, FM radio, and VHF television.

1. **Interpreting Data** In the table, what units of measurement are used for frequency?

2. **Interpreting Data** Which type of broadcast shown in the table uses the highest-frequency radio waves? Which uses the lowest-frequency waves?

3. **Calculating** Which type of broadcast uses waves with the shortest wavelength?

Broadcast Frequencies	
Type of Broadcast	**Frequency Range**
AM radio broadcast	535 kHz to 1,605 kHz
VHF television	54 MHz to 216 MHz
FM radio broadcast	88 MHz to 108 MHz
UHF television	470 MHz to 806 MHz

4. **Inferring** A broadcast uses a frequency of 100 MHz. Can you tell from this data if it is a television or a radio program? Explain.

The Radio Spectrum In addition to radio and television broadcasts, radio waves are used for many types of communication. For example, taxi drivers, firefighters, and police officers all use radio waves to do their jobs. The Federal Communications Commission, or FCC, assigns different radio frequencies for different uses. Radio stations are allowed to use one part of the radio spectrum. Television stations use other parts. Taxi and police radios are assigned separate sets of frequencies. Because the signals all have different assigned frequencies, they travel without interfering.

You probably have seen these assigned frequencies when you tune a radio. AM radio stations use frequencies measured in kilohertz (kHz), while FM radio stations use frequencies measured in megahertz (MHz). Recall that a hertz is one cycle per second. If something vibrates 1,000 times a second, it has a frequency of 1,000 Hz, or 1 kilohertz (kHz). (The prefix *kilo-* means "one thousand.") If something vibrates 1,000,000 times a second, it has a frequency of 1,000,000 Hz, or 1 megahertz (MHz). (The prefix *mega-* means "one million.")

AM radio stations range from 535 kHz to 1,605 kHz. FM radio stations range between 88 MHz and 108 MHz. A television station uses one of two sets of frequencies: Very High Frequency (VHF) or Ultra High Frequency (UHF). VHF stations range from 54 MHz to 216 MHz, corresponding to Channels 2 through 13 on your television set. UHF channels range from 470 MHz to 806 MHz, corresponding to Channels 14 through 69.

Discovery CHANNEL SCHOOL™

The Electromagnetic Spectrum

Video Preview
▶ Video Field Trip
Video Assessment

 **Reading Checkpoint** What does the term *kilohertz* stand for?

Cellular Phones

Cellular telephones have become very common, but they only work if they are in or near a cellular system. The cellular system, which is shown in Figure 15, works by dividing regions into many small cells, or geographical areas. Each cell has one or more towers that relay signals to a central hub.

Cellular phones transmit and receive signals using high-frequency microwaves. When you place a call on a cellular phone, the phone sends out microwaves. The microwaves are tagged with a number unique to your phone. A tower picks up the microwaves and transfers the signal to a hub. In turn, the hub channels and transmits the signal to a receiver. The receiver may be another tower or another hub, depending on the distance between the two phones. That tower or hub transmits the signal to the receiving cellular phone. The receiving phone rings when it picks up the microwave signal from a tower or hub. The whole exchange seems to be instantaneous.

In addition to making phone calls, you can also use some cellular phones to page someone, to send text messages, or to get information from the Internet. Some modern cellular phones can even be used as digital cameras.

 **Reading Checkpoint** What are three ways to communicate with a cellular phone?

FIGURE 15
Cellular Phone System
In the cellular phone system, cellular phones transmit and receive radio waves that travel to the nearest tower.
Predicting *What happens if a cellular phone is far away from a tower?*

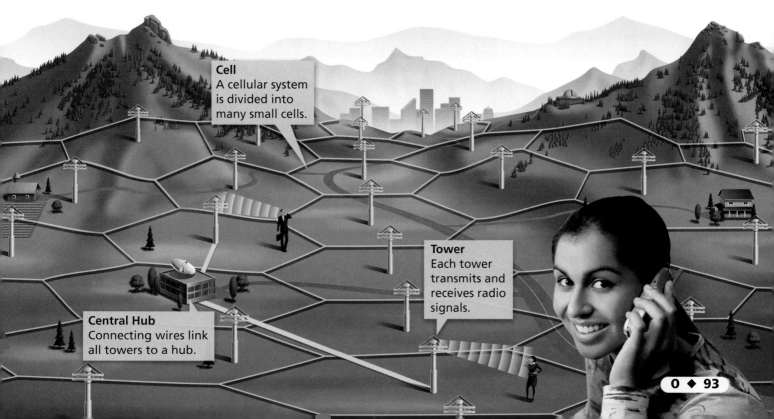

Cell
A cellular system is divided into many small cells.

Tower
Each tower transmits and receives radio signals.

Central Hub
Connecting wires link all towers to a hub.

Communications Satellites

Satellites orbiting Earth are used to send information around the world. Communications satellites work like the receivers and transmitters of a cellular phone system. **Communications satellites receive radio, television, and telephone signals and relay the signals back to receivers on Earth.** Because a satellite can "see" only part of Earth at any given time, more than one satellite is needed for any given purpose.

Satellite Phone Systems Several companies have developed satellite phone systems. The radio waves from one phone are sent up to a communications satellite. The satellite transmits the waves back to the receiving phone on Earth. With this kind of phone, you can call anywhere in the world, but the cost is greater than using a cellular phone.

Science and **History**

Wireless Communication

Since the late 1800s, many developments in communication have turned our world into a global village.

1895
First Wireless Transmission
Italian engineer and inventor Guglielmo Marconi successfully used radio waves to send a coded wireless signal a distance of more than 2 km.

1901
First Transatlantic Signals
On December 12, the first transatlantic radio signal was sent from Poldhu Cove, Cornwall, England, to Signal Hill, Newfoundland. The coded radio waves traveled more than 3,000 km through the air.

1888
Electromagnetic Waves
German scientist Heinrich Hertz proved that radio waves exist. Hertz demonstrated that the waves could be reflected, refracted, diffracted, and polarized just like light waves.

1923 Ship-to-Ship Communication
For the first time, people on one ship could talk to people on another. The signals were sent as electromagnetic waves, received by an antenna, and converted into sound.

1880   **1900**   **1920**

Television Satellites Both television networks and cable companies use communications satellites. First, the television signals are changed into AM and FM waves. These radio waves are sent up to satellites. Then the signals are relayed to local stations around the world.

Some people have their own antennas to receive signals for television programs directly from satellites. Many of the antennas are dish-shaped, so they are known as satellite dishes. Older satellite dishes were very large, more than 2 meters in diameter. But newer dishes are much smaller because the signals from satellites have become more powerful.

Television signals from satellites often are scrambled to make sure that only people who pay for the programs can use the signal. Customers need a decoding box to unscramble the signals.

Writing in Science

Research and Write Use library or Internet resources to find out more about Guglielmo Marconi. Imagine that you were hired as his assistant. Write a short letter to a friend that describes your new job.

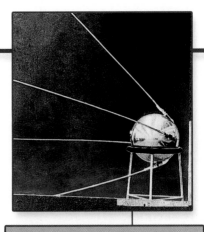

1957 *Sputnik I*
On October 4, the Soviet Union became the first country to successfully launch an artificial satellite into orbit. This development led to a new era in communications. Since then, more than 5,000 artificial satellites have been placed in orbit.

1963 Geosynchronous Orbit
Communications satellites are launched into orbits at altitudes of about 35,000 km. At this altitude, a satellite orbits Earth at the same rate as Earth rotates.

1979 Cellular Phone Network
In Japan, the world's first cellular phone network allowed people to make wireless phone calls. Today, cellular phone towers like the one above are common.

| 1960 | 1980 | 2000 |

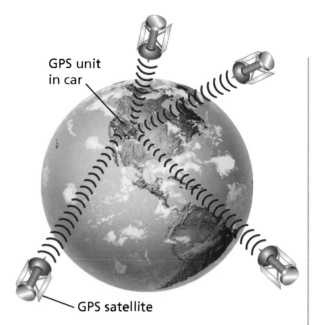

GPS unit
in car

GPS satellite

FIGURE 16
Global Positioning System
In the Global Positioning System (GPS),
signals from four satellites are used
to pinpoint a location on Earth.

Global Positioning System The Global Positioning System (GPS) is a system of navigation originally designed for the military. Now many other people use the system. GPS uses a network of satellites that broadcast radio signals to Earth. These signals carry information that tells you your exact location on Earth's surface, or even in the air. Anybody with a GPS receiver can pick up these signals.

Figure 16 shows how the signals from four GPS satellites are used to determine your position. The signals from three satellites tell you where you are on Earth's surface. The signal from the fourth satellite tells you how far above Earth's surface you are.

Today, GPS receivers are found in airplanes, boats, and cars. In a car, you can type your destination into a computer. The computer uses GPS data to map out your route. A computerized voice might even tell you when to turn right or left.

 Reading Checkpoint **What does GPS stand for?**

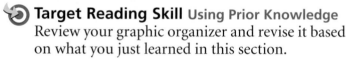

Section 4 Assessment

Target Reading Skill Using Prior Knowledge
Review your graphic organizer and revise it based on what you just learned in this section.

Reviewing Key Concepts

1. a. **Identifying** What type of wave carries signals for radio and television programs?
   b. **Sequencing** Describe the events that bring an AM broadcast into your home.
   c. **Comparing and Contrasting** How are AM waves different from FM waves? How are they the same?

2. a. **Summarizing** How does a cellular telephone work?
   b. **Interpreting Diagrams** A cellular phone transmits a signal to a receiving tower in Figure 15. How is the signal passed on to another cellular phone user?
   c. **Relating Cause and Effect** Your cellular phone transmits a signal at a specific frequency. What will happen if a cellular phone next to you also uses this frequency?

3. a. **Listing** What are three kinds of communications satellites?
   b. **Reviewing** How do communications satellites work?
   c. **Predicting** If your GPS device received signals from only three satellites, what information about your location would you be missing?

Writing in Science

Cause and Effect Paragraph Just before going to sleep one night, you search for an AM station on your radio. To your surprise, you pick up a station coming from a city 1,000 kilometers away. Your older brother tells you it is because of Earth's ionosphere. Write a paragraph explaining your brother's statement. Be sure to describe how the ionosphere affects AM radio transmissions.

Build a Crystal Radio

Problem

Can you build a device that can collect and convert radio signals?

Skills Focus

observing, drawing conclusions, making models

Materials

- cardboard tube (paper towel roll)
- 3 pieces of enameled or insulated wire, 1 about 30 m long, and 2 about 30 cm long
- wirestrippers or sandpaper
- 2 alligator clips
- scissors
- aluminum foil
- 2 pieces of cardboard (sizes can range from 12.5 cm × 20 cm to 30 cm × 48 cm)
- masking tape
- crystal diode
- earphone
- 2 pieces of insulated copper antenna wire, 1 about 30 m long, and 1 about 0.5 m long

Procedure

PART 1 Wind the Radio Coil

(*Hint*: All ends of the insulated wires need to be stripped to bare metal. If the wire is enameled, you need to sandpaper the ends.)

1. Carefully punch two holes approximately 2.5 cm apart in each end of a cardboard tube. The holes should be just large enough to thread the insulated wire through.

2. Feed one end of the 30-m piece of insulated wire through one set of holes. Leave a 50-cm lead at that end. Attach alligator clip #1 to this lead. See Figure 1.

▲ **Figure 1** Winding the Coil

3. Wind the wire tightly around the cardboard tube. Make sure the coils are close together but do not overlap one another.

4. Wrap the wire until you come to the end of the tube. Feed the end of the wire through the other set of holes, leaving a 50-cm lead as before. Attach alligator clip #2 to this lead. See Figure 2.

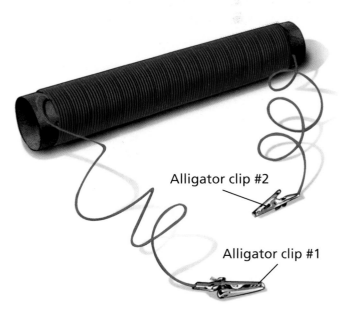

Alligator clip #2

Alligator clip #1

▲ **Figure 2** The Finished Coil

PART 2 Make the Tuning Plates

5. Without wrinkling the aluminum foil, cover one side of each piece of cardboard with the foil. Trim off any excess foil and tape the foil in place.

6. Hold the pieces of cardboard together with the foil facing inward. Tape along one edge to make a hinge. It is important for the foil pieces to be close together but not touching. See Figure 3.

▼ **Figure 3** Taping the Tuning Plates

7. Make a small hole through the cardboard and foil near a corner of one side. Feed one of the short pieces of insulated wire through the hole and tape it onto the foil as shown. Tape the other short piece of insulated wire to the corner of the other side. See Figure 4.

▼ **Figure 4** Connecting the Tuning Plates

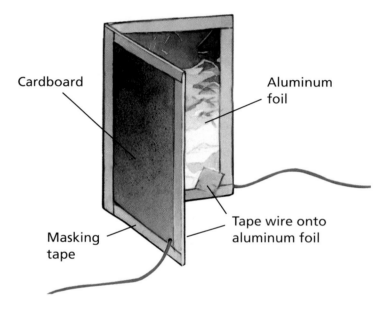

Cardboard

Aluminum foil

Masking tape

Tape wire onto aluminum foil

8. Connect one end of the wire from the foil to alligator clip #1. Connect the other wire from the foil to alligator clip #2.

PART 3 Prepare the Earphone

9. Handle the diode carefully. Connect one wire from the diode to alligator clip #1. The arrow on the diode should point to the earphone. Tape the other end of the diode wire to one of the earphone wires.

10. Connect the other wire from the earphone to alligator clip #2. See Figure 5.

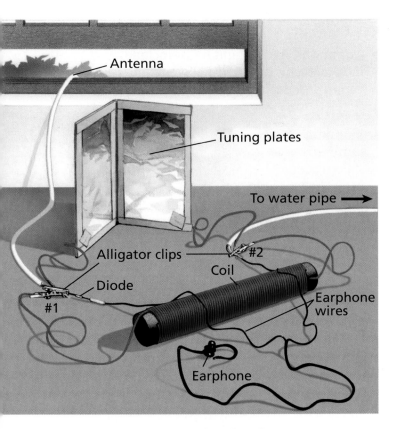

▲ Figure 5 The Completed Radio

Labels in figure: Antenna, Tuning plates, To water pipe →, Alligator clips, #2, Coil, Diode, #1, Earphone wires, Earphone

---

PART 4 Hook Up the Antenna

11. String the long piece of antenna wire along the floor to an outside window. Connect the other end of the wire to alligator clip #1.

12. Connect one end of the shorter piece of antenna wire to a cold-water pipe or faucet. Connect the other end to alligator clip #2. See Figure 5.

13. Put on the earphone and try to locate a station by squeezing the tuning plates slowly until you hear a signal. Some stations will come in when the plates are close together. Other stations will come in when the plates are opened far apart.

Analyze and Conclude

1. **Observing** How many stations can you pick up? Where are these stations located, and which station has the strongest signal? Keep a log of the stations you receive.

2. **Forming Operational Definitions** In your own words, give a definition of "signal strength." How did you compare the signal strengths of different radio stations?

3. **Drawing Conclusions** How does adjusting the tuning plates affect reception of the radio signals?

4. **Making Models** You can improve reception by having a good antenna. How can you improve your antenna?

5. **Communicating** Write a paragraph describing the various parts of the radio and how they are linked together.

Design an Experiment

Use a radio to test signal reception at various times of the day. Do you receive more stations at night or in the morning? Does weather affect reception? *Obtain your teacher's permission before carrying out your investigation.*

① The Nature of Electromagnetic Waves

Key Concepts

- An electromagnetic wave consists of vibrating electric and magnetic fields that move through space at the speed of light.

- Many properties of electromagnetic waves can be explained by a wave model. However, some properties are best explained by a particle model.

Key Terms

electromagnetic wave
electromagnetic radiation
polarized light
photoelectric effect
photon

② Waves of the Electromagnetic Spectrum

Key Concepts

- All electromagnetic waves travel at the same speed in a vacuum, but they have different wavelengths and different frequencies.

- The electromagnetic spectrum is made up of radio waves, infrared rays, visible light, ultraviolet rays, X-rays, and gamma rays.

Key Terms

electromagnetic spectrum	thermogram
radio waves	visible light
microwaves	ultraviolet rays
radar	X-rays
infrared rays	gamma rays

③ Producing Visible Light

Key Concept

- Common types of light bulbs include incandescent, tungsten-halogen, fluorescent, vapor, and neon lights.

Key Terms

illuminated
luminous
spectroscope
incandescent light
tungsten-halogen bulb
fluorescent light
vapor light
neon light

④ Wireless Communication

Key Concepts

- Transmission antennas send out, or broadcast, radio waves in all directions. Radio waves carry information from the antenna of a broadcasting station to the receiving antenna of your radio or television.

- Cellular phones transmit and receive signals using high-frequency microwaves.

- Communications satellites receive radio, television, and telephone signals, and relay the signals back to receivers on Earth.

Key Terms

amplitude modulation
frequency modulation

Review and Assessment

Go Online
PHSchool.com
For: Self-Assessment
Visit: PHSchool.com
Web Code: cga-5030

Organizing Information

Concept Mapping Copy the concept map about electromagnetic waves onto a separate sheet of paper. Then complete it and add a title. (For more on Concept Mapping, see the Skills Handbook.)

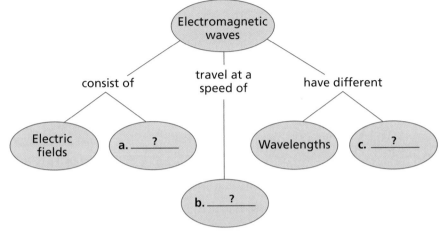

Electromagnetic waves

consist of | travel at a speed of | have different

Electric fields | **a.** ___?___ | Wavelengths | **c.** ___?___

b. ___?___

Reviewing Key Terms

Choose the letter of the best answer.

1. Electromagnetic waves are transverse waves that transfer
   a. sound energy.
   b. photons.
   c. electrical and magnetic energy.
   d. the particles of a medium.

2. Light that vibrates in only one direction is called
   a. luminous.
   b. illuminated.
   c. visible light.
   d. polarized light.

3. The electromagnetic waves with the longest wavelengths and lowest frequencies are
   a. radio waves.
   b. infrared rays.
   c. X-rays.
   d. gamma rays.

4. Radar is a system that uses reflected radio waves to
   a. detect objects and measure their speed.
   b. kill bacteria.
   c. carry AM signals.
   d. cook food.

5. A light bulb that glows when a filament inside it gets hot is a(n)
   a. vapor light.
   b. fluorescent light.
   c. incandescent light.
   d. neon light.

If the statement is true, write *true*. If it is false, change the underlined word or words to make the statement true.

6. In the <u>photoelectric effect</u>, light strikes a material and causes electrons to be ejected.

7. Electromagnetic waves that you can see are called <u>infrared rays</u>.

8. An <u>illuminated</u> object gives off its own light.

9. A(n) <u>incandescent light</u> contains a gas and is coated on the inside with a powder.

10. In <u>frequency modulation</u>, the amplitude of a wave is changed.

Writing in Science

Letter Write a letter to a friend about the rescue of a ship's crew at sea. Include details about the ship's emergency radio and the role of satellites.

Discovery CHANNEL SCHOOL™

The Electromagnetic Spectrum
Video Preview
Video Field Trip
▶ Video Assessment

Review and Assessment

Checking Concepts

11. How do you know that electromagnetic waves can travel through a vacuum?

12. Two polarizing filters overlap at right angles. Why does the area of overlap look dark?

13. Explain why the energy of infrared rays is greater than the energy of radio waves.

14. Which color of light has the longest wavelength? The shortest wavelength?

15. What damage is caused by ultraviolet rays in sunlight? How can this damage be limited?

16. Which light bulbs give off very little energy as infrared rays?

17. Which of these is most efficient: an ordinary light bulb, a tungsten-halogen bulb, or a fluorescent light? Which is least efficient?

18. Which wave shown below is an AM wave? Which is an FM wave? Explain your answers.

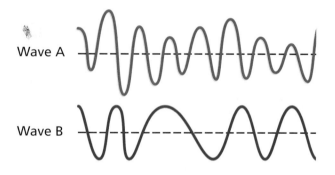

Wave A

Wave B

19. Explain how the Global Positioning System works.

Math Practice

20. **Scientific Notation** A cellular phone uses a frequency of 1.9×10^9 Hz. Write this frequency as a number without an exponent.

Thinking Critically

21. **Relating Cause and Effect** Gamma rays can cause more harm than X-rays. Explain why.

22. **Classifying** List examples of five luminous objects and five illuminated objects.

23. **Problem Solving** To build an incubator for young chicks, you need a source of heat. What type of light bulb could you use? Explain.

24. **Comparing and Contrasting** Make a table to compare the different types of wireless communication. Include headings such as type of information transmitted, frequencies, and one-way or two-way communication.

Applying Skills

Use the table below to answer Questions 25–27.

The table gives data about four radio stations.

Radio Station Frequencies

Station Name	Frequency
KLIZ	580 kHz
KMOM	103.7 MHz
WDAD	1030 kHz
WJFO	89.7 MHz

25. **Interpreting Data** Which radio station broadcasts at the longest wavelength? The shortest wavelength?

26. **Classifying** Which radio stations are AM? Which are FM?

27. **Predicting** You are going on a car trip across the United States. Which station would you expect to receive for the greater distance: KLIZ or KMOM?

Lab zone Chapter **Project**

Performance Assessment Decide how to present to your class the results of your survey about wireless communication. You might make a poster to display tables and graphs. Or you could make a computer presentation. Prepare summary statements for each table and graph. Then make your presentation to the class.

Standardized Test Prep

Test-Taking Tip

Interpreting Diagrams

When answering questions about diagrams, read all parts of the diagram carefully, including the title, captions, and labels. Make sure you understand the meanings of arrows and other symbols. Determine exactly what the question asks. Then eliminate those answer choices that are not supported by the diagram.

Sample Question

The electromagnetic waves in the diagram at right that have the shortest wavelength are

  A radio waves.
  B ultrasound waves.
  C X-rays.
  D gamma rays.

Answer

The correct answer is **D**, because gamma rays have the highest frequency and therefore the shortest wavelength. Answer **B** is wrong because ultrasound waves are not electromagnetic waves. Answers **A** and **C** are incorrect because these waves have longer wavelengths than gamma rays.

| Radio Waves | Infrared rays | Visible light | Ultraviolet rays | X-rays | Gamma rays |

Microwaves

Use the diagram to answer Questions 3 and 4.

3. The amount of energy carried by an electromagnetic wave increases with frequency. Which of the following groups of waves is listed correctly in order of increasing energy?
  A X-rays, visible light, radio waves
  B radio waves, visible light, X-rays
  C infrared rays, visible light, radio waves
  D visible light, gamma rays, X-rays

4. Microwaves are a type of
  F radio wave.
  G X-ray.
  H visible light.
  J ultraviolet ray.

5. An experiment is set up to determine the efficiency of a 60-W light bulb. The light output is measured as 6 watts. The power used is assumed to be 60 watts. The experimenter calculates the efficiency using this equation:

$$\text{Efficiency} = \frac{\text{Measured light output (watts)}}{\text{Measured power used (watts)}}$$

Why is this experiment flawed?
  A The efficiency cannot be measured.
  B The efficiency of the light bulb can only be compared to a second light bulb.
  C The light output needs to be measured more precisely.
  D The actual power used was not measured.

Constructed Response

6. Explain how a spectrum is formed when white light passes through a prism. In your answer, explain what white light is composed of.

Choose the letter of the best answer.

1. The moon does not give off its own light. You can infer that the moon
  A is luminous.
  B has no atmosphere.
  C is illuminated.
  D is incandescent.

2. Ultraviolet rays from the sun are able to reach Earth's surface because
  F they require air to travel through.
  G they have more energy than infrared rays.
  H they can travel through empty space.
  J they can penetrate through clouds.

Chapter

4

Light

interactive Textbook

These windows reflect light, but they ▶
also let light pass straight through.

Lab zone™ Chapter Project

Design and Build an Optical Instrument

You see reflections all the time—in shiny surfaces, windows, and mirrors. A camera can capture reflections on film. A telescope can capture reflected light with a curved mirror. Cameras and telescopes are optical instruments, devices that control light with mirrors or lenses. In this Chapter Project, you will design and build your own optical instrument.

Your Goal To design, build, and test an optical instrument that serves a specific purpose

Your optical instrument must

● be made of materials that are approved by your teacher

● include at least one mirror or one lens

● be built and used following the safety guidelines in Appendix A

Plan It! Start by deciding on the purpose of your optical instrument and how you will use it. Sketch your design and choose the materials you will need. Then build and test your optical instrument. Finally, make a manual that describes and explains each part of the instrument.

Light and Color

Reading Preview

Key Concepts
- What happens to the light that strikes an object?
- What determines the color of an opaque, transparent, or translucent object?
- How is mixing pigments different from mixing colors of light?

Key Terms
- transparent material
- translucent material
- opaque material
- primary colors
- secondary color
- complementary colors
- pigment

Target Reading Skill

Building Vocabulary Using a word in a sentence helps you think about how to best explain the word. As you read, carefully note the definition of each Key Term. Also note other details in the paragraph that contains the definition. Use all this information to write a sentence using the Key Term.

Discover Activity

How Do Colors Mix?

1. Cut a disk with a diameter of 10 cm out of white cardboard. Divide the disk into three equal-sized segments. Color one segment red, the next green, and the third blue.
2. Carefully punch two holes, 2 cm apart, on opposite sides of the center of the disk.
3. Thread a 1-m long string through the holes. Tie the ends of the string together to make a loop that passes through both holes.
4. With equal lengths of string on each side of the disk, tape the string in place. Turn the disk to wind up the string. Predict what color(s) you will see if the disk spins fast.
5. Spin the disk by pulling the loops to unwind the string.

Think It Over

Observing What color do you see as the wheel spins fast? Was your prediction correct?

It was hard work, but you are finally finished. You stand back to admire your work. Color is everywhere! The bright green grass rolls right up to the flower garden you just weeded. In the bright sunlight, you see patches of yellow daffodils, purple hyacinths, and red tulips. The sun's light allows you to see each color. But sunlight is white light. What makes each flower appear to be a different color?

Flowers in sunlight ▼

When Light Strikes an Object

To understand why objects have different colors, you need to know how light can interact with an object. **When light strikes an object, the light can be reflected, transmitted, or absorbed.** Think about a pair of sunglasses. If you hold the sunglasses in your hand, you can see light that reflects off the lenses. If you put the sunglasses on, you see light that is transmitted by the lenses. The lenses also absorb some light. That is why objects appear darker when seen through the lenses.

Lenses, like all objects, are made of one or more materials. Most materials can be classified as transparent, translucent, or opaque based on what happens to light that strikes the material.

Transparent Materials A **transparent material** transmits most of the light that strikes it. The light passes right through without being scattered. This allows you to see clearly what is on the other side. Clear glass, water, and air all are transparent materials. In Figure 1, you can clearly see the straw through the glass on the left.

Translucent Materials A **translucent material** (trans LOO sunt) scatters light as it passes through. You can usually see something behind a translucent object, but the details are blurred. Wax paper and a frosted glass like the middle glass in Figure 1 are translucent materials.

Opaque Materials An **opaque material** (oh PAYK) reflects or absorbs all of the light that strikes it. You cannot see through opaque materials because light cannot pass through them. Wood, metal, and tightly woven fabric all are opaque materials. You cannot see the straw through the white glass in Figure 1 because the glass is opaque.

 **Reading Checkpoint** What happens when light strikes an opaque material?

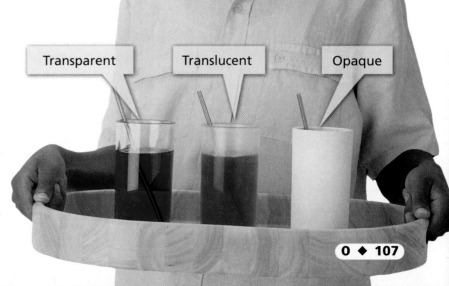

Transparent Translucent Opaque

FIGURE 1
Types of Materials
Different types of materials reflect, transmit, and absorb different amounts of light.
Comparing and Contrasting
How does a straw seen through transparent glass compare with a straw seen through translucent glass?

FIGURE 2
Colored Light
The color an apple appears to be depends on the color of the light that strikes it.
Applying Concepts *What color of light is reflected by a red apple?*

In red light, the apple appears red because it reflects the red light. But the leaves look black.

In green light, the apple appears black because no red light strikes it. But the leaves look green.

In blue light, both the apple and the leaves appear black.

The Color of Objects

If you know how light interacts with objects, you can explain why objects such as flowers have different colors. The color of any object depends on the material the object is made of and the color of light striking the object.

Color of Opaque Objects The color of an opaque object depends on the wavelengths of light that the object reflects. Every opaque object absorbs some wavelengths of light and reflects others. **The color of an opaque object is the color of the light it reflects.** For example, look at the apple shown at the top of Figure 2. The apple appears red because it reflects red wavelengths of light. The apple absorbs the other colors of light. The leaf looks green because it reflects green light and absorbs the other colors.

Objects can appear to change color if you view them in a different color of light. In red light, the apple appears red because there is red light for it to reflect. But the leaf appears black because there is no green light to reflect. In green light, the leaf looks green but the apple looks black. And in blue light, both the apple and the leaf look black.

Go Online
SCiLINKS
For: Links on colors
Visit: www.SciLinks.org
Web Code: scn-1543

FIGURE 3
Color Filters

When you look at an apple through different filters, the color of the apple depends on the color of the filter. *Interpreting Photographs Why do both the apple and the leaves appear black through the blue filter?*

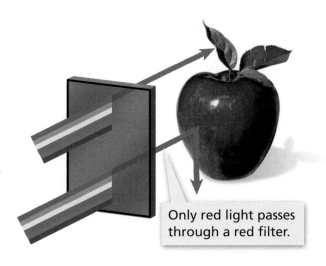

Only red light passes through a red filter.

The red filter transmits red light, so the apple looks red. But the leaf looks black.

The green filter transmits green light, so the leaf looks green. But the apple looks black.

The blue filter transmits blue light. Both the apple and the leaf look black.

Color of Transparent and Translucent Objects Materials that are transparent or translucent allow only certain colors of light to pass through them. They reflect or absorb the other colors. **The color of a transparent or translucent object is the color of the light it transmits.** For example, when white light shines through a transparent blue glass, the glass appears blue because it transmits blue light.

Transparent or translucent materials are used to make color filters. For example, a piece of glass or plastic that allows only red light to pass through is a red color filter. When you look at an object through a color filter, the color of the object may appear different than when you see the object in white light, as shown in Figure 3.

The lenses in sunglasses often are color filters. For example, lenses that are tinted yellow are yellow filters. Lenses that are tinted green are green filters. When you put on these tinted sunglasses, some objects appear to change color. The color you see depends on the color of the filter and on the color that the object appears in white light.

Reading Checkpoint **What is a color filter?**

Lab zone Skills Activity

Developing Hypotheses

1. Predict what colors you will see if you view a red, white, and blue flag through a red filter. Write a hypothesis of what the outcome will be. Write your hypothesis as an "If … then …" statement.

2. View an American flag using a red filter. What do you see? Is your hypothesis confirmed?

3. Repeat Steps 1 and 2 using a yellow filter.

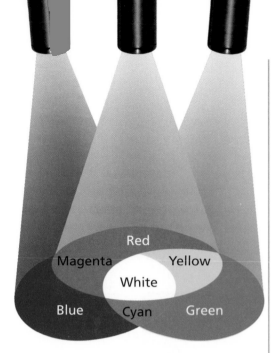

Combining Colors

Color is used in painting, photography, theater lighting, and printing. People who work with color must learn how to produce a wide range of colors using just a few basic colors. Three colors that can combine to make any other color are called **primary colors.** Two primary colors combine in equal amounts to produce a **secondary color.**

Mixing Colors of Light The primary colors of light are red, green, and blue. **When combined in equal amounts, the three primary colors of light produce white light.** If they are combined in different amounts, the primary colors can produce other colors. For example, red and green combine to form yellow light. Yellow is a secondary color of light because two primary colors produce it. The secondary colors of light are yellow (red + green), cyan (green + blue), and magenta (red + blue). Figure 4 shows the primary and secondary colors of light.

A primary and a secondary color can combine to make white light. Any two colors that combine to form white light are called **complementary colors.** Yellow and blue are complementary colors, as are cyan and red, and magenta and green.

A color television produces many colors using only the primary colors of light—red, green, and blue. Figure 5 shows a magnified view of a color television screen. The picture in the screen is made up of little groups of red, green, and blue light. By varying the brightness of each colored bar, the television can produce thousands of different colors.

FIGURE 5
Colors in Television
A television produces many colors using only the primary colors of light.
Predicting For a yellow area on a television screen, what color would you expect the bars to be?

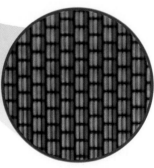

Equal amounts of red, green, and blue appear white from a distance.

Mixing Pigments How does a printer produce the many shades of colors you see in this textbook? Inks, paints, and dyes contain **pigments,** or colored substances that are used to color other materials. Pigments absorb some colors and reflect others. The color you see is the result of the colors that particular pigment reflects.

Mixing colors of pigments is different from mixing colors of light. **As pigments are added together, fewer colors of light are reflected and more are absorbed.** The more pigments that are combined, the darker the mixture looks.

Cyan, yellow, and magenta are the primary colors of pigments. These colors combine in equal amounts to produce black. By combining pigments in varying amounts, you can produce many other colors. If you combine two primary colors of pigments, you get a secondary color, as shown in Figure 6. The secondary colors of pigments are red, green, and blue.

Look at the pictures in this book with a magnifying glass. You can see tiny dots of different colors of ink. The colors used are cyan, yellow, and magenta. Black ink is also used, so the printing process is called four-color printing.

FIGURE 6
Primary Colors of Pigments
The primary colors of pigments combine in equal amounts to form black.

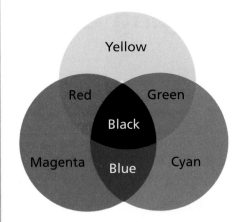

 **Reading Checkpoint** What are pigments?

Section 1 Assessment

Target Reading Skill Building Vocabulary Use your definitions to help answer the questions.

Reviewing Key Concepts

1. a. **Identifying** What three things may happen to the light that strikes an object?
   b. **Applying Concepts** What happens to light that strikes the following materials: clear plastic, aluminum foil, and tissue paper?
   c. **Problem Solving** Room-darkening window shades are used to keep sunlight out of a theater. What type of material should the shades be made of? Explain.

2. a. **Reviewing** What determines the color of an opaque object? Of a transparent or translucent object?
   b. **Drawing Conclusions** An actor's red shirt and blue pants both appear black. What color is the stage light shining on the actor?

3. a. **Describing** What are the primary colors of light? The primary colors of pigments?
   b. **Comparing and Contrasting** How does the result of mixing the primary colors of pigments compare to the result of mixing the primary colors of light?
   c. **Interpreting Diagrams** In Figure 6, which pairs of colors combine to make black?

Lab zone At-Home **Activity**

Color Mix See how many different shades of green you can make by mixing blue and yellow paint in different proportions. On white paper, paint a "spectrum" from yellow to green to blue. Show the results to your family. Then explain how magazine photos reproduce thousands of colors.

Changing Colors

Problem

How do color filters affect the appearance of objects in white light?

Skills Focus

observing, inferring, predicting

Materials

- shoe box
- scissors
- flashlight
- removable tape
- red object
  (such as a ripe tomato)
- yellow object
  (such as a ripe lemon)
- blue object
  (such as blue construction paper)
- red, green, and blue cellophane,
  enough to cover the top of the
  shoe box

Procedure ✂

1. Carefully cut a large rectangular hole in the lid of the shoe box.

2. Carefully cut a small, round hole in the center of one of the ends of the shoe box.

3. Tape the red cellophane under the lid of the shoe box, covering the hole in the lid.

4. Place the objects in the box and put the lid on.

5. In a darkened room, shine the flashlight into the shoe box through the side hole. Note the apparent color of each object in the box.

6. Repeat Steps 3–5 using the other colors of cellophane.

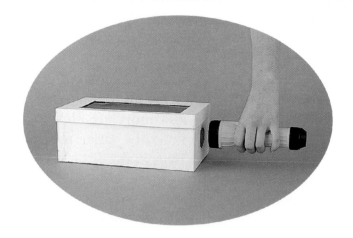

Analyze and Conclude

1. **Observing** What did you see when you looked through the red cellophane? Explain why each object appeared as it did.

2. **Observing** What did you see when you looked through the blue cellophane? Explain.

3. **Inferring** What color(s) of light does each piece of cellophane allow through?

4. **Predicting** Predict what you would see under each piece of cellophane if you put a white object in the box. Test your prediction.

5. **Predicting** What do you think would happen if you viewed a red object through yellow cellophane? Draw a diagram to support your prediction. Then test your prediction.

6. **Communicating** Summarize your conclusions by drawing diagrams to show how each color filter affects white light. Write captions to explain your diagrams.

Design an Experiment

Do color filters work like pigments or like colors of light? Design an experiment to find out what happens if you shine a light through both a red and a green filter. *Obtain your teacher's permission before carrying out your investigation.*

Reflection and Mirrors

Reading Preview

Key Concepts
• What are the kinds of reflection?
• What types of images are produced by plane, concave, and convex mirrors?

Key Terms
• ray • regular reflection
• diffuse reflection
• plane mirror • image
• virtual image
• concave mirror • optical axis
• focal point • real image
• convex mirror

Target Reading Skill
Comparing and Contrasting
As you read, compare and contrast concave and convex mirrors in a Venn diagram like the one below. Write the similarities in the space where the circles overlap and the differences on the left and right sides.

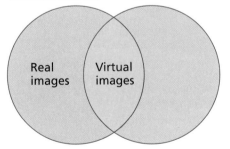

Concave Mirrors   Convex Mirrors

Real images | Virtual images

Discover **Activity**

How Does Your Reflection Wink?

1. Look at your face in a mirror. Wink your right eye. Which eye does your reflection wink?
2. Tape two mirrors together so that they open and close like a book. Open them so they form a 90-degree angle with each other. **CAUTION:** *Be careful of any sharp edges.*
3. Looking into both mirrors at once, wink at your reflection again. Which eye does your reflection wink now?

Think It Over
Observing How does your reflection wink at you? How does the second reflection compare with the first reflection?

You laugh as you and a friend move toward the curved mirror. First your reflections look tall and skinny. Then they become short and wide. At one point, your reflections disappear even though you are still in front of the mirror. Imagine what it would be like if this happened every time you tried to comb your hair in front of a mirror!

◄ Funhouse mirror

Lab zone Skills Activity

Observing

In a dark room, hold a flashlight next to a table. **CAUTION:** *Do not look directly into the flashlight.* Point its beam straight up so no light shines on the tabletop. Then hold a metal can upright 5 cm above the flashlight. Tilt the can so its flat bottom reflects light onto the table. Try this again using a white paper cup. How does the light reflected by the can compare with the light reflected by the cup?

FIGURE 7
Diffuse and Regular Reflection
The type of reflection that occurs at a surface depends on whether the surface is rough or smooth.

Reflection of Light Rays

The reflection you see in a mirror depends on how the surface reflects light. To show how light reflects, you can represent light waves as straight lines called **rays.** You may recall that light rays obey the law of reflection—the angle of reflection equals the angle of incidence.

Figure 7 shows two kinds of reflection. In the choppy water, you do not see a clear reflection of the person in the boat. But in the smooth water, you see a sharp reflection. **The two ways in which a surface can reflect light are regular reflection and diffuse reflection.**

Regular Reflection When parallel rays of light hit a smooth surface, **regular reflection** occurs. All of the light rays are reflected at the same angle because of the smooth surface. So, you see a sharp reflection.

Diffuse Reflection When parallel rays of light hit a bumpy or uneven surface, **diffuse reflection** occurs. Each light ray obeys the law of reflection but hits the surface at a different angle because the surface is uneven. Therefore, each ray reflects at a different angle, and you don't see a clear reflection.

Reading Checkpoint What kind of surface results in diffuse reflection?

Diffuse Reflection
When parallel light rays strike a rough surface, the rays are reflected at different angles.

Regular Reflection
When parallel light rays strike a smooth surface, all of the rays are reflected at the same angle.

FIGURE 8
Image in a Plane Mirror
A plane mirror forms a
virtual image. The reflected
light rays appear to come
from behind the mirror,
where the image forms.
Observing *Is the raised
hand in the image a left
hand or a right hand?*

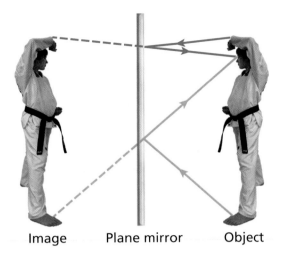

Image   Plane mirror   Object

Plane Mirrors

Did you look into a mirror this morning to comb your hair or
brush your teeth? If you did, you probably used a plane mirror.
A **plane mirror** is a flat sheet of glass that has a smooth, silver-
colored coating on one side. Often the coating is on the back
of the mirror to protect it from damage. When light strikes a
mirror, the coating reflects the light. Because the coating is
smooth, regular reflection occurs and a clear image forms. An
image is a copy of an object formed by reflected or refracted
rays of light.

What Kind of Image Forms The image you see in a plane
mirror is a **virtual image**—an upright image that forms where
light seems to come from. "Virtual" describes something that
does not really exist. Your image appears to be behind the
mirror, but you can't reach behind the mirror and touch it.

    **A plane mirror produces a virtual image that is upright
and the same size as the object.** But the image is not quite the
same as the object. The left and right of the image are reversed.
For example, when you look in a mirror, your right hand
appears to be a left hand in the image.

How Images Form Figure 8 shows how a plane mirror
forms an image. Some light rays from the karate student strike
the mirror and reflect toward his eye. Even though the rays are
reflected, the student's brain treats them as if they had come
from behind the mirror. The dashed lines show where the light
rays appear to come from. Because the light appears to come
from behind the mirror, this is where the student's image
appears to be located.

 Reading
Checkpoint   **Where does an image in a plane mirror appear to
be located?**

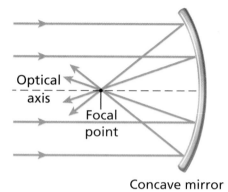

FIGURE 9

Focal Point of a Concave Mirror
A concave mirror reflects rays of light parallel to the optical axis back through the focal point.

Optical axis

Focal point

Concave mirror

Concave Mirrors

A mirror with a surface that curves inward like the inside of a bowl is a **concave mirror.** Figure 9 shows how a concave mirror can reflect parallel rays of light so that they meet at a point. Notice that the rays of light shown are parallel to the optical axis. The **optical axis** is an imaginary line that divides a mirror in half, much like the Equator that divides Earth into northern and southern halves. The point at which rays parallel to the optical axis meet is called the **focal point.** The location of the focal point depends on the shape of the mirror. The more curved the mirror is, the closer the focal point is to the mirror.

Representing How Images Form Ray diagrams are used to show where a focused image forms in a concave mirror. A ray diagram shows rays of light coming from points on the object. Two rays coming from one point on the object meet or appear to meet at the corresponding point on the image. Figure 10 shows how a ray diagram is drawn.

FIGURE 10

Drawing a Ray Diagram

Ray diagrams show where an image forms and the size of the image. The steps below show how to draw a ray diagram.

1 Draw a red ray from a point on the object (point **A**) to the mirror. Make this ray parallel to the optical axis. Then draw the reflected ray, which passes through the focal point.

2 Draw the green ray from the same point on the object to the mirror. Draw this ray as if it comes from the focal point. Then draw the reflected ray, which is parallel to the optical axis.

3 Draw dashed lines behind the mirror to show where the reflected rays appear to come from. The corresponding point on the image is located where the dashed lines cross.

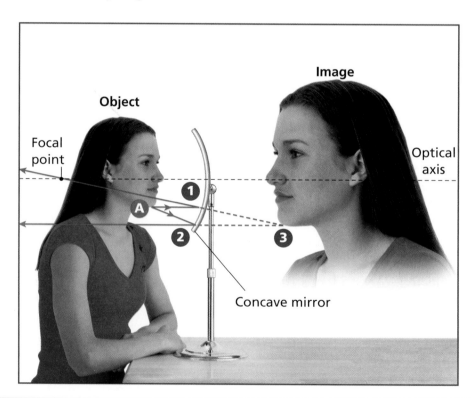

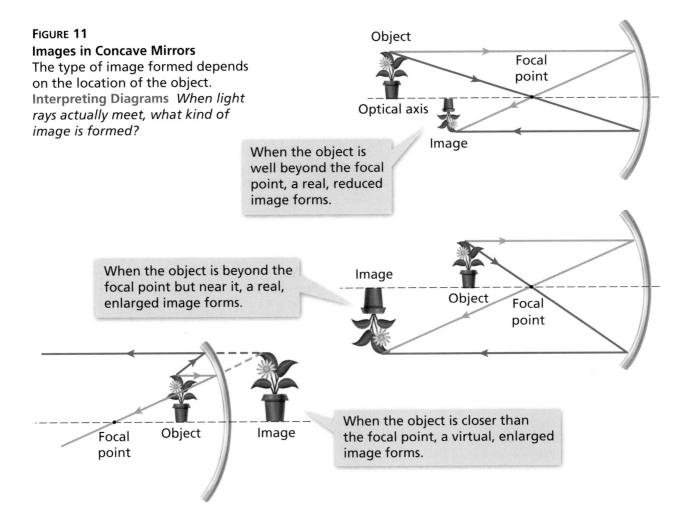

FIGURE 11
Images in Concave Mirrors
The type of image formed depends on the location of the object.
Interpreting Diagrams *When light rays actually meet, what kind of image is formed?*

Object

Focal point

Optical axis

Image

When the object is well beyond the focal point, a real, reduced image forms.

When the object is beyond the focal point but near it, a real, enlarged image forms.

Image

Object

Focal point

Focal point

Object

Image

When the object is closer than the focal point, a virtual, enlarged image forms.

Determining the Type of Image The type of image that is formed by a concave mirror depends on the location of the object. **Concave mirrors can form either virtual images or real images.** If the object is farther away from the mirror than the focal point, the reflected rays form a real image as shown in Figure 11. A **real image** forms when rays actually meet. Real images are upside down. A real image may be larger or smaller than the object.

If the object is between the mirror and the focal point, the reflected rays form a virtual image. The image appears to be behind the mirror and is upright. Virtual images formed by a concave mirror are always larger than the object. Concave mirrors produce the magnified images you see in a makeup mirror.

If an object is placed at the focal point, no image forms. But if a light source is placed at the focal point, the mirror can project parallel rays of light. A car headlight, for example, has a light bulb at the focal point of a concave mirror. Light hits the mirror, forming a beam of light that shines on the road ahead.

Go **O**nline
active art

For: Mirrors activity
Visit: PHSchool.com
Web Code: cgp-5042

Reading Checkpoint What is a real image?

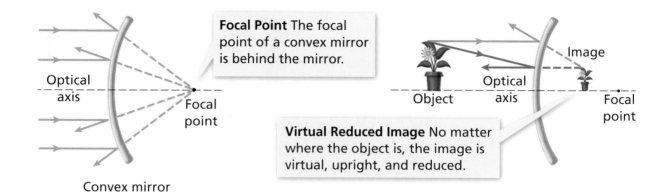

Focal Point The focal point of a convex mirror is behind the mirror.

Optical axis

Focal point

Convex mirror

Image

Object

Optical axis

Focal point

Virtual Reduced Image No matter where the object is, the image is virtual, upright, and reduced.

FIGURE 12
Convex Mirrors
Light rays parallel to the optical axis reflect as if they came from the focal point behind the mirror. The image formed by a convex mirror is always virtual.
Making Generalizations *Describe the directions of the parallel rays reflected by a convex mirror.*

Convex Mirrors

A mirror with a surface that curves outward is called a **convex mirror.** Figure 12 shows how convex mirrors reflect parallel rays of light. The rays spread out but appear to come from a focal point behind the mirror. The focal point of a convex mirror is the point from which the rays appear to come. **Because the rays never meet, images formed by convex mirrors are always virtual and smaller than the object.**

Perhaps you have seen this warning on a car mirror: "Objects in mirror are closer than they appear." Convex mirrors are used in cars as passenger-side mirrors. The advantage of a convex mirror is that it allows you to see a larger area than you can with a plane mirror. The disadvantage is that the image is reduced in size, so it appears to be farther away than it actually is.

 **Reading Checkpoint** Where are convex mirrors typically used?

Section 2 Assessment

Target Reading Skill
Comparing and Contrasting Use your Venn diagram about mirrors to help you answer Question 2 below.

Reviewing Key Concepts
1. a. **Reviewing** What are two kinds of reflection?
   b. **Explaining** Explain how both kinds of reflection obey the law of reflection.
   c. **Inferring** Why is an image clear in a shiny spoon but fuzzy in a tarnished spoon?
2. a. **Defining** What is an image?
   b. **Classifying** Which mirrors can form real images? Which can form virtual images?

   c. **Comparing and Contrasting** How are images in concave mirrors like images in convex mirrors? How are they different?

Writing in Science

Dialogue At a funhouse mirror, your younger brother notices he can make his image disappear as he walks toward the mirror. He asks you to explain, but your answer leads to more questions. Write the dialogue that might take place between you and your brother.

Refraction and Lenses

Reading Preview

Key Concepts
- Why do light rays bend when they enter a medium at an angle?
- What determines the types of images formed by convex and concave lenses?

Key Terms
- index of refraction
- mirage
- lens
- convex lens
- concave lens

Target Reading Skill

Asking Questions Before you read, preview the red headings. In a graphic organizer like the one below, ask a *what, when, where* or *how* question for each heading. As you read, write the answers to your questions.

Refraction and Lenses

Question	Answer
When does refraction occur?	Refraction occurs . . .

Lab zone Discover **Activity**

How Can You Make an Image Appear?

1. Stand about 2 meters from a window. Hold a hand lens up to your eye and look through it. What do you see? **CAUTION:** *Do not look at the sun.*

2. Move the lens farther away from your eye. What changes do you notice?

3. Now hold the lens between the window and a sheet of paper, but very close to the paper. Slowly move the lens away from the paper and toward the window. Keep watching the paper. What do you see? What happens as you move the lens?

Think It Over

Observing How is an image formed on a sheet of paper? Describe the image. Is it real or virtual? How do you know?

A fish tank can play tricks on you. If you look through the side of a fish tank, a fish seems closer than if you look over the top. If you look through the corner, you may see the same fish twice. You see one image of the fish through the front of the tank and another through the side. The two images appear in different places! How can this happen?

FIGURE 13
Optical Illusion in a Fish Tank
There is only one fish in this tank, but refraction makes it look as though there are two.

Bending Light

The index of refraction of a medium is a measure of how much light bends as it travels from air into the medium. The table shows the index of refraction of some common mediums.

1. **Interpreting Data** Which medium causes the greatest change in the direction of a light ray?

2. **Interpreting Data** According to the table, which tends to bend light more: solids or liquids?

3. **Predicting** Would you expect light to bend if it entered corn oil at an angle after traveling through glycerol? Explain.

Index of Refraction	
Medium	**Index of Refraction**
Air (gas)	1.00
Water (liquid)	1.33
Ethyl alcohol (liquid)	1.36
Quartz (solid)	1.46
Corn oil (liquid)	1.47
Glycerol (liquid)	1.47
Glass, crown (solid)	1.52
Sodium chloride (solid)	1.54
Zircon (solid)	1.92
Diamond (solid)	2.42

FIGURE 14
Refraction of Light
As light passes from a less dense medium into a more dense medium, it slows down and is refracted.

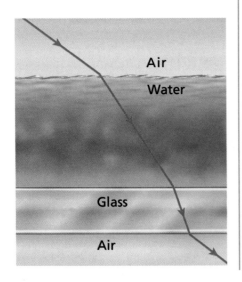

Refraction of Light

Refraction can cause you to see something that may not actually be there. As you look at a fish in a tank, the light coming from the fish to your eye bends as it passes through three different mediums. The mediums are water, the glass of the tank, and air. As the light passes from one medium to the next, it refracts. **When light rays enter a medium at an angle, the change in speed causes the rays to bend, or change direction.**

Refraction in Different Mediums Some mediums cause light to bend more than others, as shown in Figure 14. When light passes from air into water, the light slows down. Light slows down even more when it passes from water into glass. When light passes from glass back into air, the light speeds up. Light travels fastest in air, a little slower in water, and slower still in glass. Notice that the ray that leaves the glass is traveling in the same direction as it was before it entered the water.

Glass causes light to bend more than either air or water. Another way to say this is that glass has a higher index of refraction than either air or water. A material's **index of refraction** is a measure of how much a ray of light bends when it enters that material. The higher the index of refraction of a medium, the more it bends light. The index of refraction of water is 1.33, and the index of refraction of glass is about 1.5. So light is bent more by glass than by water.

Prisms and Rainbows Recall that when white light enters a prism, each wavelength is refracted by a different amount. The longer the wavelength, the less the wave is bent by a prism. Red, with the longest wavelength, is refracted the least. Violet, with the shortest wavelength, is refracted the most. This difference in refraction causes white light to spread out into the colors of the spectrum—red, orange, yellow, green, blue, and violet.

The same process occurs in water droplets suspended in the air. When white light from the sun shines through the droplets, a rainbow may appear. The water droplets act like tiny prisms, refracting and reflecting the light and separating the colors.

Mirages You're traveling in a car on a hot day, and you notice that the road ahead looks wet. Yet when you get there, the road is dry. Did the puddles dry up? No, the puddles were never there! You saw a **mirage** (mih RAHJ)—an image of a distant object caused by refraction of light. The puddles on the road are light rays from the sky that are refracted to your eyes.

Figure 16 shows a mirage. Notice the shiny white areas on the road behind the white car. The air just above the road is hotter than the air higher up. Light travels faster in hot air. So, light rays from the white car that travel toward the road are bent upward by the hot air. Your brain assumes that the rays traveled in a straight line. So the rays look as if they have reflected off a smooth surface. What you see is a mirage.

 **Reading Checkpoint** What causes a mirage?

FIGURE 15
Rainbows
A rainbow forms when sunlight is refracted and reflected by tiny water droplets. **Observing** *What is the order of colors in a rainbow?*

FIGURE 16
Mirages
The puddles and white reflections on the road are mirages. Light refracts as it goes from hot air to cool air. The refracted light appears to come from the ground.

Mirage

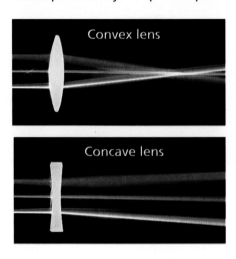

FIGURE 17
Convex and Concave Lenses
A convex lens can focus parallel rays at a focal point. A concave lens causes parallel rays to spread apart.

Convex lens

Concave lens

Lenses

Anytime you look through binoculars, a camera, or eyeglasses, you are using lenses to bend light. A **lens** is a curved piece of glass or other transparent material that is used to refract light. A lens forms an image by refracting light rays that pass through it. Like mirrors, lenses can have different shapes. The type of image formed by a lens depends on the shape of the lens and the position of the object.

Convex Lenses A **convex lens** is thicker in the center than at the edges. As light rays parallel to the optical axis pass through a convex lens, they are bent toward the center of the lens. The rays meet at the focal point of the lens and continue to travel beyond. The more curved the lens, the more it refracts light. A convex lens acts somewhat like a concave mirror, because it focuses rays of light.

An object's position relative to the focal point determines whether a convex lens forms a real image or a virtual image. Figure 18 shows that if the object is farther away than the focal point, the refracted rays form a real image on the other side of the lens. If the object is between the lens and the focal point, a virtual image forms on the same side of the lens as the object.

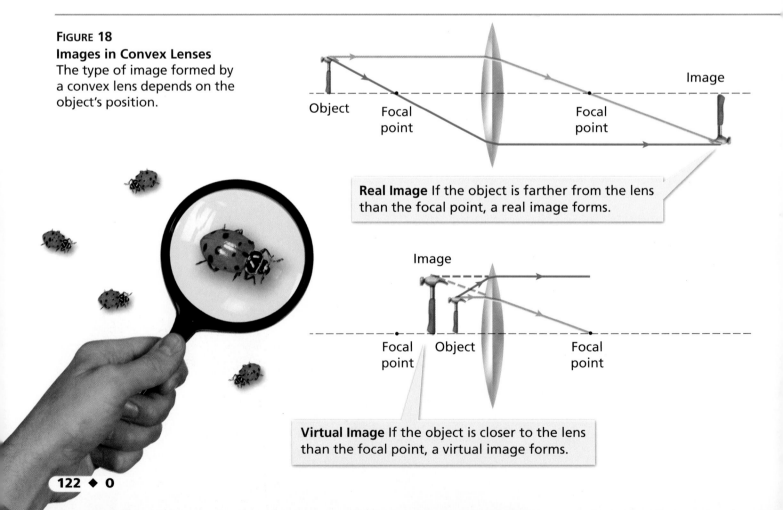

FIGURE 18
Images in Convex Lenses
The type of image formed by a convex lens depends on the object's position.

Image

Object Focal point Focal point

Real Image If the object is farther from the lens than the focal point, a real image forms.

Image

Focal point Object Focal point

Virtual Image If the object is closer to the lens than the focal point, a virtual image forms.

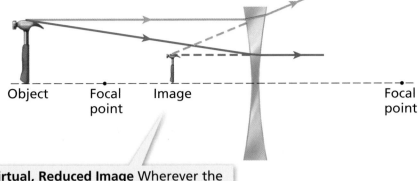

Object | Focal point | Image | Focal point

Virtual, Reduced Image Wherever the object is placed, a virtual image forms.

FIGURE 19
Images in Concave Lenses
A concave lens produces virtual images that are upright and smaller than the object.
Interpreting Diagrams *Why can a concave lens only form a virtual image?*

Go Online
active art

For: Lenses activity
Visit: PHSchool.com
Web Code: cgp-5042

Concave Lenses A **concave lens** is thinner in the center than at the edges. When light rays traveling parallel to the optical axis pass through a concave lens, they bend away from the optical axis and never meet. **A concave lens can produce only virtual images because parallel light rays passing through the lens never meet.**

Figure 19 shows how an image forms in a concave lens. The virtual image is located where the light rays appear to come from. The image is always upright and smaller than the object.

Reading Checkpoint What is the shape of a concave lens?

Section 3 Assessment

Target Reading Skill Asking Questions Use the answers to the questions you wrote about the headings to help you answer the questions below.

Reviewing Key Concepts

1. a. **Identifying** What is a material's index of refraction?
   b. **Relating Cause and Effect** What causes light rays to bend when they enter a new medium at an angle?
   c. **Predicting** If a glass prism were placed in a medium such as water, would it separate white light into different colors? Explain.
2. a. **Defining** What is a lens?
   b. **Comparing and Contrasting** Describe the shapes of a concave lens and a convex lens.

c. **Interpreting Diagrams** Use Figure 18 to explain how you can tell whether a convex lens will form a real or virtual image.

Lab zone **At-Home Activity**

Bent Pencil Here's how you can bend a pencil without touching it. Put a pencil in a glass of water so that it is half in and half out of the water. Have your family members look at the pencil from the side. Using your understanding of refraction, explain to your family why the pencil appears as it does.

Looking at Images

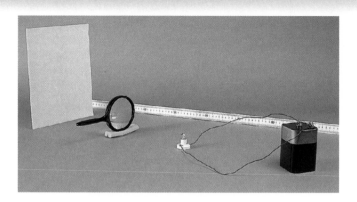

Problem

How does the distance between an object and a convex lens affect the image formed?

Skills Focus

controlling variables, interpreting data

Materials

- tape
- convex lens
- cardboard stand
- blank sheet of paper
- light bulb and socket
- clay, for holding the lens
- battery and wires
- meter stick
- centimeter ruler

Procedure 🥽 🔌

1. Tape the paper onto the cardboard stand.

2. Place a lit bulb more than 2 m from the paper. Use the lens to focus light from the bulb onto the paper. Measure the distance from the lens to the paper. This is the approximate focal length of the lens you are using.

3. Copy the data table into your notebook.

4. Now place the bulb more than twice the focal length away from the lens. Adjust the cardboard until the image is focused. Record the size of the image on the paper and note the orientation of the image. Record the distance from the bulb to the lens and from the lens to the cardboard.

5. Now, move the bulb so that it is just over one focal length away from the lens. Record the position and size of the image.

Analyze and Conclude

1. **Controlling Variables** Make a list of the variables in this experiment. Which variables did you keep constant? Which was the manipulated variable? Which were the responding variables?

2. **Observing** What happened to the position of the image as the bulb moved toward the lens?

3. **Interpreting Data** Was the image formed by the convex lens always enlarged? If not, under what conditions was the image reduced?

4. **Predicting** What would happen if you look through the lens at the bulb when it is closer to the lens than the focal point? Explain your prediction.

5. **Communicating** Write a paragraph explaining how the distance between an object and a convex lens affects the image formed. Use ray diagrams to help you summarize your results.

Design an Experiment

Design an experiment to study images formed by convex lenses with different thicknesses. How does the lens thickness affect the position and size of the images? *Obtain your teacher's permission before carrying out your investigation.*

Data Table			
Focal Length of Lens: _____ cm		Height of Bulb: _____ cm	
Distance From Bulb to Lens (cm)	Distance From Lens to Cardboard (cm)	Image Orientation (upright or upside down)	Image Size (height in cm)

Seeing Light

Reading Preview

Key Concepts
- How do you see objects?
- What types of lenses are used to correct vision problems?

Key Terms
- cornea • pupil • iris • retina
- rods • cones • optic nerve
- nearsighted • farsighted

Target Reading Skill

Sequencing A sequence is the order in which the steps in a process occur. As you read, make a flow-chart that shows how you see objects. Put the steps of the process in separate boxes in the flowchart in the order in which they occur.

How You See Objects

| Light enters the eye. |

↓

| Light focuses on the retina. |

↓

Lab zone Discover **Activity**

Can You See Everything With One Eye?

1. Write an X and an O on a sheet of paper. The O should be about 5 cm to the right of the X.
2. Hold the sheet of paper at arm's length.
3. Close or cover your left eye. Stare at the X with your right eye.
4. Slowly move the paper toward your face while staring at the X. What do you notice?
5. Repeat the activity, keeping both eyes open. What difference do you notice?

Think It Over
Posing Questions Write two questions about vision that you could investigate using the X and the O.

The pitcher goes into her windup, keeping her eye on the strike zone. The batter watches the pitcher release the ball and then swings. Crack! She drops the bat and sprints toward first base. From your seat, you watch the ball travel toward the outfield. Will it be a base hit? The left fielder watches the ball speed toward her. It's over her head for a double!

Players and spectators alike followed the first rule of baseball: Keep your eye on the ball. As the ball moves near and far, your eyes must adjust continuously to keep it in focus. Fortunately, this change in focus happens automatically.

Keep your eye on the ball! ▶

True Colors

When you stare too long at a color, the cones in your eyes get tired.

1. Stare at the bottom right star of the flag for at least 60 seconds. Do not move your eyes or blink during that time.

2. Now stare at a sheet of blank white paper.

Observing What do you see when you look at the white paper? How are the colors you see related to the colors in the original flag?

For: More on eyesight
Visit: PHSchool.com
Web Code: cgd-5044

The Human Eye

Your eyes allow you to sense light. The eye is a complex structure with many parts, as you can see in Figure 20. Each part plays a role in vision. **You see objects when a process occurs that involves both your eyes and your brain.**

Light Enters the Eye Light enters the eye through the transparent front surface called the **cornea** (KAWR nee uh). The cornea protects the eye. It also acts as a lens to help focus light rays.

After passing through the cornea, light enters the pupil, the part of the eye that looks black. The **pupil** is an opening through which light enters the inside of the eye. In dim light, the pupil becomes larger to allow in more light. In bright light, the pupil becomes smaller to allow in less light. The **iris** is a ring of muscle that contracts and expands to change the size of the pupil. The iris gives the eye its color. In most people the iris is brown; in others it is blue, green, or hazel.

An Image Forms After entering the pupil, the light passes through the lens. The lens is a convex lens that refracts light to form an image on the lining of your eyeball. Muscles, called ciliary muscles, hold the lens in place behind the pupil. When you focus on a distant object, the ciliary muscles relax, and the lens becomes longer and thinner. When you focus on a nearby object, the muscles contract, and the lens becomes shorter and fatter.

When the cornea and the lens refract light, an upside-down image is formed on the retina. The **retina** is a layer of cells that lines the inside of the eyeball. (Cells are the tiny structures that make up living things.)

The retina is made up of tiny, light-sensitive cells called rods and cones. **Rods** are cells that contain a pigment that responds to small amounts of light. The rods allow you to see in dim light. **Cones** are cells that respond to color. They may detect red light, green light, or blue light. Cones respond best in bright light. Both rods and cones help change images on the retina into signals that then travel to the brain.

A Signal Goes to the Brain The rods and cones send signals to the brain along a short, thick nerve called the **optic nerve.** The optic nerve begins at the blind spot, an area of the retina so called because it has no rods or cones. Your brain interprets the signals as an upright image. It also combines the images from each of your eyes into a single three-dimensional image.

Reading Checkpoint Where does an image form in the eye?

FIGURE 20

The Human Eye

The eye is a complex structure with many parts that allow you to see.
Relating Cause and Effect *What is the main function of each part of the eye?*

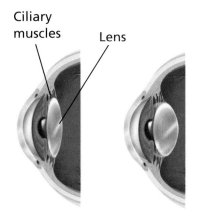

Ciliary muscles

Lens

Retina

Cornea

Iris

Pupil

Blood vessels

Optic nerve

Pupil and Iris
The iris controls the size of the pupil, which determines how much light enters the eye.

Pupil

Iris

Dim Light The iris contracts, making the pupil large.

Bright Light The iris expands, making the pupil small.

Lens and Ciliary Muscles
The ciliary muscles change the shape of the lens.

Ciliary muscles

Lens

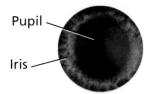

Seeing Far Away The ciliary muscles relax, making the lens thin.

Seeing Close Up The ciliary muscles contract, making the lens thick.

Retina
The retina has two kinds of cells that detect light. The rods respond to dim light. The cones respond to red, green, and blue light.

Rod

Cone

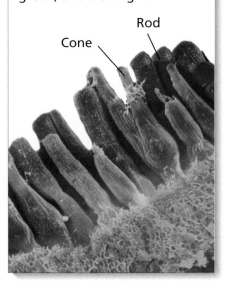

Nearsightedness (eyeball too long)

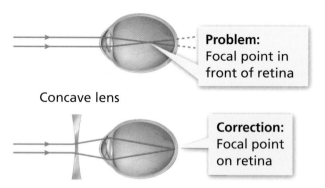

Concave lens

Farsightedness (eyeball too short)

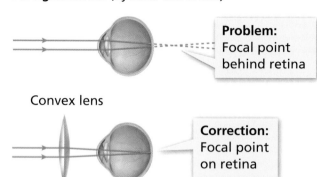

Convex lens

FIGURE 21
Vision Correction
Nearsightedness and farsightedness are caused when the eyeball is too long or too short. Both can be corrected with lenses.

Correcting Vision

If the eyeball is slightly too long or too short, the image on the retina is out of focus. Fortunately, wearing glasses or contact lenses can correct this type of vision problem. **Concave lenses are used to correct nearsightedness. Convex lenses are used to correct farsightedness.**

A **nearsighted** person can see nearby things clearly, but objects at a distance are blurred. The eyeball is too long, so the lens focuses the image in front of the retina. To correct this, a concave lens in front of the eye spreads out light rays before they enter the eye. As a result, the image forms on the retina.

A **farsighted** person can see distant objects clearly, but nearby objects appear blurry. The eyeball is too short, so the image that falls on the retina is out of focus. A convex lens corrects this by bending light rays toward each other before they enter the eye. An image then focuses on the retina.

Section 4 Assessment

Target Reading Skill Sequencing Refer to your flowchart about how you see as you answer Question 1.

Reviewing Key Concepts

1. a. **Identifying** Which parts of your body are involved in seeing objects?
   b. **Explaining** How is an image formed on the retina?
   c. **Sequencing** What happens to light after it strikes the retina?

2. a. **Reviewing** What types of lenses help correct vision problems?
   b. **Describing** Describe a nearsighted person's eye.

c. **Comparing and Contrasting** With uncorrected vision, where does an image form in a nearsighted person's eye? In a farsighted person's eye?

Lab zone At-Home **Activity**

Optical Illusion Look through a cardboard tube with your right eye. Hold your left hand against the far end of the tube with the palm facing you. Keeping both eyes open, look at a distant object. Draw what you see. What do you think causes this illusion?

Reading Preview

Key Concepts
- How are lenses used in telescopes, microscopes, and cameras?
- What makes up laser light, and how is it used?
- Why can optical fibers carry laser beams a long distance?

Key Terms
- telescope
- refracting telescope
- objective
- eyepiece
- reflecting telescope
- microscope
- camera
- laser
- hologram
- optical fiber
- total internal reflection

Target Reading Skill
Building Vocabulary A definition states the meaning of a word or a phrase by telling about its most important feature or function. Carefully read the definition of each Key Term and also read the neighboring sentences. Then write a definition of each Key Term in your own words.

Lab zone Discover **Activity**

How Does a Pinhole Viewer Work?

1. Carefully use a pin to make a tiny hole in the center of the bottom of a paper cup.
2. Place a piece of wax paper over the open end of the cup. Hold the paper in place with a rubber band.
3. Turn off the room lights. Point the end of the cup with the hole in it at a bright window. **CAUTION:** *Do not look directly at the sun.*
4. Look at the image on the wax paper.

Think It Over
Classifying Describe the image you see. Is it upside down or right-side up? Is it smaller or larger than the actual object? What type of image is it?

Have you ever seen photos of the moons of Jupiter? Have you ever thought it would be exciting to fly close to the rings of Saturn? You know that traveling in space has been done for only a few decades. But you might be surprised to know that the moons of Jupiter and the rings of Saturn had not been seen before the year 1600. It was only about 1607 that a new invention, the telescope, made those objects visible to people.

Since the 1600s, astronomers have built more powerful telescopes that allow them to see objects in space that are very far from Earth. For example, the star-forming nebula, or cloud of gas and dust in space, shown below is located trillions of kilometers from Earth. It took about 3 million years for light from this nebula to travel to Earth.

Nebula image from the Hubble Space Telescope ▶

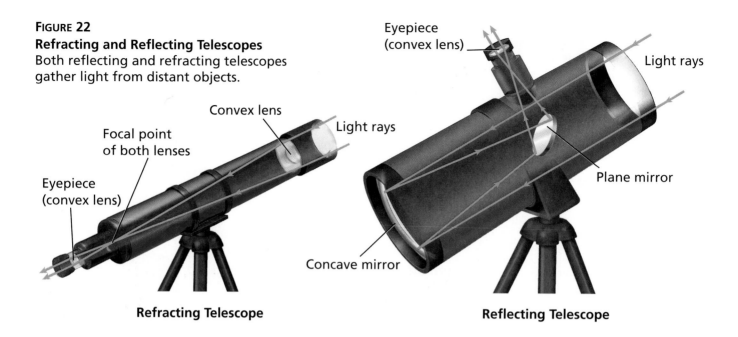

FIGURE 22
Refracting and Reflecting Telescopes
Both reflecting and refracting telescopes gather light from distant objects.

Refracting Telescope

Reflecting Telescope

Optical Instruments

A telescope helps you see objects that are far away. But another type of optical instrument, a microscope, helps you see objects that are nearby. Three common types of optical instruments are telescopes, microscopes, and cameras.

Telescopes Distant objects are difficult to see because light from them has spread out by the time it reaches your eyes. Your eyes are too small to gather much light. A **telescope** forms enlarged images of distant objects. **Telescopes use lenses or mirrors to collect and focus light from distant objects.** The most common use of telescopes is to study objects in space.

Figure 22 shows the two main types of telescopes: refracting telescopes and reflecting telescopes. A **refracting telescope** consists of two convex lenses, one at each end of a tube. The larger lens is called the objective. The **objective** gathers the light coming from an object and focuses the rays to form a real image. The lens close to your eye is called the eyepiece. The **eyepiece** magnifies the image so you can see it clearly. The image seen through the refracting telescope in Figure 22 is upside down.

A **reflecting telescope** uses a large concave mirror to gather light. The mirror collects light from distant objects and focuses the rays to form a real image. A small mirror inside the telescope reflects the image to the eyepiece. The images you see through a reflecting telescope are upside down, just like the images seen through a refracting telescope.

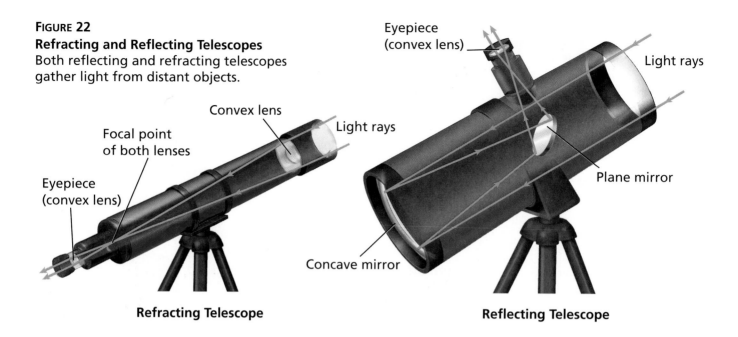

Lab zone Try This Activity

What a View!

You can use two hand lenses of different strengths to form an image.

1. Hold the stronger lens close to your eye.

2. Hold the other lens at arm's length.

3. Use your lens combination to view a distant object. **CAUTION:** *Do not look at the sun.* Adjust the distance of the farther lens until the image is clear.

Classifying What type of image do you see? What type of telescope is similar to this lens combination?

Microscopes To look at small, nearby objects, you would use a microscope. A **microscope** is an optical instrument that forms enlarged images of tiny objects. **A microscope uses a combination of lenses to produce and magnify an image.** For example, the microscope shown in Figure 23 uses two convex lenses to magnify an object, or specimen. The specimen is placed near the objective. The objective forms a real, enlarged image of the specimen. Then the eyepiece enlarges the image even more.

Cameras A **camera** uses one or more lenses to focus light, and film to record an image. Figure 24 shows the structure of a camera. Light from an object travels to the camera and passes through the lens. **The lens of the camera focuses light to form a real, upside-down image on film in the back of the camera.** In many cameras, the lens automatically moves closer to or away from the film until the image is focused.

To take a photo, you press a button that briefly opens the shutter, a screen in front of the film. Opening the shutter allows light passing through the lens to hit the film. The diaphragm is a device with a hole that can be made smaller or larger. Changing the size of the hole controls how much light hits the film. This is similar to the way the pupil of your eye changes size.

Reading Checkpoint What part of a camera controls the amount of light that enters the camera?

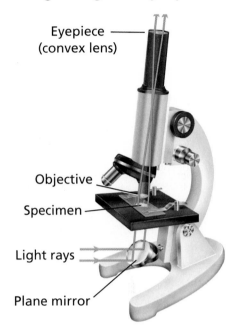

FIGURE 23
Microscope
This microscope uses a combination of lenses to form enlarged images of tiny objects.

Eyepiece (convex lens)

Objective

Specimen

Light rays

Plane mirror

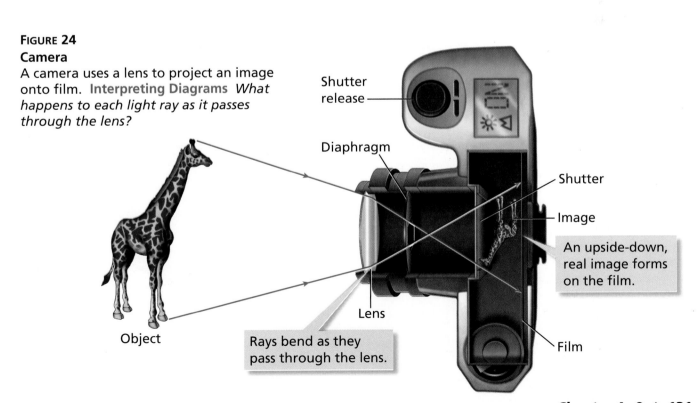

FIGURE 24
Camera
A camera uses a lens to project an image onto film. **Interpreting Diagrams** *What happens to each light ray as it passes through the lens?*

Shutter release

Diaphragm

Shutter

Image

An upside-down, real image forms on the film.

Lens

Object

Rays bend as they pass through the lens.

Film

FIGURE 25
Coherent and Incoherent Light
White light is made up of many different wavelengths. Laser light waves all have the same wavelength. *Inferring What can you infer about the color of laser light?*

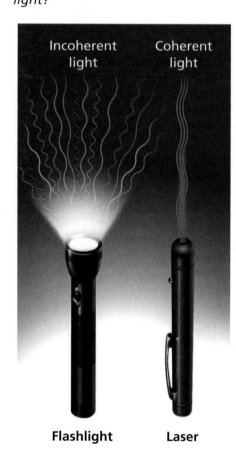

Incoherent light   Coherent light

Flashlight   **Laser**

Lasers

When you turn on a flashlight, the light spreads out as it travels. Ordinary light is made up of different colors and wavelengths. Laser light is different from ordinary light. **Laser light consists of light waves that all have the same wavelength, or color. The waves are coherent, or in step.** All of the crests of the waves align with one another, as shown in Figure 25.

What Is a Laser? A **laser** is a device that produces a narrow beam of coherent light. The word *laser* comes from a phrase that describes how it works: **l**ight **a**mplification by **s**timulated **e**mission of **r**adiation. *Light amplification* means that the light is strengthened. *Stimulated emission* means that the atoms emit light when exposed to electromagnetic radiation.

Producing Laser Light A helium-neon laser is shown in Figure 26. The laser tube contains a mixture of helium and neon gases. An electric current causes this gas mixture to emit photons. You may recall that a photon is a packet of light energy. The mirrors at both ends of the tube reflect the photons back and forth. As a photon travels back and forth, it may bump into a neon particle. This causes the neon particle to emit a photon with the same energy as the one that caused the collision. Then the two photons travel together in step with one another. This process continues until there is a stream of in-step photons traveling up and down the tube. Some of the light "leaks" through the partially reflecting mirror. This light is the laser beam.

Reading Checkpoint What is a laser?

FIGURE 26
Helium-Neon Laser
Photons travel in step up and down the laser tube. The light that comes out of the tube is laser light.

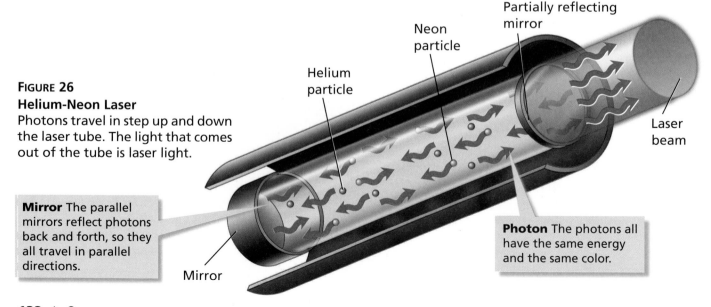

Neon particle

Partially reflecting mirror

Helium particle

Laser beam

Mirror The parallel mirrors reflect photons back and forth, so they all travel in parallel directions.

Mirror

Photon The photons all have the same energy and the same color.

Uses of Lasers

Lasers have many practical uses. Many stores use lasers to scan bar codes. The store's computer then displays the price of the item. Lasers are used in industry to cut through metal. Engineers use laser beams to make sure that surfaces are level and bridges or tunnels are properly aligned. **In addition to their use by stores, industry, and engineers, lasers are used to read information on compact discs, create holograms, and perform surgery.**

Go Online
SciLINKS

For: Links on lasers
Visit: www.SciLinks.org
Web Code: scn-1545

FIGURE 27
Using Lasers

Lasers have become commonplace in everyday living. They are found at home, in stores, and in industry.

▲ Lasers are used for precision cutting in industry.

Scientists use laser scan microscopes to study cells.

▼ Bar codes are scanned with lasers.

▲ Lasers are used in surveying.

Compact discs (CDs) are read by a laser.

Compact Discs Lasers can be used to store and read information. A compact disc is produced by converting data into electrical signals. The electrical signals are used to control a laser beam, which cuts a pattern of pits on a blank disc. When you play a compact disc or read one with a computer, a laser beam shines on the surface and is reflected. The reflection patterns vary because of the pits. The compact disc player or disc drive changes these patterns into electrical signals. The signals are then converted into sound or computer data.

Holography Check out your local video store or newsstand. Some videos and magazines have pictures that appear to move as you walk by. These pictures are called holograms. A **hologram** is a three-dimensional photograph created by using the light from a laser. The process of making these photographs is called holography.

• Tech & Design in History •

Instruments That Use Light
The development of technologies that use light has changed the way we look at the world and beyond. It has allowed major scientific discoveries.

1286 Spectacles
Italian craftsmen made small disks of glass that could be framed and worn in front of the eyes. Early spectacles consisted of convex lenses. They were used as reading glasses.

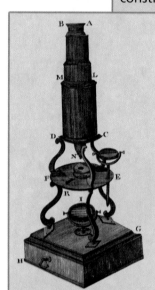

1595 Microscope
The first useful microscope is thought to have been constructed in the Netherlands by Zacharias Jansen or his father, Hans. The Jansen microscope could magnify images up to nine times the size of the object. By the mid-1600s, microscopes looked like the one shown here.

1608 Telescope
The first telescope was made of two convex lenses. From this simple invention the Italian scientist Galileo developed his more powerful telescopes shown here.

1300	1400	1500	1600

Laser Surgery A beam of laser light can be powerful enough to replace a sharp knife. For example, doctors may use lasers instead of scalpels to cut into a person's body. As the laser cuts, it seals the blood vessels. This reduces the amount of blood a patient loses. Wounds from laser surgery usually heal faster than wounds from surgery done with a scalpel.

A common use of laser surgery is to correct vision by reshaping the cornea of the eye. Doctors can also use lasers to repair detached retinas. If the retina falls away from the inside of the eye, the rods and cones can no longer send signals to the brain. This can lead to total or partial blindness. The doctor can use a laser to "weld" or burn the retina back onto the eyeball. Lasers can also be used to destroy or remove skin blemishes and cancerous growths.

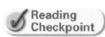 **Reading Checkpoint** What are three types of surgery done with lasers?

Writing in Science

Research and Write Find out more about early photography. Then imagine you are a newspaper reporter in 1855 asked to interview a photographer. Write a newspaper article about the photographic processes and the possible uses it might have in the future.

1826 Camera
The earliest camera, the pinhole camera, was adapted to form and record permanent images by Joseph Nicéphore Niépce and Louis-Jacques-Mandé Daguerre of France. This is one of Niépce's earliest photographic images.

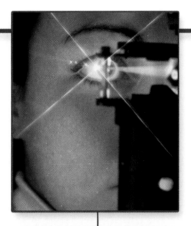

1960 Laser
The first laser, built by American Theodore Maiman, used a rod of ruby to produce light. Since then, lasers have been used in numerous ways, including in engineering, medicine, and communications.

1990 Hubble Space Telescope
This large reflecting telescope was launched by the crew of the space shuttle *Discovery*. It can detect infrared, visible, and ultraviolet rays in space and send pictures back to Earth.

1700	1800	1900	2000

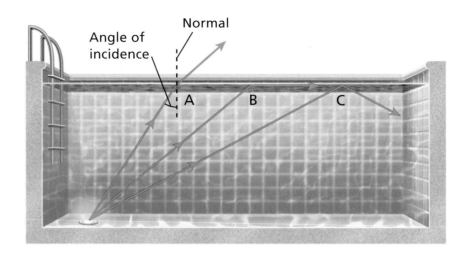

FIGURE 28
Total Internal Reflection
The floodlight in the swimming pool gives off light rays that travel to the surface. If the angle of incidence is great enough, a light ray is completely reflected back into the water.

FIGURE 28
Total Internal Reflection
The floodlight in the swimming pool gives off light rays that travel to the surface. If the angle of incidence is great enough, a light ray is completely reflected back into the water.

Optical Fibers

Laser beams, like radio waves, can carry signals from one place to another. But, laser beams are not usually sent through the air. Instead, they are sent through optical fibers. **Optical fibers** are long, thin strands of glass or plastic that can carry light for long distances without allowing the light to escape.

Optical fibers can carry a laser beam for long distances because the beam stays totally inside the fiber as it travels. Figure 28 shows how light rays can stay inside a medium and not pass through the surface to the outside. The angle of incidence determines whether or not light passes through the surface.

When ray A strikes the water's surface, some light is reflected, but most passes through and is bent. As the angle of incidence gets larger, the light is bent more and more. Ray B is bent so much that it travels parallel to the surface. If the angle of incidence is great enough, no light passes through the surface. Then all of the light is reflected back into the water, as shown by ray C. This complete reflection of light by the inside surface of a medium is called **total internal reflection.**

Figure 29 shows how total internal reflection allows light to travel a long distance in an optical fiber. Each time the light ray strikes the side of the optical fiber, the angle of incidence is large. Because the angle is large, the light ray is always completely reflected. So, no light can escape through the sides of the optical fiber.

Because the angle of incidence is large, all of the laser light reflects each time it strikes the side of the optical fiber.

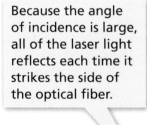

FIGURE 29
Optical Fibers
Light travels long distances through optical fibers. **Drawing Conclusions** *Why doesn't light exit through the sides of the optical fiber?*

Medicine Optical fibers are commonly used in medical instruments. Doctors can insert a thin optical fiber inside various parts of the body, such as the heart or the stomach. The optical fiber can be attached to a microscope or a camera. In this way, doctors can examine internal organs without having to perform major surgery.

Doctors often use optical fibers to repair damage to joints. In knee surgery, for example, doctors make small cuts to insert optical fibers and tiny surgical tools. Because the surgery does less damage to the knee, the recovery is easier.

Communications To send signals through optical fibers, the electrical signals that start out over copper wires are changed into pulses of light by tiny lasers. Then the signals can travel over long distances in the optical fiber. Optical fibers have led to great improvements in telephone service, computer networks, and cable television systems. Signals sent over optical fibers are usually faster and clearer than those sent over copper wire. One tiny optical fiber can carry thousands of phone conversations at the same time. Optical fibers are so much thinner than copper wire that many more fibers can be bundled together in the same space.

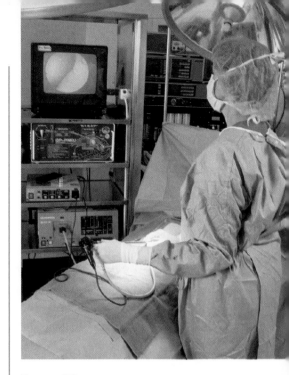

FIGURE 30
Optical-Fiber Surgery
Using optical fibers, surgeons can avoid damaging nearby healthy parts of the body.

 **Reading Checkpoint** How do optical fibers carry signals?

Section 5 Assessment

Target Reading Skill Building Vocabulary
Use your definitions to help you answer the questions below.

Reviewing Key Concepts

1. a. Reviewing How are lenses used in telescopes, microscopes, and cameras?
   b. Comparing and Contrasting Compare and contrast how images form in a refracting telescope, a reflecting telescope, and a microscope.
   c. Classifying A pair of binoculars has two lenses in each tube. Which type of optical instrument are the binoculars most similar to?
2. a. Identifying What is laser light?
   b. Summarizing How can laser light be used?
   c. Sequencing How does a laser produce laser light?

3. a. Defining What are optical fibers?
   b. Describing What are three uses of optical fibers?
   c. Relating Cause and Effect Why can optical fibers carry laser beams long distances?

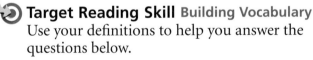 **Writing in Science**

Advertisement A company has asked you to write an advertisement for its new, easy-to-use camera. In the ad, the company wants you to describe the camera's features so that buyers will understand how the camera works. Be sure to mention the shutter, lens, and diaphragm.

① Light and Color

Key Concepts

- When light strikes an object, the light can be reflected, transmitted, or absorbed.

- An opaque object is the color of the light it reflects. A transparent or translucent object is the color of the light it transmits.

- When combined in equal amounts, the three primary colors of light produce white light. As pigments are added together, fewer colors of light are reflected and more are absorbed.

Key Terms

transparent material	secondary color
translucent material	complementary colors
opaque material	pigment
primary colors	

② Reflection and Mirrors

Key Concepts

- There are two types of reflection—regular reflection and diffuse reflection.

- A plane mirror produces a virtual image that is upright and the same size as the object.

- Concave mirrors form virtual or real images. Convex mirrors form only virtual images.

Key Terms

ray	concave mirror
regular reflection	optical axis
diffuse reflection	focal point
plane mirror	real image
image	convex mirror
virtual image	

③ Refraction and Lenses

Key Concepts

- A convex lens can form virtual images or real images. A concave lens can produce only virtual images.

Key Terms

index of refraction	convex lens
mirage	concave lens
lens	

④ Seeing Light

Key Concepts

- You see objects when a process occurs that involves both your eyes and your brain.

- Convex lenses are used to correct near-sightedness. Concave lenses are used to correct farsightedness.

Key Terms

cornea	retina	optic nerve
pupil	rods	nearsighted
iris	cones	farsighted

⑤ Using Light

Key Concepts

- Telescopes use lenses or mirrors to collect and focus light from distant objects. A microscope uses a combination of lenses to produce and magnify an image. The lens of a camera focuses light to form a real, upside-down image on film in the back of the camera.

- Laser light consists of light waves that all have the same wavelength, or color. The waves are coherent, or in step.

- In addition to their use by stores, industry, and engineers, lasers are used to read information on compact discs, create holograms, and perform surgery.

- Optical fibers can carry a laser beam for long distances because the beam stays totally inside the fiber as it travels.

Key Terms

telescope	camera
refracting telescope	laser
objective	hologram
eyepiece	optical fiber
reflecting telescope	total internal reflection
microscope	

Review and Assessment

Organizing Information

Comparing and Contrasting
Copy the graphic organizer about mirrors and lenses onto a separate sheet of paper. Then complete it and add a title. (For more on Comparing and Contrasting, see the Skills Handbook.)

Mirrors and Lenses

Type of Mirror	Effect on Light Rays	Type of Image
Plane	Regular reflection	a. ____?____
b. ____?____	c. ____?____	Real or virtual
Convex	Spread out	d. ____?____

Type of Lens	Effect on Light Rays	Type of Image
Convex	e. ____?____	f. ____?____
g. ____?____	h. ____?____	Virtual

Reviewing Key Terms

Choose the letter of the best answer.

1. A material that reflects or absorbs all of the light that strikes it is a(n)
   a. translucent material.
   b. opaque material.
   c. transparent material.
   d. polarizing filter.

2. When light bounces off an uneven surface, the result is called
   a. regular reflection.
   b. refraction.
   c. diffuse reflection.
   d. internal reflection.

3. A curved piece of glass or other transparent material that is used to refract light is a
   a. prism.   b. lens.
   c. mirage.   d. mirror.

4. A ring of muscle that changes the size of the eye's pupil is the
   a. retina.
   b. cornea.
   c. iris.
   d. ciliary muscle.

5. A device that produces coherent light is a(n)
   a. telescope.
   b. microscope.
   c. laser.
   d. optical fiber.

If the statement is true, write *true*. If it is false, change the underlined word or words to make the statement true.

6. <u>Primary colors</u> combine to make any color.

7. Lines that represent light waves are called <u>rays</u>.

8. An upright image that forms where light seems to come from is a <u>virtual</u> image.

9. For a <u>nearsighted</u> person, nearby objects appear blurry.

10. <u>Holograms</u> are long, thin strands of glass or plastic that can carry light for long distances.

Writing in Science

Persuasive Letter Write a short letter to your representative in Congress asking him or her to continue supporting telescopes in space. Include at least two advantages of space telescopes in your letter.

Discovery CHANNEL SCHOOL

Light
Video Preview
Video Field Trip
▶ Video Assessment

Review and Assessment

Checking Concepts

11. Describe transparent, translucent, and opaque materials. Give an example of each.

12. Why do you see the petals of a rose as red and the leaves as green?

13. What colors can be formed by combining complementary colors?

14. Sketch the optical axis and focal point(s) of a concave mirror and a convex mirror.

15. Describe real and virtual images. How can each type of image be formed by mirrors?

16. How is the index of refraction of a substance related to the speed of light in the substance?

17. Explain why you see a mirage on a hot road.

18. Which parts of the eye help to focus light? Which part carries a signal to the brain?

19. Explain how your eyes are able to clearly see both near and distant objects.

20. How does total internal reflection depend on the angle of incidence of light rays?

Thinking Critically

21. **Classifying** Do the colors shown below represent pigments or colors of light? Explain.

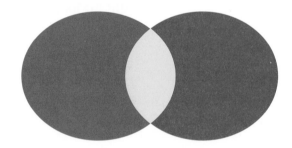

22. **Applying Concepts** Can a plane mirror produce a real image? Explain.

23. **Comparing and Contrasting** How are convex and concave mirrors alike? How are they different?

24. **Inferring** You shine a light through a convex lens so it forms a spot on an index card. Where should the lens and card be located to make the spot as small as possible?

25. **Relating Cause and Effect** Explain why your eyes can only see shades of gray in dim light.

26. **Problem Solving** A telescope produces an upside-down image. How could you modify the telescope so the image is upright?

27. **Comparing and Contrasting** How is a microscope similar to a convex lens used as a magnifying lens? How is it different?

28. **Making Generalizations** Why is laser light never white?

Applying Skills

Use the diagram to answer Questions 29–31.

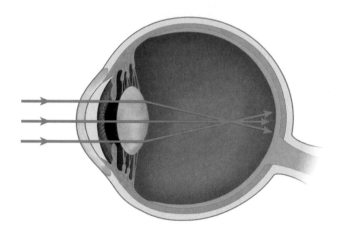

29. **Classifying** Which type of vision problem does this eye have?

30. **Problem Solving** What type of lens can correct this vision problem?

31. **Communicating** Copy the diagram above on a separate sheet of paper. Add a correcting lens to your diagram and show how the lens makes the three rays focus on the retina.

Lab zone Chapter **Project**

Performance Assessment Demonstrate your optical instrument to your class. Explain how your instrument works and how it can be used. Use diagrams that show how the mirrors or lenses in your instrument reflect or refract light.

Standardized Test Prep

Periscope

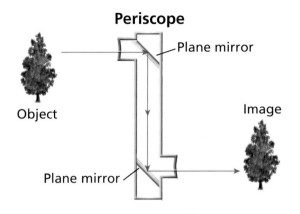

Use the diagram above and your knowledge of science to answer Question 3.

3. If you want to build a periscope, what measurement is most important?
    A the angle between the two mirrors
    B the distance between the mirrors
    C the width of the mirrors
    D the width of the tube

4. A friend hypothesizes that a periscope produces an upright image that reverses left and right. How could you test this hypothesis?
    F Test A: Draw a ray diagram to determine the type of image that is produced.
    G Test B: Look at your friend through the periscope to see if her image is upright.
    H Test C: Look at your friend through the periscope and ask her to move her right hand. Observe which hand (left or right) is moving in the image.
    J Conduct both Test B and Test C.

5. You view an American flag through sunglasses that are tinted green. What colors do you see?
    A green
    B black
    C green and black
    D red and blue

Constructed Response

6. How is a camera like a human eye? Give the function of each part of a camera and identify the part of the eye that has the same function. Use the following terms in your answer: *lens, diaphragm, film, cornea, pupil,* and *retina.*

Choose the letter of the best answer.

1. The index of refraction for water is 1.33 and for glass is 1.5. When light moves from glass into water, the speed of light
    A increases.
    B decreases.
    C remains the same.
    D depends on the angle of incidence.

2. A convex lens can produce a real or a virtual image. Which type of mirror is most similar to a convex lens?
    F plane mirror
    G convex mirror
    H concave mirror
    J none of the above

The Magic of the Movies

Lights! Camera! Action!

- A dinosaur, 12 feet tall, roars from the forest.
- An alien spaceship lands in Washington, D.C.
- A pirate leaps into the ocean to rescue a girl.

When you go to the movies, you expect to be entertained. You want a movie to make you laugh or cry or shiver. A movie is simply a series of pictures shown at tremendous speed on a flat screen. Even so, millions of people go to the movies every week.

Movies have been around for about 100 years. Until 1927, movies were silent and filmed in black and white. Then in the late 1920s and 1930s, the movie industry changed. Moviemakers added sound to make the first "talking pictures." Not long after that, they added color.

What makes movies so special? Much of the magic of the movies comes from the different ways in which directors use light, color, special effects, camera angles, editing, and computer wizardry. These techniques help to make a movie scene scary, exciting, or romantic.

Johnny Depp
Johnny plays the rogue pirate Jack Sparrow in *Pirates of the Caribbean*.

On Board the *Black Pearl*
Here camera operators film Orlando Bloom,
playing the part of Will Turner.

Choosing a Point of View

A screenwriter writes the script, or story, for a movie from one or more distinct points of view. For example, when a movie tells a story from the point of view of one main character, the audience shares that character's thoughts and feelings.

Often, the point of view shifts from one character to another in a film. In the movie *Pirates of the Caribbean: The Curse of the Black Pearl*, for instance, the story is told by alternating the point of view of three characters. They are Elizabeth Swann, the governor's daughter; Will Turner, the blacksmith; and Jack Sparrow, the pirate.

When Elizabeth is kidnapped by pirates of the ship named the *Black Pearl*, Jack leads Will on a treacherous journey to rescue her. Each of these three main characters encounters different challenges and obstacles. The "camera" follows the progress of one character for a few minutes, then shifts to follow another. Alternating these three points of view allows the audience to understand the very different experiences of each character.

The director and the film editor decide what the audience will see in each frame of the movie and which point of view will be portrayed. In choosing the point of view, the director plans the actions and conversations that will make viewers like or admire certain characters and not like others. The director and film editor skillfully weave the plot through the point of view.

Language Arts Activity

Think of a story or book you have read that you would like to see as a movie. In one or two paragraphs, write a summary of the movie plot. Then choose the point of view you will use in the movie. Explain why you chose that point of view.

How Pictures Seem to Move

The movie opens. The film rolls, and the action begins. What is happening? A movie is a fast-moving series of small photographs projected onto a screen. The pictures appear so fast—at about 24 pictures per second—that your eyes blend them together in continuous motion. But your eyes are tricking you. You are seeing an optical illusion.

When you watch a movie, your eyes see each picture for just a fraction of a second. Then the picture is replaced by the next one. The pictures move so fast that even when one image is gone, your brain continues to see it. Seeing this after-image is called "persistence of vision." It creates the illusion of motion.

Many discoveries and inventions in the 1800s combined to make the first motion picture. For example, in 1834, a toy called a zoetrope was invented. The zoetrope contained pictures inside a drumlike device with slits. People could spin the drum while looking through the slits. The motion of the zoetrope made the pictures appear to move.

By the late 1800s, American inventor Thomas Edison was working on a movie camera. It used a plastic called celluloid to make the film. Edison made the film 35 millimeters wide, a width still used today. In the late 1920s, moviemakers added another strip to the film that gave sound to movies.

Science Activity

Make your own moving picture by building a zoetrope.

- Cut a strip of white paper 45.5 cm by 7.5 cm. Mark the strip to make 8 equal picture frames.

- Near the center of the first frame, draw a picture. Your picture should be a simple outline of an object such as an animal or person.

- Draw your object again in the second frame, but change its position slightly. Repeat the step until you have drawn the object in every frame. Remember to change its position a bit each time, as shown in the illustration below.

- Cut a piece of black construction paper to measure 45.5 cm by 15 cm.

- Mark 8 vertical slits on the top half of the black paper, each 5.5 cm apart. Cut the slits, making each 4 mm wide and 7.5 cm deep.

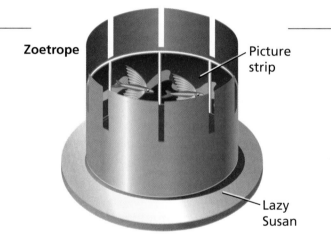

Zoetrope — Picture strip — Lazy Susan

- Tape the black paper into a circle with the slits on top.

- Tape the picture strip into a circle with the pictures on the inside. Slide the strip inside the black circle to create your zoetrope.

- Place your zoetrope on a record player or Lazy Susan. Center it. Look through the slits as you spin the zoetrope. What do you see?

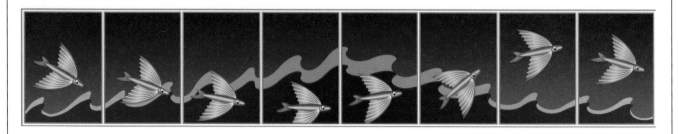

Making Models

An immense fortress under attack, a sinking luxury liner, a fiery train crash—these scenes look real on the big screen. But moviemakers don't often stage actual catastrophes such as these. Increasingly they use computers or models. A movie may use several models in different sizes.

Models must be to scale so that every detail of the model appears in proper proportion. Scale is a ratio that compares the measurements of a model to the actual size of the object. For example, if a car is 3.5 meters (350 centimeters) long, a model at a scale of 1 : 16 would be almost 22 centimeters long. A larger model of the car, at 1 : 4, would be about 88 centimeters long.

The makers of the movie *The Lord of the Rings: The Two Towers* built full-size sections of Helm's Deep, a massive fortress that is an important location in the film. They built a second model one-quarter the size of the actual set, expressed as a scale of 1 : 4. They built a third model of the fortress in a scale of 1 : 35. This small-scale model was complete in every detail so that moviegoers would be convinced they were looking at Helm's Deep.

Helm's Deep
A movie frame from *Lord of the Rings: The Two Towers* shows Helm's Deep (top). A set designer puts the finishing touches on a small-scale model of the fortress (above).

Math Activity

Sketch a simple scene, such as a room interior or a city scene. Pick four objects in the scene and estimate or measure the actual size of each. The objects could include a chair, a person, a car, or a skyscraper. (**Note:** *The height of one story in a modern building equals about 4 meters.*) Decide on a scale for your model, such as 1 : 4, 1 : 12, or 1 : 16. After determining the actual sizes of the objects, calculate the size of each scale model.

Reflecting the Times

When moviemakers look for an idea for a new movie, they think first about what people are interested in seeing. Moviemakers want to know what's important to people. Advances in science and technology and recent events in history all influence people. Movies often reflect changes in people's lives.

In the early 1900s, people were just beginning to fly airplanes. Early science fiction movies of the 1920s and 1930s were pure fantasy.

By the 1950s, space flight technology was developing. In 1957, the Soviet Union sent the first satellite, *Sputnik I*, into orbit. Soon after, the United States and the Soviet Union were competing in space exploration. Both nations also were making powerful nuclear weapons. The idea of nuclear war frightened people. Many movies of the 1950s and 1960s reflected these fears. Giant insects and other monsters appeared on movie screens. Science fiction movies featured alien invasions.

The "space race" continued in the 1960s. American astronauts and Soviet cosmonauts orbited Earth. In July 1969, three American astronauts became the first people to reach the moon. Later, space probes sent back pictures of other planets. These space flights made people dream about space travel. About the same time, people began using computers. Some people were afraid the new machines would control them. In the 1968 movie *2001: A Space Odyssey*, the computer HAL did just that.

Interest in space kept science fiction movies popular in the 1980s and 1990s. By that time, computers were part of everyday life. They were not instruments to be feared.

Tension between the United States and the Soviet Union was relaxing. Movies seemed more optimistic about the future than in the 1950s.

A Trip to the Moon, 1902
This early French movie represents an astronomer's dream. In the dream, men travel to the moon inside a capsule shot from a giant cannon.

Them!, 1954
In this 1954 movie, nuclear tests in the American Southwest create mutant giant ants.

E.T., 1982
E.T. is an alien stranded on Earth. A group of Earth children help him return home.

Jurassic Park, 1993
In this movie, dinosaurs are on the rampage. Here, *Tyrannosaurus rex* crushes a truck.

In popular movies such as *E.T.* and *Close Encounters of the Third Kind*, the human characters showed more curiosity than fear about aliens—even those that visited Earth. The movie *Men in Black* featured aliens who were more often humorous than threatening.

Social Studies Activity

Think of some recent movies that you and others may have seen. With your classmates, organize a panel discussion on the links between movies and current events. Consider changes that have occurred in the world around you. How have space probes, planet explorations, computers, video games, the Internet, and political events influenced these movies?

Tie It Together

Making a Movie

Put your movie ideas into action. With your classmates, plan a short (10–15 minute) movie. If possible, use a video camera to make your movie. Use what you've learned about point of view, the use of scale models, and editing.

- Think of a subject or event for your movie. As a class, outline the script for the movie.

- Work in small groups to make storyboards—drawings showing key scenes in the movie.

- Choose a director, actors, a camera operator, and a film editor.

- Assign groups to plan lights, sound effects, model-building, props, background painting, and photography.

- After shooting and editing your movie, present it for other students in your school.

Think Like a Scientist

Scientists have a particular way of looking at the world, or scientific habits of mind. Whenever you ask a question and explore possible answers, you use many of the same skills that scientists do. Some of these skills are described on this page.

Observing

When you use one or more of your five senses to gather information about the world, you are **observing.** Hearing a dog bark, counting twelve green seeds, and smelling smoke are all observations. To increase the power of their senses, scientists sometimes use microscopes, telescopes, or other instruments that help them make more detailed observations.

An observation must be an accurate report of what your senses detect. It is important to keep careful records of your observations in science class by writing or drawing in a notebook. The information collected through observations is called evidence, or data.

Inferring

When you interpret an observation, you are **inferring,** or making an inference. For example, if you hear your dog barking, you may infer that someone is at your front door. To make this inference, you combine the evidence—the barking dog—and your experience or knowledge—you know that your dog barks when strangers approach—to reach a logical conclusion.

Notice that an inference is not a fact; it is only one of many possible interpretations for an observation. For example, your dog may be barking because it wants to go for a walk. An inference may turn out to be incorrect even if it is based on accurate observations and logical reasoning. The only way to find out if an inference is correct is to investigate further.

Predicting

When you listen to the weather forecast, you hear many predictions about the next day's weather—what the temperature will be, whether it will rain, and how windy it will be. Weather forecasters use observations and knowledge of weather patterns to predict the weather. The skill of **predicting** involves making an inference about a future event based on current evidence or past experience.

Because a prediction is an inference, it may prove to be false. In science class, you can test some of your predictions by doing experiments. For example, suppose you predict that larger paper airplanes can fly farther than smaller airplanes. How could you test your prediction?

Activity

Use the photograph to answer the questions below.

Observing Look closely at the photograph. List at least three observations.

Inferring Use your observations to make an inference about what has happened. What experience or knowledge did you use to make the inference?

Predicting Predict what will happen next. On what evidence or experience do you base your prediction?

Classifying

Could you imagine searching for a book in the library if the books were shelved in no particular order? Your trip to the library would be an all-day event! Luckily, librarians group together books on similar topics or by the same author. Grouping together items that are alike in some way is called **classifying.** You can classify items in many ways: by size, by shape, by use, and by other important characteristics.

Like librarians, scientists use the skill of classifying to organize information and objects. When things are sorted into groups, the relationships among them become easier to understand.

Activity

Classify the objects in the photograph into two groups based on any characteristic you choose. Then use another characteristic to classify the objects into three groups.

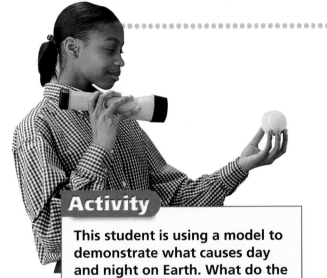

Activity

This student is using a model to demonstrate what causes day and night on Earth. What do the flashlight and the tennis ball in the model represent?

Making Models

Have you ever drawn a picture to help someone understand what you were saying? Such a drawing is one type of model. A model is a picture, diagram, computer image, or other representation of a complex object or process. **Making models** helps people understand things that they cannot observe directly.

Scientists often use models to represent things that are either very large or very small, such as the planets in the solar system, or the parts of a cell. Such models are physical models—drawings or three-dimensional structures that look like the real thing. Other models are mental models—mathematical equations or words that describe how something works.

Communicating

Whenever you talk on the phone, write a report, or listen to your teacher at school, you are communicating. **Communicating** is the process of sharing ideas and information with other people. Communicating effectively requires many skills, including writing, reading, speaking, listening, and making models.

Scientists communicate to share results, information, and opinions. Scientists often communicate about their work in journals, over the telephone, in letters, and on the Internet.

They also attend scientific meetings where they share their ideas with one another in person.

Activity

On a sheet of paper, write out clear, detailed directions for tying your shoe. Then exchange directions with a partner. Follow your partner's directions exactly. How successful were you at tying your shoe? How could your partner have communicated more clearly?

Making Measurements

By measuring, scientists can express their observations more precisely and communicate more information about what they observe.

Measuring in SI

The standard system of measurement used by scientists around the world is known as the International System of Units, which is abbreviated as SI (**Système International d'Unités,** in French). SI units are easy to use because they are based on multiples of 10. Each unit is ten times larger than the next smallest unit and one tenth the size of the next largest unit. The table lists the prefixes used to name the most common SI units.

Common SI Prefixes		
Prefix	**Symbol**	**Meaning**
kilo-	k	1,000
hecto-	h	100
deka-	da	10
deci-	d	0.1 (one tenth)
centi-	c	0.01 (one hundredth)
milli-	m	0.001 (one thousandth)

Length To measure length, or the distance between two points, the unit of measure is the **meter (m).** The distance from the floor to a doorknob is approximately one meter. Long distances, such as the distance between two cities, are measured in kilometers (km). Small lengths are measured in centimeters (cm) or millimeters (mm). Scientists use metric rulers and meter sticks to measure length.

Common Conversions	
1 km	= 1,000 m
1 m	= 100 cm
1 m	= 1,000 mm
1 cm	= 10 mm

Activity

The larger lines on the metric ruler in the picture show centimeter divisions, while the smaller, unnumbered lines show millimeter divisions. How many centimeters long is the shell? How many millimeters long is it?

Liquid Volume To measure the volume of a liquid, or the amount of space it takes up, you will use a unit of measure known as the **liter (L).** One liter is the approximate volume of a medium-size carton of milk. Smaller volumes are measured in milliliters (mL). Scientists use graduated cylinders to measure liquid volume.

Activity

The graduated cylinder in the picture is marked in milliliter divisions. Notice that the water in the cylinder has a curved surface. This curved surface is called the *meniscus.* To measure the volume, you must read the level at the lowest point of the meniscus. What is the volume of water in this graduated cylinder?

Common Conversion
1 L = 1,000 mL

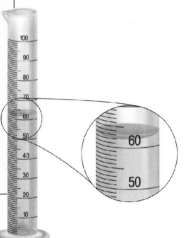

Mass To measure mass, or the amount of matter in an object, you will use a unit of measure known as the **gram (g).** One gram is approximately the mass of a paper clip. Larger masses are measured in kilograms (kg). Scientists use a balance to find the mass of an object.

Common Conversion

1 kg = 1,000 g

Activity

The mass of the potato in the picture is measured in kilograms. What is the mass of the potato? Suppose a recipe for potato salad called for one kilogram of potatoes. About how many potatoes would you need?

0.25 KG

Temperature To measure the temperature of a substance, you will use the **Celsius scale.** Temperature is measured in degrees Celsius (°C) using a Celsius thermometer. Water freezes at 0°C and boils at 100°C.

Time The unit scientists use to measure time is the **second (s).**

Activity

What is the temperature of the liquid in degrees Celsius?

Converting SI Units

To use the SI system, you must know how to convert between units. Converting from one unit to another involves the skill of **calculating,** or using mathematical operations. Converting between SI units is similar to converting between dollars and dimes because both systems are based on multiples of ten.

Suppose you want to convert a length of 80 centimeters to meters. Follow these steps to convert between units.

1. Begin by writing down the measurement you want to convert—in this example, 80 centimeters.

2. Write a conversion factor that represents the relationship between the two units you are converting. In this example, the relationship is 1 meter = 100 centimeters. Write this conversion factor as a fraction, making sure to place the units you are converting from (centimeters, in this example) in the denominator.

3. Multiply the measurement you want to convert by the fraction. When you do this, the units in the first measurement will cancel out with the units in the denominator. Your answer will be in the units you are converting to (meters, in this example).

Example

80 centimeters = ▓ meters

$$80 \text{ centimeters} \times \frac{1 \text{ meter}}{100 \text{ centimeters}} = \frac{80 \text{ meters}}{100}$$

$$= 0.8 \text{ meters}$$

Activity

Convert between the following units.

1. 600 millimeters = ▓ meters
2. 0.35 liters = ▓ milliliters
3. 1,050 grams = ▓ kilograms

Conducting a Scientific Investigation

In some ways, scientists are like detectives, piecing together clues to learn about a process or event. One way that scientists gather clues is by carrying out experiments. An experiment tests an idea in a careful, orderly manner. Although experiments do not all follow the same steps in the same order, many follow a pattern similar to the one described here.

Posing Questions

Experiments begin by asking a scientific question. A scientific question is one that can be answered by gathering evidence. For example, the question "Which freezes faster—fresh water or salt water?" is a scientific question because you can carry out an investigation and gather information to answer the question.

Developing a Hypothesis

The next step is to form a hypothesis. A **hypothesis** is a possible explanation for a set of observations or answer to a scientific question. In science, a hypothesis must be something that can be tested. A hypothesis can be worded as an *If . . . then . . .* statement. For example, a hypothesis might be *"If I add salt to fresh water, then the water will take longer to freeze."* A hypothesis worded this way serves as a rough outline of the experiment you should perform.

Designing an Experiment

Next you need to plan a way to test your hypothesis. Your plan should be written out as a step-by-step procedure and should describe the observations or measurements you will make.

Two important steps involved in designing an experiment are controlling variables and forming operational definitions.

Controlling Variables In a well-designed experiment, you need to keep all variables the same except for one. A **variable** is any factor that can change in an experiment. The factor that you change is called the **manipulated variable**. In this experiment, the manipulated variable is the amount of salt added to the water. Other factors, such as the amount of water or the starting temperature, are kept constant.

The factor that changes as a result of the manipulated variable is called the **responding variable.** The responding variable is what you measure or observe to obtain your results. In this experiment, the responding variable is how long the water takes to freeze.

An experiment in which all factors except one are kept constant is called a **controlled experiment.** Most controlled experiments include a test called the control. In this experiment, Container 3 is the control. Because no salt is added to Container 3, you can compare the results from the other containers to it. Any difference in results must be due to the addition of salt alone.

Forming Operational Definitions Another important aspect of a well-designed experiment is having clear operational definitions. An **operational definition** is a statement that describes how a particular variable is to be measured or how a term is to be defined. For example, in this experiment, how will you determine if the water has frozen? You might decide to insert a stick in each container at the start of the experiment. Your operational definition of "frozen" would be the time at which the stick can no longer move.

Experimental Procedure
1. Fill 3 containers with 300 milliliters of cold tap water.
2. Add 10 grams of salt to Container 1; stir. Add 20 grams of salt to Container 2; stir. Add no salt to Container 3.
3. Place the 3 containers in a freezer.
4. Check the containers every 15 minutes. Record your observations.

Interpreting Data

The observations and measurements you make in an experiment are called **data.** At the end of an experiment, you need to analyze the data to look for any patterns or trends. Patterns often become clear if you organize your data in a data table or graph. Then think through what the data reveal. Do they support your hypothesis? Do they point out a flaw in your experiment? Do you need to collect more data?

Drawing Conclusions

A **conclusion** is a statement that sums up what you have learned from an experiment. When you draw a conclusion, you need to decide whether the data you collected support your hypothesis or not. You may need to repeat an experiment several times before you can draw any conclusions from it. Conclusions often lead you to pose new questions and plan new experiments to answer them.

Activity

Is a ball's bounce affected by the height from which it is dropped? Using the steps just described, plan a controlled experiment to investigate this problem.

Technology Design Skills

Engineers are people who use scientific and technological knowledge to solve practical problems. To design new products, engineers usually follow the process described here, even though they may not follow these steps in the exact order. As you read the steps, think about how you might apply them in technology labs.

Identify a Need

Before engineers begin designing a new product, they must first identify the need they are trying to meet. For example, suppose you are a member of a design team in a company that makes toys. Your team has identified a need: a toy boat that is inexpensive and easy to assemble.

Research the Problem

Engineers often begin by gathering information that will help them with their new design. This research may include finding articles in books, magazines, or on the Internet. It may also include talking to other engineers who have solved similar problems. Engineers often perform experiments related to the product they want to design.

For your toy boat, you could look at toys that are similar to the one you want to design. You might do research on the Internet. You could also test some materials to see whether they will work well in a toy boat.

Drawing for a boat design ▼

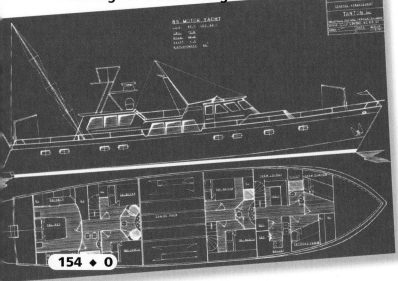

Design a Solution

Research gives engineers information that helps them design a product. When engineers design new products, they usually work in teams.

Generating Ideas Often design teams hold brainstorming meetings in which any team member can contribute ideas. **Brainstorming** is a creative process in which one team member's suggestions often spark ideas in other group members. Brainstorming can lead to new approaches to solving a design problem.

Evaluating Constraints During brainstorming, a design team will often come up with several possible designs. The team must then evaluate each one.

As part of their evaluation, engineers consider constraints. **Constraints** are factors that limit or restrict a product design. Physical characteristics, such as the properties of materials used to make your toy boat, are constraints. Money and time are also constraints. If the materials in a product cost a lot, or if the product takes a long time to make, the design may be impractical.

Making Trade-offs Design teams usually need to make trade-offs. In a **trade-off,** engineers give up one benefit of a proposed design in order to obtain another. In designing your toy boat, you will have to make trade-offs. For example, suppose one material is sturdy but not fully waterproof. Another material is more waterproof, but breakable. You may decide to give up the benefit of sturdiness in order to obtain the benefit of waterproofing.

Build and Evaluate a Prototype

Once the team has chosen a design plan, the engineers build a prototype of the product. A **prototype** is a working model used to test a design. Engineers evaluate the prototype to see whether it works well, is easy to operate, is safe to use, and holds up to repeated use.

Think of your toy boat. What would the prototype be like? Of what materials would it be made? How would you test it?

Troubleshoot and Redesign

Few prototypes work perfectly, which is why they need to be tested. Once a design team has tested a prototype, the members analyze the results and identify any problems. The team then tries to **troubleshoot,** or fix the design problems. For example, if your toy boat leaks or wobbles, the boat should be redesigned to eliminate those problems.

Communicate the Solution

A team needs to communicate the final design to the people who will manufacture and use the product. To do this, teams may use sketches, detailed drawings, computer simulations, and word descriptions.

Activity

You can use the technology design process to design and build a toy boat.

Research and Investigate

1. Visit the library or go online to research toy boats.
2. Investigate how a toy boat can be powered, including wind, rubber bands, or baking soda and vinegar.
3. Brainstorm materials, shapes, and steering for your boat.

Design and Build

4. Based on your research, design a toy boat that
   • is made of readily available materials
   • is no larger than 15 cm long and 10 cm wide
   • includes a power system, a rudder, and an area for cargo
   • travels 2 meters in a straight line carrying a load of 20 pennies
5. Sketch your design and write a step-by-step plan for building your boat. After your teacher approves your plan, build your boat.

Evaluate and Redesign

6. Test your boat, evaluate the results, and troubleshoot any problems.
7. Based on your evaluation, redesign your toy boat so it performs better.

Creating Data Tables and Graphs

How can you make sense of the data in a science experiment?
The first step is to organize the data to help you understand them.
Data tables and graphs are helpful tools for organizing data.

Data Tables

You have gathered your materials and set up your experiment. But before you start, you need to plan a way to record what happens during the experiment. By creating a data table, you can record your observations and measurements in an orderly way.

Suppose, for example, that a scientist conducted an experiment to find out how many Calories people of different body masses burn while doing various activities. The data table shows the results.

Notice in this data table that the manipulated variable (body mass) is the heading of one column. The responding variable (for

Calories Burned in 30 Minutes			
Body Mass	Experiment 1: Bicycling	Experiment 2: Playing Basketball	Experiment 3: Watching Television
30 kg	60 Calories	120 Calories	21 Calories
40 kg	77 Calories	164 Calories	27 Calories
50 kg	95 Calories	206 Calories	33 Calories
60 kg	114 Calories	248 Calories	38 Calories

Experiment 1, the number of Calories burned while bicycling) is the heading of the next column. Additional columns were added for related experiments.

Bar Graphs

To compare how many Calories a person burns doing various activities, you could create a bar graph. A bar graph is used to display data in a number of separate, or distinct, categories. In this example, bicycling, playing basketball, and watching television are the three categories.

To create a bar graph, follow these steps.

1. On graph paper, draw a horizontal, or *x*-, axis and a vertical, or *y*-, axis.

2. Write the names of the categories to be graphed along the horizontal axis. Include an overall label for the axis as well.

3. Label the vertical axis with the name of the responding variable. Include units of measurement. Then create a scale along the axis by marking off equally spaced numbers that cover the range of the data collected.

4. For each category, draw a solid bar using the scale on the vertical axis to determine the height. Make all the bars the same width.

5. Add a title that describes the graph.

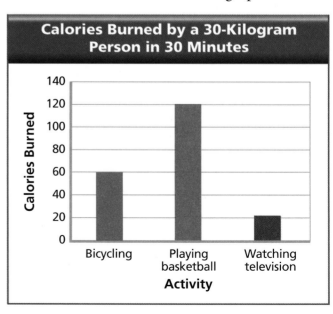

Line Graphs

To see whether a relationship exists between body mass and the number of Calories burned while bicycling, you could create a line graph. A line graph is used to display data that show how one variable (the responding variable) changes in response to another variable (the manipulated variable). You can use a line graph when your manipulated variable is **continuous,** that is, when there are other points between the ones that you tested. In this example, body mass is a continuous variable because there are other body masses between 30 and 40 kilograms (for example, 31 kilograms). Time is another example of a continuous variable.

Line graphs are powerful tools because they allow you to estimate values for conditions that you did not test in the experiment. For example, you can use the line graph to estimate that a 35-kilogram person would burn 68 Calories while bicycling.

To create a line graph, follow these steps.

1. On graph paper, draw a horizontal, or x-, axis and a vertical, or y-, axis.

2. Label the horizontal axis with the name of the manipulated variable. Label the vertical axis with the name of the responding variable. Include units of measurement.

3. Create a scale on each axis by marking off equally spaced numbers that cover the range of the data collected.

4. Plot a point on the graph for each piece of data. In the line graph above, the dotted lines show how to plot the first data point (30 kilograms and 60 Calories). Follow an imaginary vertical line extending up from the horizontal axis at the 30-kilogram mark. Then follow an imaginary horizontal line extending across from the vertical axis at the 60-Calorie mark. Plot the point where the two lines intersect.

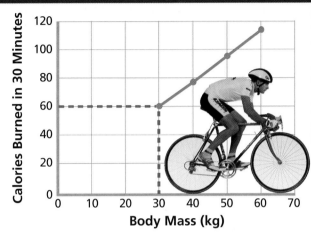

Effect of Body Mass on Calories Burned While Bicycling

5. Connect the plotted points with a solid line. (In some cases, it may be more appropriate to draw a line that shows the general trend of the plotted points. In those cases, some of the points may fall above or below the line. Also, not all graphs are linear. It may be more appropriate to draw a curve to connect the points.)

6. Add a title that identifies the variables or relationship in the graph.

Activity

Create line graphs to display the data from Experiment 2 and Experiment 3 in the data table.

Activity

You read in the newspaper that a total of 4 centimeters of rain fell in your area in June, 2.5 centimeters fell in July, and 1.5 centimeters fell in August. What type of graph would you use to display these data? Use graph paper to create the graph.

Circle Graphs

Like bar graphs, circle graphs can be used to display data in a number of separate categories. Unlike bar graphs, however, circle graphs can only be used when you have data for *all* the categories that make up a given topic. A circle graph is sometimes called a pie chart. The pie represents the entire topic, while the slices represent the individual categories. The size of a slice indicates what percentage of the whole a particular category makes up.

The data table below shows the results of a survey in which 24 teenagers were asked to identify their favorite sport. The data were then used to create the circle graph at the right.

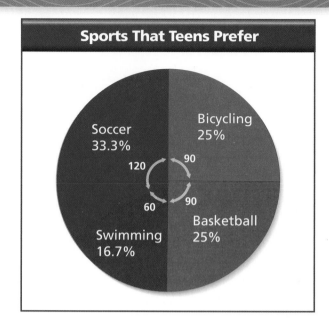

Sports That Teens Prefer

Soccer 33.3%
Bicycling 25%
Basketball 25%
Swimming 16.7%

Favorite Sports	
Sport	**Students**
Soccer	8
Basketball	6
Bicycling	6
Swimming	4

To create a circle graph, follow these steps.

1. Use a compass to draw a circle. Mark the center with a point. Then draw a line from the center point to the top of the circle.

2. Determine the size of each "slice" by setting up a proportion where x equals the number of degrees in a slice. (*Note:* A circle contains 360 degrees.) For example, to find the number of degrees in the "soccer" slice, set up the following proportion:

$$\frac{\text{Students who prefer soccer}}{\text{Total number of students}} = \frac{x}{\text{Total number of degrees in a circle}}$$

$$\frac{8}{24} = \frac{x}{360}$$

Cross-multiply and solve for x.

$$24x = 8 \times 360$$
$$x = 120$$

The "soccer" slice should contain 120 degrees.

3. Use a protractor to measure the angle of the first slice, using the line you drew to the top of the circle as the 0° line. Draw a line from the center of the circle to the edge for the angle you measured.

4. Continue around the circle by measuring the size of each slice with the protractor. Start measuring from the edge of the previous slice so the wedges do not overlap. When you are done, the entire circle should be filled in.

5. Determine the percentage of the whole circle that each slice represents. To do this, divide the number of degrees in a slice by the total number of degrees in a circle (360), and multiply by 100%. For the "soccer" slice, you can find the percentage as follows:

$$\frac{120}{360} \times 100\% = 33.3\%$$

6. Use a different color for each slice. Label each slice with the category and with the percentage of the whole it represents.

7. Add a title to the circle graph.

Activity

In a class of 28 students, 12 students take the bus to school, 10 students walk, and 6 students ride their bicycles. Create a circle graph to display these data.

Math Review

Scientists use math to organize, analyze, and present data.
This appendix will help you review some basic math skills.

Mean, Median, and Mode

The **mean** is the average, or the sum of the data divided by the number of data items. The middle number in a set of ordered data is called the **median.** The **mode** is the number that appears most often in a set of data.

> **Example**
>
> A scientist counted the number of distinct songs sung by seven different male birds and collected the data shown below.
>
> | Male Bird Songs | | | | | | | |
> |---|---|---|---|---|---|---|---|
> | **Bird** | A | B | C | D | E | F | G |
> | **Number of Songs** | 36 | 29 | 40 | 35 | 28 | 36 | 27 |
>
> To determine the mean number of songs, add the total number of songs and divide by the number of data items—in this case, the number of male birds.
>
> $$\text{Mean} = \frac{231}{7} = 33 \text{ songs}$$
>
> To find the median number of songs, arrange the data in numerical order and find the number in the middle of the series.
>
> **27 28 29 35 36 36 40**
>
> The number in the middle is 35, so the median number of songs is 35.
>
> The mode is the value that appears most frequently. In the data, 36 appears twice, while each other item appears only once. Therefore, 36 songs is the mode.

> **Practice**
>
> Find out how many minutes it takes each student in your class to get to school. Then find the mean, median, and mode for the data.

Probability

Probability is the chance that an event will occur. Probability can be expressed as a ratio, a fraction, or a percentage. For example, when you flip a coin, the probability that the coin will land heads up is 1 in 2, or $\frac{1}{2}$, or 50 percent.

The probability that an event will happen can be expressed in the following formula.

$$P(\text{event}) = \frac{\text{Number of times the event can occur}}{\text{Total number of possible events}}$$

> **Example**
>
> A paper bag contains 25 blue marbles, 5 green marbles, 5 orange marbles, and 15 yellow marbles. If you close your eyes and pick a marble from the bag, what is the probability that it will be yellow?
>
> $$P(\text{yellow marbles}) = \frac{15 \text{ yellow marbles}}{50 \text{ marbles total}}$$
>
> $$P = \frac{15}{50}, \text{ or } \frac{3}{10}, \text{ or } 30\%$$

> **Practice**
>
> Each side of a cube has a letter on it. Two sides have *A*, three sides have *B*, and one side has *C*. If you roll the cube, what is the probability that *A* will land on top?

Area

The **area** of a surface is the number of square units that cover it. The front cover of your textbook has an area of about 600 cm^2.

Area of a Rectangle and a Square To find the area of a rectangle, multiply its length times its width. The formula for the area of a rectangle is

$$A = \ell \times w, \text{ or } A = \ell w$$

Since all four sides of a square have the same length, the area of a square is the length of one side multiplied by itself, or squared.

$$A = s \times s, \text{ or } A = s^2$$

Example

A scientist is studying the plants in a field that measures 75 m $\times$ 45 m. What is the area of the field?

$$A = \ell \times w$$
$$A = 75 \text{ m} \times 45 \text{ m}$$
$$A = 3,375 \text{ m}^2$$

Area of a Circle The formula for the area of a circle is

$$A = \pi \times r \times r, \text{ or } A = \pi r^2$$

The length of the radius is represented by r, and the value of π is approximately $\frac{22}{7}$.

Example

Find the area of a circle with a radius of 14 cm.

$$A = \pi r^2$$
$$A = 14 \times 14 \times \frac{22}{7}$$
$$A = 616 \text{ cm}^2$$

Practice

Find the area of a circle that has a radius of 21 m.

Circumference

The distance around a circle is called the circumference. The formula for finding the circumference of a circle is

$$C = 2 \times \pi \times r, \text{ or } C = 2\pi r$$

Example

The radius of a circle is 35 cm. What is its circumference?

$$C = 2\pi r$$
$$C = 2 \times 35 \times \frac{22}{7}$$
$$C = 220 \text{ cm}$$

Practice

What is the circumference of a circle with a radius of 28 m?

Volume

The volume of an object is the number of cubic units it contains. The volume of a wastebasket, for example, might be about 26,000 cm^3.

Volume of a Rectangular Object To find the volume of a rectangular object, multiply the object's length times its width times its height.

$$V = \ell \times w \times h, \text{ or } V = \ell w h$$

Example

Find the volume of a box with length 24 cm, width 12 cm, and height 9 cm.

$$V = \ell w h$$
$$V = 24 \text{ cm} \times 12 \text{ cm} \times 9 \text{ cm}$$
$$V = 2,592 \text{ cm}^3$$

Practice

What is the volume of a rectangular object with length 17 cm, width 11 cm, and height 6 cm?

Fractions

A **fraction** is a way to express a part of a whole. In the fraction $\frac{4}{7}$, 4 is the numerator and 7 is the denominator.

Adding and Subtracting Fractions To add or subtract two or more fractions that have a common denominator, first add or subtract the numerators. Then write the sum or difference over the common denominator.

To find the sum or difference of fractions with different denominators, first find the least common multiple of the denominators. This is known as the least common denominator. Then convert each fraction to equivalent fractions with the least common denominator. Add or subtract the numerators. Then write the sum or difference over the common denominator.

> **Example**
>
> $$\frac{5}{6} - \frac{3}{4} = \frac{10}{12} - \frac{9}{12} = \frac{10 - 9}{12} = \frac{1}{12}$$

Multiplying Fractions To multiply two fractions, first multiply the two numerators, then multiply the two denominators.

> **Example**
>
> $$\frac{5}{6} \times \frac{2}{3} = \frac{5 \times 2}{6 \times 3} = \frac{10}{18} = \frac{5}{9}$$

Dividing Fractions Dividing by a fraction is the same as multiplying by its reciprocal. Reciprocals are numbers whose numerators and denominators have been switched. To divide one fraction by another, first invert the fraction you are dividing by—in other words, turn it upside down. Then multiply the two fractions.

> **Example**
>
> $$\frac{2}{5} \div \frac{7}{8} = \frac{2}{5} \times \frac{8}{7} = \frac{2 \times 8}{5 \times 7} = \frac{16}{35}$$

> **Practice**
>
> Solve the following: $\frac{3}{7} \div \frac{4}{5}$.

Decimals

Fractions whose denominators are 10, 100, or some other power of 10 are often expressed as decimals. For example, the fraction $\frac{9}{10}$ can be expressed as the decimal 0.9, and the fraction $\frac{7}{100}$ can be written as 0.07.

Adding and Subtracting With Decimals To add or subtract decimals, line up the decimal points before you carry out the operation.

> **Example**
>
> | 27.4 | 278.635 |
> |------|---------|
> | + 6.19 | − 191.4 |
> | 33.59 | 87.235 |

Multiplying With Decimals When you multiply two numbers with decimals, the number of decimal places in the product is equal to the total number of decimal places in each number being multiplied.

> **Example**
>
> 46.2 (one decimal place)
> × 2.37 (two decimal places)
> 109.494 (three decimal places)

Dividing With Decimals To divide a decimal by a whole number, put the decimal point in the quotient above the decimal point in the dividend.

> **Example**
>
> $15.5 \div 5$
>
> $$\frac{3.1}{5 \overline{)15.5}}$$

To divide a decimal by a decimal, you need to rewrite the divisor as a whole number. Do this by multiplying both the divisor and dividend by the same multiple of 10.

> **Example**
>
> $1.68 \div 4.2 = 16.8 \div 42$
>
> $$\frac{0.4}{42 \overline{)16.8}}$$

> **Practice**
>
> Multiply 6.21 by 8.5.

Ratio and Proportion

A **ratio** compares two numbers by division. For example, suppose a scientist counts 800 wolves and 1,200 moose on an island. The ratio of wolves to moose can be written as a fraction, $\frac{800}{1,200}$, which can be reduced to $\frac{2}{3}$. The same ratio can also be expressed as 2 to 3 or 2 : 3.

A **proportion** is a mathematical sentence saying that two ratios are equivalent. For example, a proportion could state that $\frac{800 \text{ wolves}}{1,200 \text{ moose}} = \frac{2 \text{ wolves}}{3 \text{ moose}}$. You can sometimes set up a proportion to determine or estimate an unknown quantity. For example, suppose a scientist counts 25 beetles in an area of 10 square meters. The scientist wants to estimate the number of beetles in 100 square meters.

Example

1. Express the relationship between beetles and area as a ratio: $\frac{25}{10}$, simplified to $\frac{5}{2}$.

2. Set up a proportion, with x representing the number of beetles. The proportion can be stated as $\frac{5}{2} = \frac{x}{100}$.

3. Begin by cross-multiplying. In other words, multiply each fraction's numerator by the other fraction's denominator.

   $$5 \times 100 = 2 \times x, \text{ or } 500 = 2x$$

4. To find the value of x, divide both sides by 2. The result is 250, or 250 beetles in 100 square meters.

Practice

Find the value of x in the following proportion: $\frac{6}{7} = \frac{x}{49}$.

Percentage

A **percentage** is a ratio that compares a number to 100. For example, there are 37 granite rocks in a collection that consists of 100 rocks. The ratio $\frac{37}{100}$ can be written as 37%. Granite rocks make up 37% of the rock collection.

You can calculate percentages of numbers other than 100 by setting up a proportion.

Example

Rain falls on 9 days out of 30 in June. What percentage of the days in June were rainy?

$$\frac{9 \text{ days}}{30 \text{ days}} = \frac{d\%}{100\%}$$

To find the value of d, begin by cross-multiplying, as for any proportion:

$$9 \times 100 = 30 \times d \qquad d = \frac{900}{30} \qquad d = 30$$

Practice

There are 300 marbles in a jar, and 42 of those marbles are blue. What percentage of the marbles are blue?

Significant Figures

The **precision** of a measurement depends on the instrument you use to take the measurement. For example, if the smallest unit on the ruler is millimeters, then the most precise measurement you can make will be in millimeters.

The sum or difference of measurements can only be as precise as the least precise measurement being added or subtracted. Round your answer so that it has the same number of digits after the decimal as the least precise measurement. Round up if the last digit is 5 or more, and round down if the last digit is 4 or less.

Example

Subtract a temperature of 5.2°C from the temperature 75.46°C.

75.46 − 5.2 = 70.26

5.2 has the fewest digits after the decimal, so it is the least precise measurement. Since the last digit of the answer is 6, round up to 3. The most precise difference between the measurements is 70.3°C.

Practice

Add 26.4 m to 8.37 m. Round your answer according to the precision of the measurements.

Significant figures are the number of nonzero digits in a measurement. Zeroes between nonzero digits are also significant. For example, the measurements 12,500 L, 0.125 cm, and 2.05 kg all have three significant figures. When you multiply and divide measurements, the one with the fewest significant figures determines the number of significant figures in your answer.

Example

Multiply 110 g by 5.75 g.

110 × 5.75 = 632.5

Because 110 has only two significant figures, round the answer to 630 g.

Scientific Notation

A **factor** is a number that divides into another number with no remainder. In the example, the number 3 is used as a factor four times.

An **exponent** tells how many times a number is used as a factor. For example, $3 \times 3 \times 3 \times 3$ can be written as 3^4. The exponent 4 indicates that the number 3 is used as a factor four times. Another way of expressing this is to say that 81 is equal to 3 to the fourth power.

Example

$$3^4 = 3 \times 3 \times 3 \times 3 = 81$$

Scientific notation uses exponents and powers of ten to write very large or very small numbers in shorter form. When you write a number in scientific notation, you write the number as two factors. The first factor is any number between 1 and 10. The second factor is a power of 10, such as 10^3 or 10^6.

Example

The average distance between the planet Mercury and the sun is 58,000,000 km. To write the first factor in scientific notation, insert a decimal point in the original number so that you have a number between 1 and 10. In the case of 58,000,000, the number is 5.8.

To determine the power of 10, count the number of places that the decimal point moved. In this case, it moved 7 places.

58,000,000 km = 5.8 × 10^7 km

Practice

Express 6,590,000 in scientific notation.

Reading Comprehension Skills

Each section in your textbook introduces a Target Reading Skill. You will improve your reading comprehension by using the Target Reading Skills described below.

Using Prior Knowledge

Your prior knowledge is what you already know before you begin to read about a topic. Building on what you already know gives you a head start on learning new information. Before you begin a new assignment, think about what you know. You might look at the headings and the visuals to spark your memory. You can list what you know. Then, as you read, consider questions like these.

• How does what you learn relate to what you know?

• How did something you already know help you learn something new?

• Did your original ideas agree with what you have just learned?

Asking Questions

Asking yourself questions is an excellent way to focus on and remember new information in your textbook. For example, you can turn the text headings into questions. Then your questions can guide you to identify the important information as you read. Look at these examples:

    Heading: Using Seismographic Data

    Question: How are seismographic data used?

    Heading: Kinds of Faults

    Question: What are the kinds of faults?

    You do not have to limit your questions to text headings. Ask questions about anything that you need to clarify or that will help you understand the content. *What* and *how* are probably the most common question words, but you may also ask *why*, *who*, *when*, or *where* questions.

Previewing Visuals

Visuals are photographs, graphs, tables, diagrams, and illustrations. Visuals contain important information. Before you read, look at visuals and their labels and captions. This preview will help you prepare for what you will be reading.

    Often you will be asked what you want to learn about a visual. For example, after you look at the normal fault diagram below, you might ask: What is the movement along a normal fault? Questions about visuals give you a purpose for reading—to answer your questions.

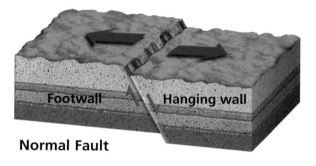

Footwall   **Hanging wall**

Normal Fault

Outlining

An outline shows the relationship between main ideas and supporting ideas. An outline has a formal structure. You write the main ideas, called topics, next to Roman numerals. The supporting ideas, called subtopics, are written under the main ideas and labeled A, B, C, and so on. An outline looks like this:

Technology and Society
I. Technology through history
II. The impact of technology on society
A.
B.

Identifying Main Ideas

When you are reading science material, it is important to try to understand the ideas and concepts that are in a passage. Each paragraph has a lot of information and detail. Good readers try to identify the most important—or biggest—idea in every paragraph or section. That's the main idea. The other information in the paragraph supports or further explains the main idea.

Sometimes main ideas are stated directly. In this book, some main ideas are identified for you as key concepts. These are printed in bold-face type. However, you must identify other main ideas yourself. In order to do this, you must identify all the ideas within a paragraph or section. Then ask yourself which idea is big enough to include all the other ideas.

Comparing and Contrasting

When you compare and contrast, you examine the similarities and differences between things. You can compare and contrast in a Venn diagram or in a table.

Venn Diagram A Venn diagram consists of two overlapping circles. In the space where the circles overlap, you write the characteristics that the two items have in common. In one of the circles outside the area of overlap, you write the differing features or characteristics of one of the items. In the other circle outside the area of overlap, you write the differing characteristics of the other item.

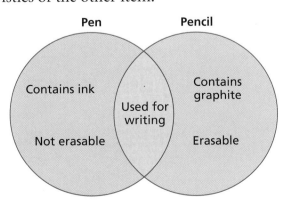

Table In a compare/contrast table, you list the characteristics or features to be compared across the top of the table. Then list the items to be compared in the left column. Complete the table by filling in information about each characteristic or feature.

Blood Vessel	Function	Structure of Wall
Artery	Carries blood away from heart	
Capillary		
Vein		

Identifying Supporting Evidence

A hypothesis is a possible explanation for observations made by scientists or an answer to a scientific question. Scientists must carry out investigations and gather evidence that either supports or disproves the hypothesis.

Identifying the supporting evidence for a hypothesis or theory can help you understand the hypothesis or theory. Evidence consists of facts—information whose accuracy can be confirmed by testing or observation.

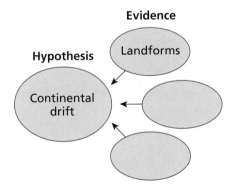

Sequencing

A sequence is the order in which a series of events occurs. A flowchart or a cycle diagram can help you visualize a sequence.

Flowchart To make a flowchart, write a brief description of each step or event in a box. Place the boxes in order, with the first event at the top of the page. Then draw an arrow to connect each step or event to the next.

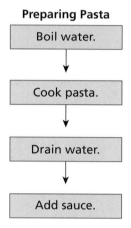

Preparing Pasta

Boil water.

Cook pasta.

Drain water.

Add sauce.

Cycle Diagram A cycle diagram shows a sequence that is continuous, or cyclical. A continuous sequence does not have an end because when the final event is over, the first event begins again. To create a cycle diagram, write the starting event in a box placed at the top of a page in the center. Then, moving in a clockwise direction, write each event in a box in its proper sequence. Draw arrows that connect each event to the one that occurs next.

Seasons of the Year

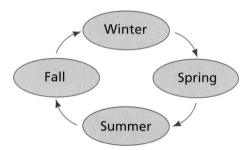

Winter

Spring

Summer

Fall

Relating Cause and Effect

Science involves many cause-and-effect relationships. A cause makes something happen. An effect is what happens. When you recognize that one event causes another, you are relating cause and effect.

Words like *cause, because, effect, affect,* and *result* often signal a cause or an effect. Sometimes an effect can have more than one cause, or a cause can produce several effects.

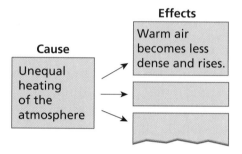

Cause

Unequal heating of the atmosphere

Effects

Warm air becomes less dense and rises.

Concept Mapping

Concept maps are useful tools for organizing information on any topic. A concept map begins with a main idea or core concept and shows how the idea can be subdivided into related subconcepts or smaller ideas.

You construct a concept map by placing concepts (usually nouns) in ovals and connecting them with linking words (usually verbs). The biggest concept or idea is placed in an oval at the top of the map. Related concepts are arranged in ovals below the big idea. The linking words connect the ovals.

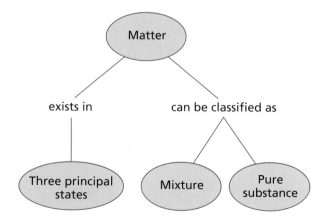

Matter

exists in

can be classified as

Three principal states

Mixture

Pure substance

Building Vocabulary

Knowing the meaning of these prefixes, suffixes, and roots will help you understand the meaning of words you do not recognize.

Word Origins Many science words come to English from other languages, such as Greek and Latin. By learning the meaning of a few common Greek and Latin roots, you can determine the meaning of unfamiliar science words.

Prefixes A prefix is a word part that is added at the beginning of a root or base word to change its meaning.

Suffixes A suffix is a word part that is added at the end of a root word to change the meaning.

Greek and Latin Roots		
Greek Roots	**Meaning**	**Example**
ast-	star	astronaut
geo-	Earth	geology
metron-	measure	kilometer
opt-	eye	optician
photo-	light	photograph
scop-	see	microscope
therm-	heat	thermostat
Latin Roots	**Meaning**	**Example**
aqua-	water	aquarium
aud-	hear	auditorium
duc-, duct-	lead	conduct
flect-	bend	reflect
fract-, frag-	break	fracture
ject-	throw	reject
luc-	light	lucid
spec-	see	inspect

Prefixes and Suffixes		
Prefix	**Meaning**	**Example**
com-, con-	with	communicate, concert
de-	from; down	decay
di-	two	divide
ex-, exo-	out	exhaust
in-, im-	in, into; not	inject, impossible
re-	again; back	reflect, recall
trans-	across	transfer
Suffix	**Meaning**	**Example**
-al	relating to	natural
-er, -or	one who	teacher, doctor
-ist	one who practices	scientist
-ity	state of	equality
-ology	study of	biology
-tion, -sion	state or quality of	reaction, tension

Safety Symbols

These symbols warn of possible dangers in the laboratory and remind you to work carefully.

 Safety Goggles Wear safety goggles to protect your eyes in any activity involving chemicals, flames or heating, or glassware.

 Lab Apron Wear a laboratory apron to protect your skin and clothing from damage.

 Breakage Handle breakable materials, such as glassware, with care. Do not touch broken glassware.

 Heat-Resistant Gloves Use an oven mitt or other hand protection when handling hot materials such as hot plates or hot glassware.

 Plastic Gloves Wear disposable plastic gloves when working with harmful chemicals and organisms. Keep your hands away from your face, and dispose of the gloves according to your teacher's instructions.

 Heating Use a clamp or tongs to pick up hot glassware. Do not touch hot objects with your bare hands.

 Flames Before you work with flames, tie back loose hair and clothing. Follow instructions from your teacher about lighting and extinguishing flames.

 No Flames When using flammable materials, make sure there are no flames, sparks, or other exposed heat sources present.

 Corrosive Chemical Avoid getting acid or other corrosive chemicals on your skin or clothing or in your eyes. Do not inhale the vapors. Wash your hands after the activity.

 Poison Do not let any poisonous chemical come into contact with your skin, and do not inhale its vapors. Wash your hands when you are finished with the activity.

 Fumes Work in a ventilated area when harmful vapors may be involved. Avoid inhaling vapors directly. Only test an odor when directed to do so by your teacher, and use a wafting motion to direct the vapor toward your nose.

 Sharp Object Scissors, scalpels, knives, needles, pins, and tacks can cut your skin. Always direct a sharp edge or point away from yourself and others.

 Animal Safety Treat live or preserved animals or animal parts with care to avoid harming the animals or yourself. Wash your hands when you are finished with the activity.

 Plant Safety Handle plants only as directed by your teacher. If you are allergic to certain plants, tell your teacher; do not do an activity involving those plants. Avoid touching harmful plants such as poison ivy. Wash your hands when you are finished with the activity.

 Electric Shock To avoid electric shock, never use electrical equipment around water, or when the equipment is wet or your hands are wet. Be sure cords are untangled and cannot trip anyone. Unplug equipment not in use.

 Physical Safety When an experiment involves physical activity, avoid injuring yourself or others. Alert your teacher if there is any reason you should not participate.

 Disposal Dispose of chemicals and other laboratory materials safely. Follow the instructions from your teacher.

 Hand Washing Wash your hands thoroughly when finished with the activity. Use antibacterial soap and warm water. Rinse well.

 General Safety Awareness When this symbol appears, follow the instructions provided. When you are asked to develop your own procedure in a lab, have your teacher approve your plan before you go further.

Science Safety Rules

General Precautions

Follow all instructions. Never perform activities without the approval and supervision of your teacher. Do not engage in horseplay. Never eat or drink in the laboratory. Keep work areas clean and uncluttered.

Dress Code

Wear safety goggles whenever you work with chemicals, glassware, heat sources such as burners, or any substance that might get into your eyes. If you wear contact lenses, notify your teacher.

Wear a lab apron or coat whenever you work with corrosive chemicals or substances that can stain. Wear disposable plastic gloves when working with organisms and harmful chemicals. Tie back long hair. Remove or tie back any article of clothing or jewelry that can hang down and touch chemicals, flames, or equipment. Roll up long sleeves. Never wear open shoes or sandals.

First Aid

Report all accidents, injuries, or fires to your teacher, no matter how minor. Be aware of the location of the first-aid kit, emergency equipment such as the fire extinguisher and fire blanket, and the nearest telephone. Know whom to contact in an emergency.

Heating and Fire Safety

Keep all combustible materials away from flames. When heating a substance in a test tube, make sure that the mouth of the tube is not pointed at you or anyone else. Never heat a liquid in a closed container. Use an oven mitt to pick up a container that has been heated.

Using Chemicals Safely

Never put your face near the mouth of a container that holds chemicals. Never touch, taste, or smell a chemical unless your teacher tells you to.

Use only those chemicals needed in the activity. Keep all containers closed when chemicals are not being used. Pour all chemicals over the sink or a container, not over your work surface. Dispose of excess chemicals as instructed by your teacher.

Be extra careful when working with acids or bases. When mixing an acid and water, always pour the water into the container first and then add the acid to the water. Never pour water into an acid. Wash chemical spills and splashes immediately with plenty of water.

Using Glassware Safely

If glassware is broken or chipped, notify your teacher immediately. Never handle broken or chipped glass with your bare hands.

Never force glass tubing or thermometers into a rubber stopper or rubber tubing. Have your teacher insert the glass tubing or thermometer if required for an activity.

Using Sharp Instruments

Handle sharp instruments with extreme care. Never cut material toward you; cut away from you.

Animal and Plant Safety

Never perform experiments that cause pain, discomfort, or harm to animals. Only handle animals if absolutely necessary. If you know that you are allergic to certain plants, molds, or animals, tell your teacher before doing an activity in which these are used. Wash your hands thoroughly after any activity involving animals, animal parts, plants, plant parts, or soil.

During field work, wear long pants, long sleeves, socks, and closed shoes. Avoid poisonous plants and fungi as well as plants with thorns.

End-of-Experiment Rules

Unplug all electrical equipment. Clean up your work area. Dispose of waste materials as instructed by your teacher. Wash your hands after every experiment.

English and Spanish Glossary

acoustics The study of how sounds interact with each other and the environment. (p. 52)
acústica Estudio de cómo interactúan los sonidos entre ellos y con el medio ambiente.

amplitude The maximum distance the particles of a medium move away from their rest positions as a wave passes through the medium. (p. 12)
amplitud Distancia máxima a la que se separan las partículas de un medio de sus posiciones de reposo, cuando una onda atraviesa el medio.

amplitude modulation A method of transmitting signals by changing the amplitude of a wave. (p. 91)
amplitud modulada Método de transmisión de señales por el cual se cambia la amplitud de una onda.

antinode A point of maximum amplitude on a standing wave. (p. 22)
antinodo Punto de máxima amplitud en una onda estacionaria.

camera An optical instrument that uses lenses to focus light, and film to record an image of an object. (p. 131)
cámara Instrumento óptico que usa lentes para enfocar la luz, y película para grabar la imagen de un objeto.

cochlea A fluid-filled cavity in the inner ear that is shaped like a snail shell. (p. 55)
cóclea Cavidad llena de líquido en el oído interno que tiene forma de caracol.

complementary colors Any two colors that combine to form white light or black pigment. (p. 110)
colores complementarios Dos colores cualesquiera que se combinan para crear luz blanca o pigmento negro.

compression The part of a longitudinal wave where the particles of the medium are close together. (p. 9)
compresión Parte de una onda longitudinal donde las partículas del medio están muy juntas.

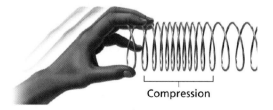
Compression

concave lens A lens that is thinner in the center than at the edges. (p. 123)
lente cóncava Lente que es más fina en el centro que en los extremos.

concave mirror A mirror with a surface that curves inward. (p. 116)
espejo cóncavo Espejo cuya superficie se curva hacia dentro.

cones Cells in the retina that respond to and detect color. (p. 126)
conos Células en la retina que responden y detectan el color.

constructive interference The interference that occurs when waves combine to make a wave with a larger amplitude. (p. 20)
interferencia constructiva Interferencia que ocurre cuando las ondas se combinan para crear una onda con una amplitud mayor.

convex lens A lens that is thicker in the center than at the edges. (p. 122)
lente convexa Lente que es más gruesa en el centro que en los extremos.

convex mirror A mirror with a surface that curves outward. (p. 118)
espejo convexo Espejo cuya superficie se curva hacia fuera.

cornea The transparent front surface of the eye. (p. 126)
córnea Superficie frontal transparente del ojo.

crest The highest part of a transverse wave. (p. 8)
cresta Parte más alta de una onda transversal.

decibel (dB) A unit used to compare the loudness of different sounds. (p. 44)
decibelio (dB) Unidad usada para comparar el volumen de diferentes sonidos.

density The ratio of the mass of a substance to its volume. (p. 40)
densidad Razón de la masa de una sustancia a su volumen.

destructive interference The interference that occurs when two waves combine to make a wave with a smaller amplitude. (p. 21)
interferencia destructiva Interferencia que ocurre cuando dos ondas se combinan para crear una onda con una amplitud más pequeña.

diffraction The bending of waves as they move around a barrier or pass through an opening. (p. 20)
difracción Cambio de dirección de las ondas cuando rodean una barrera o pasan por una abertura.

diffuse reflection Reflection that occurs when parallel rays of light hit a rough surface and all reflect at different angles. (p. 114)
reflexión difusa Reflexión que ocurre cuando rayos de luz paralelos tocan una superficie rugosa y se reflejan en diferentes ángulos.

Doppler effect The change in frequency of a wave as its source moves in relation to an observer. (p. 46)
efecto Doppler Cambio en la frecuencia de una onda a medida que se mueve su fuente en relación al observador.

E

ear canal A narrow region leading from the outside of the human ear to the eardrum. (p. 54)
canal auditivo Región estrecha que va desde el exterior del oído humano hasta el tímpano.

eardrum A small, tightly stretched, drumlike membrane in the ear. (p. 54)
tímpano Membrana pequeña muy tensa con forma de tambor que está en el oído.

echo A reflected sound wave. (p. 38)
eco Onda sonora reflejada.

echolocation The use of reflected sound waves to determine distances or to locate objects. (p. 61)
ecolocación Uso de ondas sonoras reflejadas para determinar distancias o para localizar objetos.

elasticity The ability of a material to bounce back after being disturbed. (p. 40)
elasticidad Capacidad de un material para volver a su forma original después de verse alterada.

electromagnetic radiation The energy transferred through space by electromagnetic waves. (p. 71)
radiación electromagnética Energía transferida por ondas electromagnéticas a través del espacio.

electromagnetic spectrum The complete range of electromagnetic waves placed in order of increasing frequency. (p. 75)
espectro electromagnético Gama completa de ondas electromagnéticas colocadas en orden de menor a mayor frecuencia.

electromagnetic wave Transverse waves that transfer electrical and magnetic energy. (p. 71)
ondas electromagnéticas Ondas transversales que transfieren energía eléctrica y magnética.

energy The ability to do work. (p. 7)
energía Capacidad para realizar trabajo.

eyepiece A lens that magnifies the image formed by the objective. (p. 130)
ocular Lente que aumenta la imagen formada por el objetivo.

F

farsightedness A condition that causes a person to see nearby objects as blurry. (p. 128)
hipermetropía Condición que causa que una persona vea borrosos los objetos cercanos.

fluorescent light Light bulb that glows when an electric current causes ultraviolet rays to strike a coating inside a tube. (p. 86)
luz fluorescente Lámpara que se ilumina cuando una corriente eléctrica causa que los rayos ultravioleta choquen con el recubrimiento interior de un tubo.

focal point The point at which light rays parallel to the optical axis meet, or appear to meet, after being reflected (or refracted) by a mirror (or a lens). (p. 116)
punto de enfoque Punto en el que se encuentran, o parecen encontrarse, los rayos de luz paralelos al eje óptico después de reflejarse (o refractarse) en un espejo (o lente).

frequency The number of complete waves that pass a given point in a certain amount of time. (p. 13)
frecuencia Número de ondas completas que pasan por un punto dado en cierto tiempo.

frequency modulation A method of transmitting signals by changing the frequency of a wave. (p. 91)
frecuencia modulada Método de transmisión de señales por el cual se cambia la frecuencia de una onda.

fundamental tone The lowest natural frequency of an object. (p. 49)
tono fundamental Frecuencia natural más baja de un objeto.

gamma rays Electromagnetic waves with the shortest wavelengths and highest frequencies. (p. 80)
rayos gamma Ondas electromagnéticas con la menor longitud de onda y la mayor frecuencia.

hertz (Hz) Unit of measurement for frequency. (p. 13)
hercio (Hz) Unidad de media de frecuencia.

hologram A three-dimensional photograph created using lasers. (p. 134)
holograma Fotografía tridimensional creada usando rayos láser.

illuminated Word used to describe an object that can be seen because it reflects light. (p. 84)
iluminado Palabra que se usa para describir un objeto que se puede ver porque refleja la luz.

image A copy of an object formed by reflected or refracted rays of light. (p. 115)
imagen Copia de un objeto formado por rayos de luz que se reflejan y se refractan.

incandescent light Light bulb that glows when a filament inside it gets white hot. (p. 84)
luz incandescente Lámpara que se ilumina cuando un filamento interior se calienta tanto que se pone blanco.

index of refraction A measure of the amount a ray of light bends when it passes from one medium to another. (p. 120)
índice de refracción Medida de la inclinación de un rayo de luz cuando pasa de un medio a otro.

infrared rays Electromagnetic waves with wavelengths shorter than radio waves, but longer than visible light. (p. 77)
rayos infrarrojos Ondas electromagnéticas con longitud de onda menor que las ondas de radio, pero mayor que la de la luz visible.

infrasound Sound waves with frequencies below 20 Hz. (p. 45)
infrasonido Ondas sonoras con frecuencias menores de 20 Hz.

intensity The amount of energy per second carried through a unit area by a wave. (p. 43)
intensidad Cantidad de energía por segundo que lleva una onda a través de una unidad de área.

interference The interaction between waves that meet. (p. 20)
interferencia Interacción entre ondas que se encuentran.

iris The ring of muscle that controls the size of the pupil and gives the eye its color. (p. 126)
iris Anillo muscular que controla el tamaño de la pupila y da el color al ojo.

larynx Two folds of tissue that make up the human voice box. (p. 45)
laringe Dos pliegues de tejido que forman la caja sonora humana.

laser A device that producesa narrow beam of coherent light. (p. 132)
láser Aparato que produce un delgado rayo de luz coherente.

law of reflection The rule that the angle of reflection equals the angle of incidence. (p. 18)
ley de reflexión Regla que enuncia que el ángulo de reflexión es igual al ángulo de incidencia.

lens A curved piece of glass or other transparent material that is used to refract light. (p. 122)
lente Trozo de cristal u otro material transparente curvado que se usa para refractar la luz.

longitudinal wave A wave that moves the medium in a direction parallel to the direction in which the wave travels. (p. 9)
onda longitudinal Onda que mueve el medio en dirección paralela a la dirección en la que viaja la onda.

loudness Perception of the energy of a sound. (p. 42)
volumen Percepción de la energía de un sonido.

luminous Word used to describe an object that can be seen because it emits light. (p. 84)
luminoso Palabra que se usa para describir un objeto que se puede ver porque emite luz.

mechanical wave A wave that requires a medium through which to travel. (p. 7)
onda mecánica Onda que necesita un medio por el cual viajar.

medium The material through which a wave travels. (p. 7)
medio Material a través del cual viaja una onda.

microscope An optical instrument that forms enlarged images of tiny objects. (p. 131)
microscopio Instrumento óptico que forma imágenes aumentadas de objetos diminutos.

microwaves Radio waves with the shortest wavelengths and the highest frequencies. (p. 76)
microondas Ondas de radio con la menor longitud de onda y la mayor frecuencia.

mirage An image of a distant object caused by refraction of light as it travels through air of varying temperature. (p. 121)
espejismo Imagen de un objeto distante causado por la refracción de la luz cuando viaja por el aire a temperaturas cambiantes.

music A set of tones and overtones combined in ways that are pleasing. (p. 48)
música Conjunto de tonos y sobretonos combinados de manera agradable.

nearsightedness A condition that causes a person to see distant objects as blurry. (p. 128)
miopía Condición que causa que una persona vea borrosos los objetos lejanos.

neon light Glass tube containing neon gas that produces light. (p. 87)
luz de neón Tubo de vidrio que contiene gas neón que produce luz.

node A point of zero amplitude on a standing wave. (p. 22)
nodo Punto de amplitud cero en una onda estacionaria.

objective A lens that gathers light from an object and forms a real image. (p. 130)
objetivo Lente que reúne la luz de un objeto y forma una imagen real.

opaque material A material that reflects or absorbs all of the light that strikes it. (p. 107)
material opaco Material que refleja o absorbe toda la luz que llega a él.

optic nerve Short, thick nerve that carries signals from the eye to the brain. (p. 126)
nervio óptico Nervio corto y grueso que lleva señales del ojo al cerebro.

optical axis An imaginary line that divides a mirror in half. (p. 116)
eje óptico Recta imaginaria que divide un espejo por la mitad.

optical fiber A long, thin strand of glass or plastic that can carry light for long distances without allowing the light to escape. (p. 136)
fibra óptica Filamento largo y delgado de vidrio o plástico que puede transportar luz a través de largas distancias sin dejarla escapar.

overtone A natural frequency that is a multiple of the fundamental tone's frequency. (p. 49)
armónico Frecuencia natural que es un múltiplo de la frecuencia del tono fundamental.

photoelectric effect The ejection of electrons from a substance when light is shined on it. (p. 73)
efecto fotoeléctrico Expulsión de electrones de una sustancia cuando le da la luz.

photon A tiny particle or packet of light energy. (p. 73)
fotón Partícula diminuta o paquete de energía luminosa.

pigment A colored substance used to color other materials. (p. 111)
pigmento Sustancia con color que se usa para colorear otros materiales.

pitch Perception of the frequency of a sound. (p. 44)
tono Percepción de la frecuencia de un sonido.

plane mirror A flat mirror that produces an upright, virtual image the same size as the object. (p. 115)
espejo plano Espejo liso que produce una imagen virtual vertical del mismo tamaño que el objeto.

polarized light Light that vibrates in only one direction. (p. 72)
luz polarizada Luz que vibra en una sola dirección.

primary colors Three colors that can be used to make any other color. (p. 110)
colores primarios Tres colores que se pueden usar para hacer cualquier color.

pupil The opening in the center of the iris through which light enters the inside of the eye. (p. 126)
pupila Abertura en el centro del iris a través de la cual entra la luz en el ojo.

P wave A longitudinal seismic wave. (p. 27)
onda P Onda sísmica longitudinal.

radar A system that uses reflected radio waves to detect objects and measure their distance and speed. (p. 76)
radar Sistema que usa ondas de radio reflejadas para detectar objetos y medir su distancia y velocidad.

radio waves Electromagnetic waves with the longest wavelengths and lowest frequencies. (p. 76)
ondas de radio Ondas electromagnéticas con la mayor longitud de onda y la menor frecuencia.

rarefaction The part of a longitudinal wave where the particles of the medium are far apart. (p. 9)
rarefacción Parte de una onda longitudinal donde las partículas del medio están alejadas.

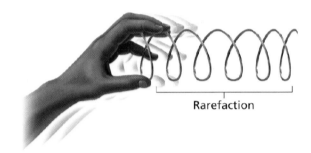
Rarefaction

ray A straight line used to represent a light wave. (p. 114)
rayo Línea recta que se usa para representar una onda de luz.

real image An upside-down image formed where rays of light meet. (p. 117)
imagen real Imagen invertida formada donde se encuentran los rayos de luz.

reflecting telescope A telescope that uses a concave mirror to gather light from distant objects. (p. 130)
telescopio reflector Telescopio que usa un espejo cóncavo para reunir luz de los objetos distantes.

reflection The bouncing back of an object or a wave when it hits a surface through which it cannot pass. (p. 18)
reflexión Rebote de un objeto o una onda cuando golpea una superficie por la cual no puede pasar.

refracting telescope A telescope that uses two convex lenses to form images. (p. 130)
telescopio refractor Telescopio que usa dos lentes convexas para formar imágenes.

refraction The bending of waves as they enter a new medium at an angle. (p. 19)
refracción Cambio de dirección de las ondas cuando entran en un nuevo medio en un determinado ángulo.

regular reflection Reflection that occurs when parallel rays of light hit a smooth surface and all reflect at the same angle. (p. 114)
reflexión regular Reflexión que ocurre cuando rayos de luz paralelos chocan contra una superficie lisa y se reflejan en el mismo ángulo.

resonance The increase in the amplitude of a vibration that occurs when external vibrations match an object's natural frequency. (p. 23)
resonancia Aumento en la amplitud de vibración que ocurre cuando vibraciones externas se corresponden con la frecuencia natural de un objeto.

retina The layer of cells that lines the inside of the eyeball. (p. 126)
retina Capa de células que recubre el interior del globo ocular.

reverberation The echoes of a sound that are heard after a sound source stops producing sound waves. (p. 52)
reverberación Ecos de un sonido que son oídos después de que la fuente sonora deja de producir ondas sonoras.

rods Cells in the retina that detect dim light. (p. 126)
bastones Células de la retina que detectan la luz tenue.

secondary color Any color produced by combining equal amounts of any two primary colors. (p. 110)
color secundario Color producido al combinar iguales cantidades de dos colores primarios cualesquiera.

seismic wave A wave produced by an earthquake. (p. 27)
onda sísmica Onda producida por un terremoto.

seismograph An instrument used to detect and measure earthquake waves. (p. 29)
sismógrafo Instrumento que se usa para detectar y medir ondas de terremotos.

sonar A system that uses reflected sound waves to detect and locate objects underwater. (p. 62)
sonar Sistema que usa ondas sonoras reflejadas para detectar y localizar objetos debajo del agua.

sonogram An image formed using reflected ultrasound waves. (p. 63)
sonograma Imagen creada usando ondas de ultrasonido reflejadas.

spectroscope An instrument used to view the different colors of light produced by different light sources. (p. 84)
espectroscopio Instrumento que se usa para ver los diferentes colores de la luz producidos por fuentes de luz diferentes.

standing wave A wave that appears to stand in one place, even though it is really two waves interfering as they pass through each other. (p. 22)
onda estacionaria Onda que parece que permanece en un lugar, aunque en realidad son dos ondas que interfieren cuando se cruzan.

surface wave A combination of a longitudinal wave and a transverse wave that travels along the surface of a medium. (p. 28)
onda superficial Combinación de una onda longitudinal con una onda transversal que viaja por la superficie de un medio.

S wave A transverse seismic wave. (p. 27)
onda S Onda sísmica transversal.

telescope An optical instrument that forms enlarged images of distant objects. (p. 130)
telescopio Instrumento óptico que forma imágenes aumentadas de los objetos lejanos.

thermogram An image that shows regions of different temperatures in different colors. (p. 77)
termografía Imagen que muestra regiones de diferentes temperaturas en diferentes colores.

total internal reflection The complete reflection of light by the inside surface of a medium. (p. 136)
reflexión interna total Reflexión completa de la luz en la superficie interna de un medio.

translucent material A material that scatters light as it passes through. (p. 107)
material traslúcido Material que dispersa la luz cuando ésta lo atraviesa.

transparent material A material that transmits light without scattering it. (p. 107)
material transparente Material que transmite luz sin dispersarla.

transverse wave A wave that moves the medium in a direction perpendicular to the direction in which the wave travels. (p. 8)
onda transversal Onda que mueve el medio en dirección perpendicular a la dirección en la que viaja la onda.

trough The lowest part of a transverse wave. (p. 8)
valle Parte más baja de una onda transversal.

tsunami A huge surface wave on the ocean caused by an underwater earthquake. (p. 28)
tsunami Gran ola superficial del océano causado por un terremoto subterráneo.

tungsten-halogen bulb Incandescent light bulb containing a tungsten filament and a halogen gas. (p. 85)
lámpara de tungsteno-halógeno Lámpara de luz incandescente que contiene un filamento de tungsteno y gas halógeno.

ultrasound Sound waves with frequencies above 20,000 Hz. (p. 45)
ultrasonido Ondas sonoras con frecuencias mayores de 20,000 Hz.

ultraviolet rays Electromagnetic waves with wavelengths shorter than visible light, but longer than X-rays. (p. 78)
rayos ultravioletas Ondas electromagnéticas con longitud de onda menor que la luz visible, pero mayor que la de los rayos X.

vapor light Light bulb containing neon or argon gas along with a small amount of solid sodium or mercury. (p. 86)
luz de vapor Lámpara que contiene gas neón o argón y una pequeña cantidad de sodio sólido o mercurio.

vibration A repeated back-and-forth or up-and-down motion. (p. 8)
vibración Movimiento repetido hacia delante y hacia atrás o hacia arriba y hacia abajo.

virtual image An upright image formed where rays of light appear to meet or come from. (p. 115)
imagen virtual Imagen vertical que se forma desde donde parecen provenir los rayos de luz.

visible light Electromagnetic waves that are visible to the human eye. (p. 78)
luz visible Ondas electromagnéticas visibles al ojo humano.

wave A disturbance that transfers energy from place to place. (p. 7)
onda Perturbación que transfiere energía de un lugar a otro.

wavelength The distance between two corresponding parts of a wave. (p. 13)
longitud de onda Distancia entre dos partes correspondientes de una onda.

X-rays Electromagnetic waves with wavelengths shorter than ultraviolet rays, but longer than gamma rays. (p. 79)
rayos X Ondas electromagnéticas con longitud de onda menor que la de los rayos ultravioleta, pero mayor que la de los rayos gamma.

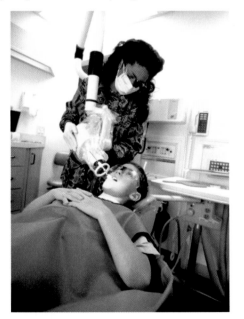

Index

Index

Page numbers for key terms are printed in **boldface** type.
Page numbers for illustrations, maps, and charts are printed in *italics*.

Index

Page numbers for key terms are printed in **boldface** type.
Page numbers for illustrations, maps, and charts are printed in *italics*.

Index

Acknowledgments

Staff Credits

Diane Alimena, Scott Andrews, Jennifer Angel, Michele Angelucci, Laura Baselice, Carolyn Belanger, Barbara A. Bertell, Suzanne Biron, Peggy Bliss, Stephanie Bradley, James Brady, Anne M. Bray, Sarah M. Carroll, Kerry Cashman, Jonathan Cheney, Joshua D. Clapper, Lisa J. Clark, Bob Craton, Patricia Cully, Patricia M. Dambry, Kathy Dempsey, Leanne Esterly, Emily Ellen, Thomas Ferreira, Jonathan Fisher, Patricia Fromkin, Paul Gagnon, Kathy Gavilanes, Holly Gordon, Robert Graham, Ellen Granter, Diane Grossman, Barbara Hollingdale, Linda Johnson, Anne Jones, John Judge, Kevin Keane, Kelly Kelliher, Toby Klang, Sue Langan, Russ Lappa, Carolyn Lock, Rebecca Loveys, Constance J. McCarty, Carolyn B. McGuire, Ranida Touranont McKneally, Anne McLaughlin, Eve Melnechuk, Natania Mlawer, Janet Morris, Karyl Murray, Francine Neumann, Baljit Nijjar, Marie Opera, Jill Ort, Kim Ortell, Joan Paley, Dorothy Preston, Maureen Raymond, Laura Ross, Rashid Ross, Siri Schwartzman, Melissa Shustyk, Laurel Smith, Emily Soltanoff, Jennifer A. Teece, Elizabeth Torjussen, Amanda M. Watters, Merce Wilczek, Amy Winchester, Char Lyn Yeakley. **Additional Credits:** Tara Alamilla, Louise Gachet, Allen Gold, Andrea Golden, Terence Hegarty, Etta Jacobs, Meg Montgomery, Stephanie Rogers, Kim Schmidt, Adam Teller, Joan Tobin.

Illustration

David Corrente: 141; **John Edwards and Associates:** 18; **Ray Goudey:** 70; **Phillip Guzy:** 43, 45, 49, 50, 51l, 51r, 55, 79, 85, 86, 87, 110, 117, 121, 131, 132; **Matt Mayerchak:** 6, 8, 17, 24, 26, 28, 31, 36, 39, 42, 44, 48, 53, 54, 57, 60, 65, 89, 92, 101, 102, 113, 119, 120, 124, 125, 138; **Steve McEntee:** 8, 9, 10, 12–13, 19, 21, 30, 37t, 44, 61, 75, 93; **Richard McMahon:** 40, 50–51, 54, 71, 73, 90b, 94, 108, 109, 111, 114, 117, 123, 134–135, 136, 140l; **Robert Roper:** 38l, 38r, 46; **Roberta Warshaw:** 66l, 66r, 67.

Photography

Photo Research Paula Wehde

Cover Image bottom, Brian Sytnyk/Masterfile; **top,** Mark Lewis/Picturesque

Page iii, Washington University Photo Department; **vi,** E.R. Degginger/Color Pic; **vii,** Richard Haynes; **viii,** Richard Haynes; **x,** Courtesy of Christine Darden; **x-1,** NASA; **1b,** Courtesy of Christine Darden.; **2,** Matthew Pippen; **3,** Courtesy of Christine Darden.

Chapter 1
Pages 4–5, Paul Friedlander; **5 inset,** Lon C. Diehl/PhotoEdit; **6b,** Image Bank/Getty Images, Inc.; **6t,** Richard Haynes; **11b,** Chris Cole/Duomo; **11t,** Richard Haynes; **14,** Jim Zuckerman/Corbis; **16,** Richard Haynes; **17b,** Alese & Mort Pechter/Corbis; **17t,** Richard Haynes; **18,** Reno Tucillo; **19,** Fundamental Photographs; **20 both,** Coastal Inlets Research Program; **22 both,** Richard Megna/Fundamental Photographs; **23,** EERC; **24,** Richard Haynes; **25,** Richard Haynes; **26b,** Courtesy National Information Service for Earthquake Engineering, University of California, Berkeley; **29,** Getty Images, Inc.; **29 inset,** Getty Images, Inc.; **30,** Chris Cole/Duomo.

Chapter 2
Pages 34–35, Paul Arthur/Getty Images; **35 inset,** Jon Chomitz; **36b,** Corbis; **36t,** Richard Haynes; **37,** Richard Haynes; **40,** Richard Haynes; **41,** The Granger Collection, NY; **42,** Richard Haynes; **43 ear image,** Index Stock Imagery; **44 both,** Jack Vartoogian; **45,** Richard Haynes; **47,** Reuters/Corbis; **48b,** Michael Newman/PhotoEdit; **48t,** Richard Haynes; **50l,** Photo Disc/Getty Images, Inc.; **50–51m,** Doug Martin/Photo Researchers, Inc.; **51r,** Getty Images, Inc.; **52,** Ted Soqui/Corbis; **53,** Richard Haynes; **55,** Quest/Dorling Kindersley; **56l,** SPL/Photo Researchers, Inc.; **56r,** Russ Lappa; **58b,** Michael Newman/PhotoEdit; **58t,** Firefly Productions/Corbis; **59b,** David Madison/Getty Images, Inc.; **60b,** Dale Spartas/Corbis; **60t,** Getty Images, Inc.; **61l,** Minden Pictures; **61r,** Corbis; **63b,** Philippe Saada/Phototake; **63t,** CMSP; **64,** Reuters/Corbis.

Chapter 3
Pages 68–69, Roger Ressmeyer/Corbis; **69 inset,** Richard Haynes; **70,** Richard Haynes; **72l,** Clive Streeter/Dorling Kindersley; **72r,** Diane Schiumo/Fundamental Photographs; **74,** Richard Haynes; **76,** Corbis; **77,** Alfred Pasieska/SPL/Photo Researchers, Inc.; **78,** Peter A. Simon/Corbis; **79l,** Science VU/Visuals Unlimited; **79r,** Tom Stewart/Corbis; **82,** Richard Haynes; **84,** Photo Researchers, Inc.; **86,** Phil Degginger; **87,** Will & Deni McIntyre/Corbis; **89,** Richard Haynes; **90 TV,** TRBfoto/Getty Images, Inc.; **90 picture on TV,** Shaun Botterill/Getty Images, Inc.; **93,** Thinkstock/Index Stock Imagery, Inc.; **94l,** John Jenkins/American Museum of Radio & Electricity; **94r,** Science Photo Library; **95l,** AP/Wide World Photos; **95m,** David Ducros/SPL/Photo Researchers, Inc.; **95r,** Tony Freeman Photographs; **98,** Richard Haynes; **99,** Richard Haynes; **100b,** Alfred Pasieska/SPL/Photo Researchers, Inc.; **100t,** Photo Researchers.

Chapter 4
Pages 104–105, Dan McCoy/Rainbow; **105 inset,** Richard Haynes; **106b,** E.R. Degginger/Color Pic; **106t,** Richard Haynes; **107,** Richard Haynes; **108, 109,** PhotoDisc/Gettty Images, Inc.; **110 parrot,** Getty Images, Inc.; **110 TV,** Russ Lappa; **110br,** Jerome Wexler/Photo Researchers, Inc.; **112,** Richard Haynes; **113b,** Tony Freeman/PhotoEdit; **113t,** Richard Haynes; **114,** Michael D. Gardner; **115 all,** Sergio Piumatti; **116,** Richard Haynes; **119b,** Russ Lappa; **119t,** Richard Haynes; **121b,** E.R. Degginger/Color Pic; **121t,** Getty Images, Inc.; **122b, all,** Getty Images, Inc.; **122t,** David Parker/Photo Researchers, Inc.; **124,** Richard Haynes; **125,** David Young-Wolf/PhotoEdit; **127r,** Omnikron/Photo Researchers, Inc.; **127l,** Photo Researchers, Inc.; **129b,** NASA, Hui Yang University of Illinois Nursery of New Stars; **129t,** Richard Haynes; **133bl,** Tony Freeman/PhotoEdit; **133bm,** John Goell/The Picture Cube; **133br,** Getty Images, Inc.; **133tl,** Patrick Bennett/Corbis; **133tr,** Corbis; **134l,** Corbis; **134r,** Scala/Art Resource, NY; **135l,** Hulton-Deutsch Collection/Corbis; **135m,** Phototake; **135r,** Grant Heilman Photography, Inc.; **136,** Corbis; **137,** Custom Medical Stock Photo; **138,** Corbis.

Pages 142, Kobal Collection; **143,** Photofest; **145b,** "The Lord of the Rings: The Two Towers" (c) MMII, New Line Productions, Inc. TM Tolkien Ent. Licensed to New Line Productions, Inc. All rights Reserved, Photo appears courtesy of New Line Productions, Inc.; **145t,** Everett Collection; **146l,** The Kobal Collection; **146r,** Photofest; **147b,** Richard Haynes; **147tl,** Kobal Collection; **147tr,** Everett Collection; **148,** Tony Freeman/PhotoEdit; **149b,** Russ Lappa; **149m,** Richard Haynes; **149t,** Russ Lappa; **150,** Richard Haynes; **152,** Richard Haynes; **154,** Tanton Yachts; **155,** Richard Haynes; **157b,** Richard Haynes; **157t,** Dorling Kinderlsey; **159,** Image Stop/Phototake; **162,** Richard Haynes; **169,** Richard Haynes; **172,** Tony Freeman/PhotoEdit; **173,** Will & Deni McIntyre/Corbis; **175,** Philippe Saada/Phototake; **176l,** Dale Spartas/Corbis; **176r,** Tom Stewart/Corbis.